EXTREME
PRODUCTIVITY

EXTREME PRODUCTIVITY

BOOST YOUR RESULTS, REDUCE YOUR HOURS

ROBERT C. POZEN

HARPER
BUSINESS

An Imprint of HarperCollins*Publishers*
www.harpercollins.com

FIRST EDITION

Designed by Michael Correy

Library of Congress Cataloging-in-Publication Data has been applied for.

ISBN 978-0-06-218853-3

12 13 14 15 16   OV/RRD   10 9 8 7 6 5 4 3 2 1

To my children, Joanna and David, who have given me so much love and support

CONTENTS

ACKNOWLEDGMENTS

I would like to give my sincere thanks to my friends and colleagues who took time out of their busy schedules to read some early drafts of this book. Their feedback and specific suggestions were truly helpful in shaping the book's final version. Those seven readers are Beth Argy, Lena Goldberg, Theresa Hamacher, Jeremy Kagan, Peter Kaufman, Lauren Pyle, and Rich Weitzel. James Levine not only was a helpful reader of drafts but also did an excellent job as my literary agent.

I want to give special thanks to Kathy Holub, who helped edit the book. Through her efforts, the book is shorter, better organized, and more fun to read.

I would also like to thank the following people for reviewing a late-stage draft of the manuscript: Sara Petras, Rachel Branwen, Kathleen Miskiewicz, Maureen Leary-Jago, and Mary Ellen Hammond.

I want to express my special appreciation to MFS Investment Management, and especially Courtney Mahoney, for providing me with excellent administrative support for the book.

Finally, and most important, I am very grateful to Lucas Goodman, my brilliant research assistant. Lucas did a great job in researching a diverse array of topics, writing initial drafts of many sidebars, and integrating my many revisions into the manuscript. And he did all this quickly with great dedication and diplomacy—a wonderful example of personal productivity.

INTRODUCTION

P eople often ask me how I get so much done. During most of the last five years, I've held two full-time jobs—serving as full-time chairman of MFS Investment Management and carrying a full teaching load at Harvard Business School. I've also served on the governing boards of two publicly traded companies (Medtronic and Nielsen), a health care foundation (the Commonwealth Fund), and a medical research center (the Harvard NeuroDiscovery Center). At the same time, I've managed to write three books (including this one) and publish roughly a hundred articles in newspapers and magazines. Through all this, I've maintained a strong relationship with my wife of thirty-five years and our two children, as well as a wide network of friends and relatives.

Though these multiple roles did not seem unusual to me, the editors of the *Harvard Business Review* (*HBR*) were intrigued and asked if they could interview me about the secret recipe for my productivity sauce. When these interviews elicited a large positive response in the blogosphere, the *HBR* editors asked me to write a short article distilling my principles of productivity. I got even more enthusiastic reactions to that article. Strangers stopped me in airports to talk about productivity, and an MIT professor thanked me for improving his reading habits.

However, because the article only skimmed the surface of what can be said about personal productivity, I decided to write this book. In reflecting upon productivity over my career, I can point to a number of habits and methods that have helped me become successful. But even more critical was the realization early in my career that success comes not just from hard work and careful planning—though those are both important. Success depends in large part on a proper mind-set: focusing on the results you plan to achieve, rather than the number of hours you work. The results are what matter most to your employer, clients, and colleagues.

WHAT IS PERSONAL PRODUCTIVITY?

Let's begin with what I mean by "personal productivity." I mean *the quantity and quality of your results in achieving your own objectives*. I won't attempt to dictate what those objectives should be, only that you should clearly articulate them and their relative priority. You may be looking to climb the corporate ladder as quickly as possible or seeking a better balance between your professional and personal lives. In either case, you will benefit by getting more done in the hours you work.

This book does not ask you to embrace a new philosophy of life in order to be successful. It does not even require you to adopt a totally integrated system for personal productivity. It contains specific and practical suggestions on how to increase your productivity at work. You can pick and choose whichever suggested techniques seem most helpful to you.

The suggestions in this book are much broader than those in the typical manual on time management, with its emphasis on mundane tasks such as organizing your files. Although time management is a significant component of productivity, it is not the only one. A useful set of recommendations on productivity should cover a wider range of topics, as this book does—for example, on setting goals for your career and developing skills such as effective writing.

Most fundamentally, the book urges you to adopt a different mind-set as well as to follow concrete techniques. As I previously noted, in order to be productive, you have to focus on the results you want to achieve, not the time you spend at work. Unfortunately, this mind-set is directly at odds with the system of billable hours in accounting or law firms and the emphasis on hours logged at the office in most occupations.

Last, this book is not selling snake oil. In the 1830s, some authors suggested that one could succeed only by following a special diet, sleeping on a hard bed, or abstaining from masturbation![1] More recently, others have urged quick fixes like holding many short meetings or working only a few hours per week. There are no miracle cures in this book. Most of my recommendations call for rigorous thinking and disciplined behavior sustained over long time periods.

SPECIFIC AND PRACTICAL ADVICE

This book is organized into five main parts, each with two or three chapters. The end of each chapter includes specific and practical "takeaways"—lessons to be learned.

- Part I tells you the three big ideas underlying the rest of the book—setting goals with explicit priorities, focusing on the final results, and not sweating the small stuff.

- Part II helps you implement your short-term priorities in a disciplined manner. It contains chapters on organizing your daily routine, managing your travel schedule, and running efficient meetings.

- Part III helps you develop three key personal skills that are critical to becoming a successful professional. It contains chapters on improving your reading comprehension, writing abilities, and effectiveness in public speaking.

- Part IV helps you navigate through the organizational challenges of personal productivity. It contains chapters on managing down by delegating functions and managing up by working well with your boss.

- Part V provides you with a framework for making long-term decisions about your career. It contains chapters on maximizing your options, succeeding in a rapidly changing world, and achieving a satisfying work-life balance.

THE KNOWLEDGE WORKER'S GUIDE TO PRODUCTIVITY

I've written this book for all types of professionals—those who primarily use their brains in their work. This includes accountants, computer programmers, doctors, engineers, investment bankers, lawyers, marketers, psychologists, real estate brokers, retailers, scientists, teachers, and so on. Although the majority of the book's examples are drawn from the commercial world, most of its lessons apply to professionals in other types of organizations: not-for-profit institutions, academia, and government. No matter where you work, you probably face many of the same challenges in allocating your time, running meetings, and dealing with difficult bureaucracies.

Though each of the book's five parts addresses all professionals, some chapters are particularly relevant to groups at certain stages of their careers. Those beginning their professional career may be particularly interested in the chapters on career planning and business writing. Those climbing the corporate ladder may be particularly interested in the chapters on managing up and down. Senior executives may be particularly interested in the chapters on efficient travel and effective speeches. To get the most out of this book, concentrate on the sections that are most relevant to you.

MY PATH TO PRODUCTIVITY: HOW I
LEARNED TO BE PRODUCTIVE

Before we get into the first part of this book, I want to share with you my own history of learning how to be productive. Unlike many productivity gurus, I have not been a consultant on the subject; I've developed my productivity techniques by working in various types of organizations and at various levels. Later in my career, when I was the boss, I could draw upon the resources of a large organization. But early in my career, I worked alone or with peers, and sometimes had to deal with difficult bosses.

I was raised in a family with a high degree of discipline and organization. My father dropped out of high school and worked as a traveling salesman for men's underwear and shirts. The highlight of his career was his stint as an army officer during World War II. After a week on the road as a traveling salesman, he would carefully inspect our house to ensure that everything was in its proper place, harkening back to his old days in the army.

Whereas my father represented order to the point of excess, my mother was a better role model for productivity. She kept our household running smoothly and worked as a bookkeeper at an equipment-leasing company. In fact, she was a brilliant manager, although she never had the money to attend college. My mother pushed hard for higher education for me and my two brothers (who both became cardiologists).

FROM BRIDGEPORT TO HARVARD

After attending a bland elementary school, I was forced to deal with a much tougher environment in junior high school. There I learned to handle with street smarts and tact a number of situations that threatened my productivity and personal health. Standing on the playground one day, I was approached by Al—a fifteen-year-old bully from my seventh-grade homeroom. Al told me that I would have to bring a chocolate bunny to homeroom every Friday for "protection." When I naively raised the question "Protection from what?" he responded, "Protection from me—since there are lots of hammers in shop class on Friday."

So I said, "Al, I bet you're a great basketball player." When Al began to boast about his abilities, I challenged him to a one-on-one game of playground basketball. Here's the deal I made with him: "If you win, I bring you a chocolate bunny every Friday. But if I win, you bring me the bunnies." Luckily, I won that game, and Al left me alone, though I never did find the nerve to ask him for the chocolate bunnies.

When I was a freshman in high school, my father was laid off for the first of several times. It was painful to see that proud man with little formal education searching for jobs. So I tried to make some financial contribution. Through most of high school, I worked two jobs while playing on basketball and tennis teams. On Tuesday, Thursday, and Sunday, I taught Hebrew school at the local synagogue. On Monday, Wednesday, and Friday, I worked as a stock boy at a local bookstore.

With all those obligations, I had to learn how to use my time efficiently. Fortunately or unfortunately, my high school was not academically demanding. Since I was so busy after school, I learned to multitask early, quietly doing my homework as I sat through boring classes.

My high school was a rough-and-tumble place where most of the students were not college-bound and the quality of the teaching was generally low. As a result, I was forced to learn how to learn by myself. That turned out to be an extremely useful skill later in my university and working years. I figured out how to analyze problems and generate potential solutions without much guidance from supervisors or teachers.

For example, the same teacher taught all the sciences at my high school: biology, chemistry, and physics. In each course, he followed the same methodology: At the start of each class, he assigned ten or twenty problems that were due by the end of that school day. Then he would leave the room for the remainder of the class. Left to our own devices, we students reviewed the relevant pages in our textbook, debated the issues, and tried to solve the assigned problems. It seems that we had inadvertently stumbled upon a productive learning model:

small interactive groups applying general concepts to specific factual situations.

There was one inspiring teacher at my high school, an English teacher named Ms. Helen Scinto. She taught me the importance of finding a mentor to help me think about my career. She suggested books for me to read and closely edited my papers. She gave me the confidence and courage to apply for admission to Harvard College, where I was lucky enough to be accepted with a generous package of scholarships and loans.

When I arrived at Harvard, I directly confronted social class for the first time. Roughly half of the student body had gone to private schools, and many of the other students came from high schools in wealthy suburbs. I was intimidated by the academic preparation and material resources of my classmates, so I stepped up my educational game.

While many of my classmates had lots of free time to pursue their intellectual and social interests, I needed to hold a job during all of my college years. I worked as a night librarian, marketed a computerized dating service, and researched housing for a Boston consulting firm. To cope with those jobs and pursue a multidisciplinary major, I learned how to read and write quickly by always focusing on the final product. I graduated summa cum laude, while writing for the editorial page of the *Harvard Crimson* and captaining the basketball team at Lowell House.

After graduation, I was not keen on a business career. I was more interested in the two big social movements of the 1960s: advancing civil rights and stopping the Vietnam War. To pursue those interests, I enrolled at Yale Law School, which I financed through a teaching job along with scholarships and loans. I served on the editorial board of the *Yale Law Journal* and worked with a nonprofit housing group. I also became enthused about the fledging field of "Law and Economics," which sparked my interest in financial regulation. With such a heavy schedule, I became an expert at managing my time efficiently.

After graduate school, I went directly into teaching Law and Economics at Georgetown and New York Universities. During almost four years in academia, I published two books and several scholarly articles on financial regulation. Though I enjoyed teaching, it seemed that my scholarly output had little practical impact. When the footnotes became longer than the text in my last article, I decided to move to Washington, D.C., to become associate general counsel of the Securities and Exchange Commission (SEC).

That was my first experience with a government bureaucracy, where lots of people wanted a say on every significant decision. In response, I helped develop practical procedures for coordinating every division's input on rule proposals. And I learned how to skim lengthy memoranda to pick out the critical issues requiring discussion among the commissioners.

Needing to support a growing family, I then became a partner at the Washington, D.C., law firm of Caplin & Drysdale. Although I established a successful practice advising financial institutions, I was appalled by the system of billing by the hour. The faster I solved problems, the less I was paid! The clients seemed to have more interesting work, and they could build up stock ownership in their companies. By contrast, the compensation of lawyers was limited by the hours they could log, and their schedules were controlled by the whims of their clients.

In late 1986, I got a big break. Fidelity Investments was looking for a new general counsel, and I had family reasons for wanting to live in Boston. After a number of interviews, I came back for a private dinner with Ned Johnson, Fidelity's chairman. Near dessert, I finally asked Ned if it would be possible to obtain a description of my potential job. Ned replied, "You want a job description? It's very simple: figure out what needs to be done and do it!" I signed on immediately.

At Fidelity I rose through the ranks, becoming president and vice chairman before retiring at the end of 2001. There I learned about productivity in a highly decentralized organization that maintained a strong entrepreneurial spirit. When Ned decided to start a new business, such as telecoms, he would create a new company so its managers would have an ownership interest in the company. I followed Ned's example: as the investment team grew larger and larger, I divided it into smaller and smaller groups: growth and value stocks, small and large companies, and so on.

Toward the end of my Fidelity career, I wanted to have more of a voice in public policy debates. But I still had to cope with a stressful day job. So I started to multitask during the day and work on policy projects on the weekends. In my last year at Fidelity, I wrote a textbook on the mutual fund industry and served on the President's Commission to Strengthen Social Security.

Over the last decade, I've gone from multiple tasks to multiple jobs. In 2003, I taught at Harvard Law School and served as secretary of economic affairs for Mitt Romney, who was governor of Massachusetts at the time. Faced with a $3 billion budget deficit, the governor asked me to oversee the economic-related agencies in what was called a "supersecretary" role. I learned many lessons about state government, including that a crisis is a good catalyst for change. In one year, we eliminated the budget deficit primarily by reducing spending; we also raised revenue, without changing tax rates, by increasing user fees and closing tax loopholes.

In 2004, I finished teaching at Harvard Law School, as I became the full-time chairman of MFS Investment Management. I was recruited by the new CEO of MFS, Rob Manning, who was coping with the fallout of a major SEC enforcement action against the firm. Rob and I formed a great partnership with a clear allocation of functions. He was Mr. Internal, running the core operations of the firm—the investment professionals, the back office, the budget, and so on. I was Mr. External, dealing with the concerns of regulators, fund directors, and institutional clients. That was a truly effective combination. With the help of an excellent management team, MFS's assets under management nearly doubled in eight years.

During my tenure at MFS, as things calmed down, I found time to participate actively in the public debates on certain policies. In 2005, for example, I formulated a progressive proposal for restoring Social Security to solvency. In 2007–2008, I chaired the SEC Advisory Committee on Improvements to Financial Reporting, which issued a unanimous report with many recommendations that were actually adopted. The secret to our success: we issued an interim report at the halfway mark and obtained useful feedback from the relevant regulators on our draft proposals.

Now that you know about my journey to productivity, it's time to start yours. Wherever you are in your career, I hope this book can help you produce more and better-quality results for the time that you spend. I will continue to blog on my Web page, www.bobpozen.com, which will also include my future articles.

Part I

THREE BIG IDEAS

Based on what I've learned over the course of my career, I believe that you can maximize your productivity by applying three related ideas:

- Articulate your goals and rank them in order of priority. This helps you align your time allocations with your priorities.

- Focus on the final product. In tackling high-priority projects, quickly formulate tentative conclusions to guide your work.

- Don't sweat the small stuff. Deal with low-priority items in a way that allows you to spend as little time on them as possible.

1

SET AND PRIORITIZE
YOUR GOALS

Many executives are whirlwinds of activity, racing from meeting to meeting or crisis to crisis without giving much thought to the rationale for their hectic schedules. Many of those professionals like the feeling of *doing* something; they are not comfortable reflecting on their priorities. Their typical approach can be described as "Ready, fire, aim!" Others get bogged down in a schedule dictated by their company or spend most of their time responding to "urgent" requests from others.

As a result, those energetic, ambitious people end up spending too little time on activities that support their highest goals. Despite their talent, they often report a serious mismatch between their work priorities and time allocations.

No matter what your career aspirations are, you should begin by thinking carefully about why you are engaging in any activity and what you expect to get out of it. In this chapter, I will walk you through an exercise to establish your highest-ranking goals and to determine whether your actual schedule is consistent with this ranking. This process has six steps:

1. Write down everything you are doing, or are planning to do, in order to achieve your professional goals.

2. Organize the items by time horizon: Career Aims, yearly Objectives, and weekly Targets.

3. Rank your Objectives by their relative importance, taking into account what the world needs as well as what you want.

4. Rank your Targets by their relative importance—both those serving your Objectives and those assigned to you.

5. Estimate how you actually spend your time, and compare that with your prioritized set of Objectives and Targets.

6. Understand and address the reasons for mismatches between your goals and your time allocations.

1. WRITE EVERYTHING DOWN

On one or two sheets of paper, write down everything you are required to do in your professional life. This includes all those routine tasks in your job description that you have to do on a daily or weekly basis, such as filing reports or reviewing documents. It also includes any longer-term projects assigned to you.

But don't stop there; if you spend all your time responding to crises and tasks assigned by others, you can only tread water. To get ahead, you also need to think about what you *want* to do. These may be long-term goals, such as advancing your career. Or they could be short-term goals, such as developing a new skill or meeting more people in your industry. On the same sheet of paper as your assigned tasks, add these aspirations for your work. Don't worry about separating tasks and goals; just jot them all down. We'll organize them in step 2.

To illustrate, I've completed this exercise from the perspective of the manager of one retail outlet of a consumer electronics chain. I'll call him "Joshua." The list below contains thirteen tasks that Joshua must do—or wants to do—at work. Throughout this chapter, I'll use Joshua's example to illustrate the concept of setting your priorities.

Joshua's List

Hire more sales staff.

Increase profits by 15 percent.

Participate in "community history day."

Become a top executive at chain.

Attend a tech expo.

Create a pleasant customer experience.

Write weekly sales report for boss.

Hire an interior designer.

Meet people in retail industry.

Meet with area store managers.

Get fancier offices.

Develop a local marketing strategy.

Refine performance standards for sales staff.

Please be as broad as possible with your list. The point is for you to capture *all* your tasks and goals here; you'll evaluate whether they are significant later in the chapter. If you get stuck, keep reading. The rest of the chapter should help prod your memory.

2. ORGANIZE BY TIME HORIZON

The next step is to divide your list into three time categories: Career Aims (5+ years), Objectives (3–24 months), and Targets (1 week or less). Some goals won't fall neatly into one category; consider each on a case-by-case basis. If it's a relatively quick and simple goal, assign it to the shorter time period. If it's long and requires many cumbersome steps, make it part of the longer time period.

- *Career Aims*: These are long-term goals over at least five years. For example, a young law school graduate might have a Career Aim of becoming a U.S. attorney, the general counsel of a company, or a partner in a large firm. Or perhaps even all three.

- *Objectives*: These are the goals for your professional life over the next three months to two years. They typically require many intermediate steps. Objectives could include completing a systems project, doubling the sales of a product, or developing a new organizational structure.

- *Targets*: These are "action steps" that should guide your work on a weekly or daily basis. For example, your Targets could involve writing a short report, resolving a client's problem, or finishing one part of a larger project.

Next, make sure that each of your Objectives has one or two associated Targets. If any of your Objectives lacks a Target, think hard about the next actionable step you can take to advance that Objective, and then add it to your list of Targets. For example, if one of your Objectives is to double the sales of a product, a Target for the next week might be meeting with a large vendor to make a sales pitch. If an Objective is to publish a research paper by the end of next year, a Target may be to start writing a grant request that could get your experiment funded.

Here is Joshua's list of Career Aims, Objectives, and Targets:

Figure 1: TIME DIMENSION

Career Aims	Objectives	Targets
Become a top executive at chain.	Increase profits by 15 percent. Create a pleasant customer experience. Meet people in retail industry. Get fancier offices.	Hire more sales staff. Meet with area store managers. Participate in "community history day." Attend a tech expo. Write weekly sales report for boss. Hire an interior designer. Develop a local marketing strategy. Refine performance standards for sales staff.

Once you have sorted your goals into these three categories, put your Career Aims aside. Planning your career as a whole is a complicated process, and I'll talk about it at length in part V of this book. For now, let's focus on the medium-term and short-term goals—your Objectives and Targets. These will determine how you should be spending time on a daily basis.

3. RANK YOUR OBJECTIVES

At the end of this section, you'll rank your Objectives, but don't try to do that yet. Start by thinking about what you want to do, what you're good at, and what the world needs from you. These are three distinctly different things—and there may be some conflict among them.

What You Want to Do: As I've said, your personal preferences are critical to your ranking decisions. For instance, if you have a burning desire to invent your company's newest product, you should rank that Objective higher. But your preferences do not tell the whole story.

What You're Good At: I call this the principle of comparative advantage. Ask yourself, "What am I better at doing than others?" "Which Objectives play to my strengths?" Even if you really want to invent new products for your company, you may not have the scientific background to succeed; you may be more of a "people person," skilled at motivating others and resolving problems with clients. You should be willing to rank an Objective higher if you have a comparative advantage in accomplishing it due to your personality or skills.

What the World Needs from You: Unfortunately, you cannot be fully productive by looking only at the supply side—what you want to do and what you are best at doing. You must also consider the demand side—what the world, your organization, or your boss needs most from you. For example, even if you *have* the skills to invent new products, it may be a poor use of your time from the organization's perspective—fixing a problem with an existing product may be a more pressing need. So you also need to ask, "What are the Objectives my organization most needs me to achieve?"

Answering this question may require some thought. Grab another sheet of paper and write down two or three top Objectives for your organization or department. Think about whatever metric is used to evaluate its performance—its profits, say, or the new drugs it puts into the research pipeline. Ask yourself what one change you could make in your current job to help your department achieve success by this metric, directly or indirectly. Is it spending more time visiting clients? Recruiting a talented professional to replace a retiring employee?

For senior executives, this ranking of Objectives should be closely aligned with those of their organization. If a firm has an Objective to expand into Latin America by next year, that should be a high-ranking Objective of its senior managers. But even at junior levels, an employee's Objectives should be reasonably consistent with the needs of the organization. For instance, a middle manager may be a talented writer of sales literature, but her organization needs her unit to revise compliance manuals. If she wants to thrive at this company, she would be wise to give a higher ranking to revising compliance manuals than to developing new sales literature. (If she finds this hard to do, perhaps because she despises working on compliance manuals and has a passion for writing sales literature, she may be working in the wrong unit or company. In that case, she might want to add to her list an Objective of changing jobs.)

You should also consider what your boss wants and needs. At all levels of the organization, your boss will be under pressure from above—for instance, to cut costs or to expand globally. These Objectives of your boss should influence the way you prioritize the Objectives of your organization or unit. If your boss gives special weight to an Objective, you should too—with certain exceptions.

On occasion, you may think that some of your boss's Objectives are off base. Your boss may be overly motivated by his or her own personal agenda; as a result, his or her goals may conflict with those of your organization. At other times, you may feel that your boss is making a strategic blunder, so you might want to persuade him or her to change course. In chapter 11, "Managing Your Boss," I'll suggest ways for you to address such conflicts.

Once you've considered both the supply and demand factors, rank your own list of Objectives on a scale of 1 to 10, with 10 being the highest and 1 the lowest. You should review the ranking of your Objectives on an annual basis, or whenever you experience a major change in your professional life.

In figure 2, I have completed this exercise from Joshua's perspective. His four Objectives for the year are, from highest to lowest priority:

- Increase profits by 15 percent.

- Create a pleasant customer experience.

- Meet people in retail industry.

- Get fancier offices.

You'll notice that I have assigned the highest priority to Objectives that Joshua and his organization share. His personal Objective that is less important to his organization—"Meet people in retail industry"—is ranked lower. His boss's Objective—"Get fancier offices"—is ranked even lower; in Joshua's opinion, this Objective would not meaningfully support his or his organization's goals.

Figure 2: OBJECTIVES

WHAT YOU WANT
- Meet people in retail industry.
- Create a pleasant customer experience.
- Increase profits by 15 percent.

WHAT ORGANIZATION WANTS
- Create a pleasant customer experience.
- Increase profits by 15 percent.

WHAT BOSS WANTS
- Increase profits by 15 percent.
- Get fancier offices.

IMPORTANCE

10: Increase profits by 15 percent.
- What Organization Wants
- What Boss Wants
- What You Want

8: Create a pleasant customer experience.
- What Organization Wants
- What You Want

5: Meet people in retail industry.
- What You Want

1: Get fancier offices,
- What Boss Wants

IMPORTANCE ↑

4. RANK YOUR TARGETS

Now it's time to focus on your Targets—your action steps. Your Targets will typically fall into one of two categories: *Enabling Targets* that help you accomplish your Objectives and *Assigned Targets* that are given to you. So you should first decide which Targets belong in which category and then try to rank them.

Enabling Targets (Tasks That Further Your Objectives)

Some Targets will obviously belong in this category. Here's a simple example: last year, finishing this book was a very high Objective for me, so writing the first draft of a particular chapter tended to be my highest-ranked Enabling Target during each week.

An Enabling Target can further an Objective in more subtle ways. Suppose that you've been told that next Monday you will be assigned a major project (i.e., an Objective) that will require your full attention. So, this week, you would like to get as many of your small tasks as possible out of the way to allow you to focus on this new project once next week begins. Completing these lower-priority Enabling Targets supports this new Objective by clearing away all distractions.

An Enabling Target can also advance an Objective by addressing the needs of those you manage. For instance, as I'll discuss in chapter 10, "Managing Your Team," managers should use their influence to acquire resources (money, time, and manpower) for their subordinates. Since you and your subordinates should generally be working toward the same goals, helping them reach their Objectives should help you achieve your own.

So list your Enabling Targets and rank them—with 10 the highest and 1 the lowest—based on the importance of the Objective in question and how effectively the Enabling Target furthers that particular Objective. As an illustration, I have ranked five of Joshua's Enabling Targets in figure 3.

Figure 3: ENABLING TARGETS

Target	Which Objective(s) Does the Target Advance?	Objective's Importance	How Effectively Does the Target Advance the Objective?	Overall Importance
Refine performance standards for sales staff	Increase profits by 15 percent	10	Very well	**10**
Develop a local marketing strategy	Increase profits by 15 percent	10	Somewhat	**7**
Hire more sales staff	Create a pleasant customer experience	8	Somewhat	**6**
Attend a tech expo	Meet people in retail industry	5	Somewhat	**3**
Hire an interior designer	Get fancier offices	1	Very Well	**2**

IMPORTANCE

Assigned Targets (Required Tasks)

These are the chores that pile up on a daily and weekly basis, but often seem unrelated to the bigger picture—*your* bigger picture. They include answering emails, responding to requests, and dealing with bureaucratic procedures. Technically, Assigned Targets could be considered "enabling"—they support your unstated Objective of "not getting fired." Still, they are very different from those that support your own specific Objectives, so it's useful to separate them out like this.

Although Assigned Targets are typically immediate and concrete, that doesn't mean they are important enough to consume you and your schedule. In many cases, you should consider them low priority and spend as little time on them as possible. In chapter 3, "Don't Sweat the Small Stuff," I will show you how to minimize the amount of time you devote to them. (Ideally, you might be able to delegate them to subordinates if you have them—see chapter 10 for a step-by-step guide to effective delegation.) For now, let's just focus on ranking these Assigned Targets. Here are some rules of thumb.

Generally, a request from your boss is more important than a request from elsewhere. If you perform poorly on your boss's requests, he or she will have serious doubts about your competence. By contrast, if you fail to answer a request from a random person in your organization, or if you dash off a superficial email in response, he or she may ask someone else for help and not judge you too harshly.

Among the tasks given to you by your boss, some of them have higher priorities than others. An effective manager will indicate the level of importance he or she gives to a specific project—whether he or she expects a "detailed report" or a "brief memo," for instance. Be alert for clues like these. If the priority of a specific Assigned Target is at all unclear, ask your boss directly.

In figure 4, I have ranked Joshua's three Assigned Targets, with 10 the highest and 1 the lowest. As you'll see, the rankings depend on who made the request and the level of indicated importance. Now put together your list of Assigned Targets and rank them according to these criteria.

Figure 4: ASSIGNED TARGETS

Target	Whose Request?	Implied Importance?	Overall Importance
Write weekly sales report for boss	Boss	High	9
Meet with area store managers	Peers	High	4
Participate in "community history day"	Boss	Low	2

IMPORTANCE ↑

5. ESTIMATE HOW YOU ACTUALLY SPEND YOUR TIME

Once you've ranked your Objectives and both types of Targets, you'll be ready to determine how effectively your actual schedule matches your high-priority goals.

However, most professionals have a much better grasp of how they spend their money than their time. Suppose you won $100,000 on a game show and I asked you after one year what you had done with that money. You would probably be able to tell me how much you had spent on what and how much you had saved. But unless you bill your time by the hour, you probably have only a vague sense of how much time you've devoted to various tasks and functions over the last year.

For example, once when I was giving a speech in Cleveland, I met a sales manager for a wealth management firm. He told me his sales reps all thought they spent more than two-thirds of their time visiting clients. But when he took a careful look at his reps' calendars, phone records, and travel logs, he found that those crucial visits to customers accounted for only *one-third* of the sales reps' time.

To get a good grasp of how you actually spend your time, take out your calendar or whatever tool you use to keep track of time. Then answer the six questions on the next page.

Your Work Schedule Now

How many hours do you spend at work versus other activities?

At work, what are the three main activities on which you spend the most time?

How many hours each week do you spend on company meetings, filling out forms or reports, or responding to emails?

Your Work Schedule Next Year

Do you expect your weekly schedule to be similar or different a year from now, as compared with today?

What will be your three main activities during the next year? Will they change over the course of the year?

How will you measure your success over the next year? What would constitute a failure in this time period?

Now go back and compare your allocations of time with your ranked list of Objectives and Targets. What percentage of your time do you spend on activities that help you meet your highest Objectives and Targets? How much time do you spend on lower-ranking items? Are you spending time on activities that didn't even make it onto your list?

6. ADDRESS THE MISMATCH BETWEEN PRIORITIES AND TIME SPENT

If you are like most professionals, you will find that you are spending no more than half of your time on your highest priorities. In a recent survey of 1,400 senior executives, the consulting firm McKinsey found that only

9 percent said they were "very satisfied" with the match between how they used their time and what they hoped to accomplish. Almost one-third said they were dissatisfied to some extent.[1] Furthermore, only 48 percent of the survey's respondents felt that their allocations of time were aligned to a great extent with the strategic priorities of their organizations. Those executives weren't goofing off; they were apparently *trying* to match their time allocation to their top priorities, but there was a lot of room for improvement.

Some professionals have not carefully thought about their Objectives and Targets. As a result, they often neglect an important goal—until it becomes a crisis, demanding their full time and effort. This pattern of reacting to crises—rather than proactively achieving priorities—was highly associated with McKinsey respondents' poor use of time. Those who were unsatisfied with their time allocation spent 30 percent of their workdays responding to crises—more than twice as much as those who said they were happy with how they spend their time.

CONCENTRATE ON YOUR PRIORITIES

To help align your time allocation with your priorities, put together a to-do list that drives them home. Start by integrating all your Objectives and Targets into one tiered list with the highest-priority items on the top half of the page. For each of those items, write down a precise deadline for completion. On the bottom of the page, keep track of all your lower-priority items and roughly estimate when you would like to finish each one.

The construction of this tiered to-do list is a dynamic process. I make minor adjustments each day; each weekend, I do a detailed review of my list and reconsider my priorities. I often add priority items to reflect new projects or current events, and I usually drop a few items that have become less important to me or are being done by others. In any case, you should keep your to-do list to one or two pages. If your to-do list is much longer than that, it won't be very useful.

Though I write my to-do list in longhand, various software products can help you manage your to-do list. These include Microsoft Outlook and a smartphone app called "Remember the Milk," which has more than 3.7 million subscribers.[2] These software packages have the advantage of allowing you to organize your list by due date or various other categories (such as work, study, or personal) at the touch of a button.

At higher levels in an organization, an executive's ego often causes him or her to spend too much time on certain activities. Personally, I used to struggle with invitations to speak at conferences. Because I like to talk and those speaking opportunities were flattering to my ego, I found myself constantly traveling long distances to make short speeches that hardly justified the travel time. As I continued my career, I reluctantly came to see that many of those speaking engagements furthered neither my Objectives nor my Targets. So I learned to politely refuse a good number of invitations by saying that my speaking calendar was already full. No offense was taken by the hosts, and I had more time to spend on more productive activities.

This discrepancy between top priorities and time allocation can occur at all levels of an organization. When I was a trustee of a Boston hospital, I had the pleasure of meeting a young employee named Cynthia, who worked in the hospital's financial department. In January one year, she described to me her three top Objectives for the year: understanding how the health care industry operates, learning how to manage people, and expanding her network of contacts.

At the end of the year, she reported that she had been too busy dealing with day-to-day tasks to make meaningful progress toward any of her Objectives. "I spent every day answering phone calls from insurance companies, dealing with budget requests from other units, and preparing the next quarter's financial statement," she complained. "I was so absorbed in responding to the needs of others that I didn't have time to focus on my own goals."

Although Cynthia has less discretion over her use of time than a senior executive, she still could have done a better job matching her time to her most important goals. I suggested to her that over the next year, she should devote less time to some of her daily Targets, either by doing them more efficiently or by recognizing that certain tasks require only a quick-and-dirty effort. I then suggested that she use the time gained to take practical steps to pursue her Objectives—by signing up for a course, asking to manage a small group, and meeting professionals working in other parts of the hospital.

FIX THE MISMATCH

Throughout the rest of this book, I'm going to try to address the causes of this mismatch and offer strategies to resolve them. Broadly, my solutions fit into two categories: personal and organizational.

On the personal side, I will suggest some specific techniques for focusing on your highest priorities. For instance, I will explain how to use a daily calendar to make sure your appointments support your Objectives and Targets (chapter 4). I will also show you how to better focus on your Objectives and Targets through a productive daily routine at the office (chapter 4) and while you're traveling (chapter 5).

You may also need to make deeper changes in your own personal habits. In particular, those who procrastinate tend to avoid working on important activities in favor of pleasant distractions. Others are perfectionists who don't know when to stop working on an assignment and move on. I offer strategies for dealing with both types of unproductive behaviors (chapters 2 and 3). Furthermore, many managers spend too much time involved in the projects of their subordinates. These micromanagers should learn how to delegate more responsibility to those who report to them (chapter 10).

On the organizational side, I'll discuss additional roadblocks to your productive use of time. Poorly run internal meetings, for example (chapter 6), can take up a huge portion of your workday—often without meaningfully contributing to achieving any of your Objectives or Targets. You might be spending too much time and effort dealing with a bloated bureaucracy and burdensome procedures (chapter 3). In later chapters, I will show you some strategies for dealing with these organizational barriers.

TAKEAWAYS

1. To be productive, you need to articulate your goals clearly and prioritize them.

2. You should try hard to match how you spend your time to your top priorities.

3. To enhance this match, write down your long-term Career Aims (5+ years), your medium-range Objectives (3–24 months), and your short-term Targets (1 week or less).

4. For each type of goal, develop a clear rank order of priorities.

5. To rank your Objectives, consider both supply (what you are good at and like to do) and demand (what your organization and your boss need from you).

6. To rank your Targets, consider the extent to which they further your high-ranked Objectives, either directly or indirectly.

7. A high-ranked Target can also be a task that your boss considers to be very important, if it is consistent with an organizational Objective.

8. Compare these rankings with how you currently allocate your time. If you find a mismatch, diagnose it. What's the cause?

9. Some solutions will require changes in your personal habits; many professionals procrastinate or micromanage too much.

10. Other solutions will require changes in your organization's procedures—or the way you deal with them.

2

FOCUS ON THE
FINAL PRODUCT

I recently asked a researcher at Harvard Business School to evaluate the strategy of a Chinese insurance company that had purchased a Chinese bank. She thoroughly scoured several books and methodically searched hundreds of Internet pages to compile every detail about the company she could find. After a week, she presented me with a lengthy report on the history of the company, its management team, and its financial performance. But what did all that data mean in terms of the company's strategy? She couldn't answer—she was lost in a flood of information.

So I suggested that she stop researching and instead formulate a tentative set of conclusions about the Chinese company's strategy. After taking some time to think, she hypothesized that the company was trying to become a "financial supermarket" by offering an array of insurance, banking, and securities services to its wealthy customers. With those tentative conclusions in mind, she was able to focus on the critical issues for the success of the company's strategy: its cross-marketing plan, techno-logical platform, and employee training.

This story illustrates my second big idea: focusing on the final product. This idea is critical to efficiently completing your high-priority projects, which often are broad in scope and complex in content. I'm going to teach you how to quickly formulate a set of tentative conclusions to guide your work. The key word here is "tentative"—you should stop midway to re-assess the final product in light of what you've learned so far. However, to apply this idea to your high-priority projects, you'll probably have to overcome two constraints: your own tendency to procrastinate and your organization's emphasis on hours worked.

START AT THE END

I have seen many professionals waste days or weeks at the beginning of a knowledge-based project by gathering reams of information without a clear sense of the key questions to be answered. Although extensive re-search might seem a logical first step, it's actually very inefficient. There are literally thousands of facts that *could* be relevant to any project; do you really want to collect them all? No, because most of them won't be sig-nificant to your conclusions and some won't even make it into your report.

Instead, think hard at the start of a project about where it's going: what are the critical issues, and how are they likely to be resolved? After a day or so of gathering relevant information, write down your tentative conclusions for the project. These will allow you to more quickly engage in analysis—rather than description—by providing a focus for your subsequent research. Write the conclusions in the form of a rebuttable hypothesis that can be revised as the project progresses. You might even have to scrap your conclusions completely as you learn new facts. That's fine. This approach is similar to the scientific method: you generate a set of hypotheses; *then* you test them out, not the other way around.

Let's take a simple example. Imagine that your boss needs you to pick a new location for your organization's main office in your city. You could spend weeks researching all of the commercial buildings in the city and then make a comprehensive presentation to your boss. Alternatively, you could start by formulating, with your boss's help, the realistic parameters for your new offices. What neighborhoods would be desirable, and which would be out of bounds? What is the range of rent your organization would be willing to pay? With these guidelines in hand, you could narrow down your search and get to a better result more quickly.

This same methodology increases the productivity of any project involving interviews. A few years ago, I asked a graduate student to interview the executives of foundations that had made mission-related investments in private commercial ventures—for example, a cancer foundation buying stock in a small biotech company that was testing out a new cancer therapy. She carefully put together a standard set of questions for interviewing the participants in the investing process—the trustees of the foundations and the investment analysts selecting the companies to invest in.

Although her questions would have generated a great deal of information, they were overly broad in scope. At my direction, she developed a set of rebuttable hypotheses about the key constraints on such mission-related investments, such as the trustees' concerns about the legal risks of such investments. With these hypotheses in hand, she revised her questionnaires to focus on these critical constraints and strategies.

I use this method constantly at Harvard Business School, where I often work with students to research, write, and publish cases for the school's courses. The students are always surprised when I ask them to begin by formulating a teaching plan for a class session based on the case. I explain that it's impossible to write a good case until you decide what the students should get out of the class. Are you trying to teach the students how to motivate employees? Deal with a shifting customer base? Evaluate a new business opportunity? In order to avoid hours of wasted time and effort in writing a case, you've got to focus on the end result first.

THE MIDFLIGHT CHECK

Though you should start by generating tentative conclusions, you should give them another look midway through the project—and make revisions in light of what you've learned so far. In other words, you need to start with rebuttable hypotheses to guide your research, but you should not wait until the end to evaluate them. By pausing and reflecting midway through the project, you will be able to focus the second half of your work on a better set of hypotheses.

Let's go back to the graduate student conducting the interviews about foundations buying stock in mission-related companies. By generating tentative conclusions at the start, she was able to design questionnaires aimed at what she believed was the most critical issue: the legal risks of mission-related investing. However, after conducting a few interviews, she found that trustees faced a bigger problem: recruiting and paying talented investment professionals. So she formulated new interview questions to explore those challenges. In other words, she revised the questionnaires so they were better aimed at the critical issues as they became apparent.

The midflight check is particularly useful when a project involves pro-fessionals from different parts of an organization. I remember an effort to develop an annuity product (which accepts premiums from customers during their working years and pays them monthly during their retirement years). In conducting their initial survey, the marketing experts found that most customers wanted a guaranteed monthly payment, plus a higher payment whenever the stock market rose. During our midflight check, the marketing group shared those results with the portfolio managers who would be invest-ing these premiums. The managers explained that this combination was not practical since the potential for realizing an upside stock gain generally en-tails the possibility of incurring a significant stock loss. It was a useful reality check for the marketing experts, who revised their survey to reflect products that the company could actually deliver.

This ongoing process of formulating tentative conclusions and revising them is especially critical to software development projects. At the start of such projects, the business users typically meet with the software developers to agree on general specifications. Then the business users expect to sit back, wait a few months, and receive a completed software package. During those months, however, the developers are making hundreds of decisions to implement the general specifications—*without checking in with the end users*. As a result, the process often takes much more time and money than anticipated and the end users are often unhappy with the final product.

I've learned to avoid many of these problems by having a monthly meeting between the business users and software developers to refine the project specifications and resolve new issues as they arise. When a software project starts to run over time and budget, I personally attend the next monthly meeting and ask the developers: *what three changes in the project specifications would most significantly reduce the time and cost of the project?* The developers often suggest deleting certain features. In my experience, the business users always agree to make at least two of the three suggested changes, saying that the features would be "nice to have" but aren't essential. This critical input, which the developers have no other way of getting, can have a dramatic effect on the project.

STOP PROCRASTINATING TODAY!

In order to quickly formulate tentative conclusions, you need to be ready to jump right into the meat of the project. Unfortunately, many professionals have trouble getting started on their highest priorities. Instead, they procrastinate by distracting themselves with more pleasant tasks.

Procrastination is easy enough to recognize when it takes its stereotypical form—say, if you're browsing Facebook instead of responding to your boss's emails. But sometimes it's not so obvious. Instead of working on your highest Target, you may be working on something less important because it seems easier. For instance, a professor may put off creating a teaching plan for tomorrow's class by grading yesterday's multiple-choice exam. Some commentators refer to this practice as "structured procrastination" and suggest it as a remedy for those who can't start projects.[1] I disagree. Although this practice is better than procrastinating to the point of doing nothing, it's still an unproductive strategy.

I myself have unwittingly engaged in "structured procrastination." For instance, when I became president of Fidelity Investments, I found myself attending many presentations by officials of various public companies as they marched through Fidelity's offices. Although the presentations were more fascinating than reviewing budgets or systems projects, they did not help me accomplish my high-priority Objectives and Targets. Those meetings were not meant for me—they were designed primarily to allow Fidelity analysts to ask tough questions of executives before investing in their companies. Soon I stopped going to those presentations.

Though all of us put off difficult tasks to some extent, others literally cannot finish a project without a deadline, and they cannot work hard on a project until near the deadline. As one young professional told me, "I wish I could get motivated and do a little advance planning. But I just can't get going until the due date is really close." This professional is not alone: researchers estimate that roughly 15 percent of adults are chronic procrastinators.[2]

Chronic procrastinators pay a high personal price for their habit. They are very anxious in the early days of a project—when they are thinking about what needs to be done but not actually doing anything except avoiding work. As the deadline nears, they go into panic mode: they eliminate all other aspects of their lives and work through the night in the final days or weeks before the deadline. This roller-coaster rhythm not only produces shoddy work but also alienates their friends and families, who get tired of watching the same bad movie over and over again.

If you are a chronic procrastinator, here are a few suggestions.

1.   Some projects may be difficult to start because their size and complexity seem overwhelming. To counteract this feeling, break the project into smaller pieces and get going on the first steps. Once you get started, it is easier to continue.

2. If you are easily distracted and constantly find other things to do, you'll have to be merciless in controlling your work environment. Clear your docket, set aside time to concentrate on the big project, and cut off access to distractions such as social networking websites and video games.

3. If you are a severe procrastinator, you may suffer from a deep-seated fear of failure; you may not believe that the final product will be any good.[3] If you think this may be a factor in your tendency to procrastinate, I strongly recommend seeking the help of a psychotherapist who can help you deal with this fear.

No matter what type of procrastinator you are, you can help yourself by creating evenly spaced, minideadlines—interim dates for completing specific stages of the project. In other words, if you can't work without a deadline, create more deadlines.

When Professor Dan Ariely studied a group of MIT students, he found that there is considerable value to setting your own deadlines.[4] But when given the chance, many of his subjects skewed the deadlines toward the end of the project, which gave them time to procrastinate. Don't make the same mistake: if you want to be most productive, set your deadlines so they create an evenly paced schedule for work, with similar amounts of times allotted to comparable tasks.

For slight to moderate procrastinators, I suggest that each of these minideadlines be tied to a personal reward for completing tasks, such as allowing yourself to eat an ice cream sundae or watch a favorite TV show. Such rewards, especially if "enforced" by a friend or spouse, can make minideadlines a significant boost to productivity.

For severe procrastinators, however, or for complex tasks that are particularly daunting, rewards may not be enough. In that case, *make yourself accountable to someone else*—preferably your boss, although a colleague whose work is connected with yours may do the trick. Give your boss a list of your minideadlines and agree in writing to meet them—making the minideadline real in every respect. Don't be embarrassed to confess your procrastination habit to your boss. For starters, your boss is probably well aware of your habit. Second, you are taking concrete steps to address it, which benefits everyone you work with. Any boss who doesn't welcome your initiative is, in my view, a very poor manager.

FOCUS ON RESULTS, NOT HOURS

If you can avoid procrastination and quickly home in on the final product, you will be able to get your work done in much less time. Unfortunately, your newly increased efficiency may put you at odds with your organization's culture if it places too much emphasis on hours worked.

In some professions, the misplaced emphasis on time arises from the hourly billing system—which infuriated me when I was a practicing lawyer. But even without a distortive billing system, many managers in other sectors wrongly assume, sometimes subconsciously, that spending more hours in the office leads to a better product. If you're going to succeed in such organizations while working fewer hours, you will need strategies to manage this tension between hours and results.

Billable Hours

I recently overheard a conversation between two young professionals, a New York lawyer and a Chicago consultant. The lawyer proudly announced that he had billed three thousand hours the previous year. In practice, that means working twelve hours a day, six days a week, because not every hour is billable. By any measure, that's a brutal workload. But the consultant immediately topped him. She had worked fifteen hours a day, she boasted, and most of that time had been on the road!

Although the two of them seemed to find this conversation entertaining, I doubt their clients were impressed by their long hours. To a client, the key measures of success are results and costs. If those young professionals could produce the same results in fewer hours, their clients would be happier and the professionals would have more time for their personal lives.

Unfortunately, the cultures of many professional service firms—legal, accounting, and consulting—strongly promote the virtues of long hours over results. Young professionals are under tremendous pressure to meet annual billable hour targets; they receive bonuses and personal recognition for burning the midnight oil.

However, billing by the hour creates a potential conflict of interest between professionals and their clients—which should be a subject of concern on both sides of the fence. Lawyers have little incentive to be efficient with their time, and clients worry about that. Conversely, when lawyers charge $600 an hour, clients may be reluctant to call their lawyer to discuss a significant issue, and lawyers are constantly cleaning up the messes created when clients call them too late.

When I was a partner at a Washington, D.C., law firm, I quickly came to despise the system of billable hours because it punished me for being efficient. I specialized in complex transactions for financial institutions, and I was often able to answer clients' questions quickly. As a result, my billable hours on each transaction were relatively low; my expert knowledge and efficient approach were working against me. So I wrote to my clients that in the future I would be sharply increasing my hourly rate unless they objected. Not a single client objected—and one even told me that I was the "fastest lawyer on the East Coast"!

Nevertheless, high hourly rates don't really solve the problem. So how can this model be fundamentally changed? If you're the client of a professional services firm, you have by far the most leverage to implement more productive ways to get legal work done. Large organizations can build an internal legal department (based on annual salaries) for all but the most complex matters. And organizations of any size can solicit competitive bids from qualified law firms on a value-oriented basis—i.e., arrangements *not* based on hours.

Indeed, in the tough economic climate following the 2008 financial crisis, more clients began insisting on value-oriented billing—and law firms responded. Between 2008 and 2012, according to one survey, law firms reported that revenue from non-hourly-fee arrangements nearly doubled.[5] These alternatives have always existed in the legal world, and I'm glad to see them used more widely. They include a fixed fee for an entire legal episode, such as a patent application; a contingent fee on a successful legal result, such as a verdict for damages; and a monthly retainer for repeat work, such as real estate closings.

Though associates have less power than clients or partners, they can still play a role in reforming the billing system of their firm. As pressures from clients mount, partners may become more receptive to similar pressure from associates, who are known to be miserable under the current system. In a survey of associates at top law firms, 85 percent responded that they would like to reduce their hours by an average of 15 percent and most would be willing to take a proportionate pay cut.[6] So if you want your firm to change its pricing model, you are not alone; this chorus of dissatisfaction could help motivate your firm to adopt a more sensible billing system.

If you're really unhappy and can't reform the billing practices at your firm, you can always leave. In-house legal departments don't generally base pay on hours worked. And if you decide that it's more fun to be a client, as I did, you can try to move from the practice of law to another type of work, such as starting your own business.

Face Time

Even organizations that don't bill by the hour often place too much emphasis on time spent at work.[7] Punching a time clock made sense in the industrial age, when assembly lines moved at a constant speed and workers performed simple, repeated actions. And it still may make sense for standardized kinds of work. But it makes no sense for professionals. Their contribution is not the time they spend on their work but the value they create through their knowledge.

Consider Fred and Ashley, who work in an insurance company. Fred always comes in early and stays late. Ashley sometimes shows up to work at 10 a.m., after a morning jog. You might assume that Fred is more productive and hardworking than Ashley, but how do you really know? Fred may be spending half his day managing his fantasy football team or attending meetings that waste his time. Ashley may be ruminating on new ideas during her jog—and then implementing them in a disciplined manner once she gets to the office. You can't measure a professional's value simply by counting how many hours he or she spends sitting at a desk.

Unfortunately, research suggests that corporate managers still confuse "face time" with quality of results.[8] In a 2010 study involving thirty corporate offices in northern California, managers indicated that they highly respected their subordinates who were seen at the office during normal business hours as well as on the weekend and in the evening. The researchers also found that their opinions were often formed subconsciously. That is, managers in their study *believed* that they cared only about results, but subconsciously they placed a large emphasis on the hours their employees spent at work.[9]

If you are a manager, you can counter this subconscious bias by making it clear to your subordinates that you care about their getting the work done, rather than the hours they spend at the office. Set clear goals and metrics, and trust your subordinates to do their work (see chapter 10, "Managing Your Team," for a detailed discussion). Reinforce the message when schedules need to be changed. The head of a Chicago financial firm, who uses this method, told me about a typical conversation he had with an employee who asked for time off to go to his child's birthday party. When the employee promised that he would make up the hours missed, the boss protested, "I want you to get a really good result on this project, in terms of the metrics that we've agreed upon. But it's up to you how many hours that takes and when to work them."

If you are lower on the totem pole and work for a boss who watches the clock, you'll have to start by earning your boss's trust. As you gain a track record for producing high-quality results, you may be able to negotiate more freedom. Chapter 11, "Managing Your Boss," will provide you with some tools for developing such a collaborative relationship with your superiors.

In the meantime, you may be able to reduce your hours by taking advantage of your firm's work flow. For instance, at many investment banks, the daily assignments from managing directors don't come down to the associates until close to noon. That leaves many associates hanging around in the morning without much to do. If those associates were to schedule medical appointments ending at 11 a.m. or regularly hit the gym for an extended morning workout, their productivity would not be significantly impaired.

No matter where you stand in the hierarchy, you can contribute to changing the culture of your organization by avoiding snide remarks on the subject of time. If a colleague is leaving at 4 p.m., don't make a joke about "banker's hours." If someone shows up twenty minutes "late" in the morning, don't derisively comment, "Look who's here."

Seemingly innocuous comments such as these can reinforce a culture that values face time. Trust that your colleague is getting his or her work done. If you need something from a colleague who is leaving early, say so directly—e.g., "Michael, could I ask you a quick question about those numbers before you go?" If you find that a subordinate's work is not up to par, don't focus the discussion on the hours he or she spends at work. Give feedback about the final product.

TAKEAWAYS

1. Focus on achieving the best results, not spending the highest number of hours at work.

2. Write out the tentative conclusions of a complex problem before gathering too much data. This will focus your research.

3. Formulate your conclusions in the form of rebuttable

hypotheses, which can be changed by evidence and new insights.

4. Stop midway through any project to revise your methods and conclusions in light of what you've learned so far.

5. If a project involves teams from multiple parts of a large organization, use the midflight check as a chance for all teams to share their intermediate results and coordinate approaches.

6. To help you get started, reward yourself when you complete a task—say, with ice cream or a TV show.

7. Set minideadlines before the actual deadline if you find yourself unable to get started. If necessary, make the minideadlines official by submitting them to your boss.

8. If you're a professional whose work is charged by the billable hour—or if you're a client of such a firm— encourage the firm's partners to reform their billing systems to better reflect value produced rather than hours logged.

9. Don't assume that your colleagues' productivity can be measured by the number of hours they spend at work.

10. Don't support the office culture of "face time"; avoid snide comments when someone leaves early or arrives late.

3

DON'T SWEAT THE SMALL STUFF

In every organization, some employees spend an inordinate amount of time on tasks that don't really matter. For instance, I once worked with an accountant whose job included preparing quarterly sales reports for a firm's top executives. Although the executives told him that they needed only ballpark estimates, he devoted almost a week to analyzing each quarter's sales data and making sure that the numbers were perfectly correct. As a result, his boss was reluctant to give him any new major projects—if it took him a week to estimate quarterly sales, how long would it take him to evaluate the financial statements of a merger candidate?

Though attention to detail is usually considered a positive attribute, your time commitment should vary according to the importance of a project and the needs of your audience. It may take you one day to do B+ work, but it may take the rest of the week to bump it up to an A. For your highest-ranked Objectives and Targets, it is usually worth spending that extra time and effort. But for most of your low-priority tasks, B+ is quite often "good enough."

In this chapter, I will tell you about my key techniques for "not sweating the small stuff" to help you spend more time on your highest priorities. Then I'll show you how to mitigate personal and bureaucratic forces that lead you to spend excessive time on low-priority tasks.

OHIO (ONLY HANDLE IT ONCE)

Once I received a letter with a deficiency notice from a state tax agency. Since the deficiency was small and I was busy, I put the letter on a shelf of a bookcase in my office. A week later I remembered that letter and wanted to send a response. But where had I left it? I wasted an hour searching for that letter—and then I had to read it again to remember what the deficiency was about in the first place.

Countless mistakes like that made me a convert to the principle of OHIO. This has nothing to do with the Buckeye State; it stands for "Only Handle It Once." This means tackling your low-priority items immediately when you receive them, if possible. If you let a backlog develop, you will waste a lot of time and increase your anxiety level.

For example, every day you receive a barrage of requests for your time and knowledge—from your coworkers, your family, your friends, and people you don't know. When you get a request, decide promptly whether you should ignore it or offer a response. As a general guideline, you should probably decide *not* to respond to 80 percent of all requests. These include spam from advertisers, daily reports from national groups, and even emails from your own organization, where you're just one of hundreds of recipients and don't need to take action. But they also include personalized requests that are not worth your time.

My general guideline is based on the 80-20 rule: that you get 80 percent of your benefit from 20 percent of your input. For instance, many sales reps make 80 percent of their money from 20 percent of their clients, but they spend most of their time dealing with the other 80 percent. Unless they can divert their less profitable clients to an assistant or website, they may be better off "firing" those clients and focusing on the 20 percent that actually drive their earnings.[1] Apply a similar ratio to your personalized mail. You may need to be ruthless in determining which requests merit your time and which can be delegated or ignored.

If you determine that you need or want to respond to a request, figure out whether the request can be answered immediately or needs more information for a thoughtful response. If you can respond immediately, do so. If you need to wait a few days to gather information, put a reminder in your calendar to respond to the request on a specific date in the future.

Waiting—for an hour, a day, or a week—to respond to a legitimate request will double or triple the time involved. In the best case, you will have to reread the request and think again about the issues it raises. In the worst case, you will spend a significant amount of time trying to find the request again—before you can reread it and think again about the issues. Furthermore, if you delay a week before responding, that will lead the requester to think you don't care about him or her.

Suppose you receive an email invitation to attend a conference on a subject directly relevant to your work. Under the principle of OHIO, you can see if the date and location are convenient and then immediately accept the invitation and book a flight if you decide to go.

Alternatively, you can wait a few days to turn your attention to this invitation. To begin with, you will have to search through your past emails to find the invitation. Then you will have to reread it, reconsult your calendar, and decide if you want to accept. These time-consuming extra steps can be avoided if you respond immediately to the conference invitation. Although the time you save seems minimal for each individual request, these are the sorts of behaviors that free up *hours* over the long run. By responding immediately to important requests, you will also impress the person making the request.

MANAGING YOUR INBOX

Aside from the OHIO principle, here are a few tips to help you deal efficiently with emails:

- Don't get addicted to your email by checking it constantly! You'll only distract yourself when you should be doing something else more productive. Instead, check your email on a set schedule— every hour or so. One caveat: if your boss insists that you reply to his or her emails immediately, you may grudgingly have to meet his or her time demands.

- If you want to be more ambitious in kicking your email addiction, you'll need the cooperation of your colleagues. Work collectively with your firm to call an "email holiday"—a set hour (or more) each week when emails are banned.[2]

- If there's a long thread of emails back and forth, look at the most recent reply first. The latest reply may have resolved whatever issues were brought up earlier in the conversation.

- Your inbox may be overflowing with "FYI" emails copied to you from your subordinates. If you are overwhelmed by such emails, ask your colleagues and employees to be more selective about what they send along.

- Similarly, think before you hit "reply all." Does everyone really need to see your latest response?

- Lastly, a big pet peeve of mine: resist the urge to send a one-word reply saying, "Thanks!" Instead, show your thankfulness by minimizing the flow of emails to your helper.

MULTITASK CAUTIOUSLY

As you apply the OHIO principle, you will find tasks that *can't* be done immediately. Some are complex and important and require your full concentration; for such projects, you should quickly formulate a set of tentative conclusions, as I discussed in the previous chapter. Other tasks are simply long and tedious; you can't finish them immediately, but you don't need to devote much brainpower to them.

You can efficiently accomplish many of these low-priority chores by multitasking. I regularly take advantage of this strategy. I check—and sometimes respond to—my email on a BlackBerry as I stand in elevators or sit in taxis. I write short memos while listening to conference calls. In meetings where my full brainpower isn't needed, I discreetly catch up on my reading. Being a compulsive multitasker has significantly boosted my productivity. Nevertheless, from personal experience, I can also tell you to beware of the cognitive and social limitations of multitasking.

How to Divide Your Brainpower

Executives dream of attending an important meeting while simultaneously reading an in-depth analysis of a possible acquisition. However, this is not feasible if you want to devote anything close to your full attention to both activities. The brain (specifically the prefrontal cortex) is simply not capable of fully focusing on more than one activity at the same time. So when people say that they are "multitasking," their brains are really toggling back and forth among two or more activities—focusing on the acquisition analysis for ten seconds, then the meeting for five seconds, and so forth. This constant switching is quite inefficient. At every switch, your brain has to restart and refocus, wasting time and energy. You would be much better off doing one task at a time if either is critically important to you, as many researchers have pointed out.[3]

However, most people don't multitask by trying to perform two important and strenuous mental tasks. Rather, they multitask by eating a sandwich while listening to a long conference call or checking email while attending a boring meeting. The key here is that neither activity really requires your full attention—you're not trying to absorb and analyze all the information you receive. Instead, you're monitoring one activity and waiting for cues that you should switch your attention to the other activity. When used this way, multitasking is a terrific method of accomplishing low-priority tasks.

I frequently multitask when I listen to conference calls that cover current political events in Washington. These calls cover many subjects of minimal interest to me, such as agricultural subsidies or political fundraising. When those subjects are being discussed, I might also be skimming a report from my "to do" pile. But when I hear the conference call turning to a subject of significance to me, such as pension reform or securities regulation, I stop reading to give my full attention to the Washington developments in those two fields.

Similarly, at many board meetings, the first five or ten minutes are devoted to routine matters: approving the minutes from the prior meeting and reviewing the current meeting's agenda. Since I'm well prepared for the meeting, those five or ten minutes are a waste of my time. I prefer to use the time to quietly catch up with my reading on my iPad—since all the board materials are also on my iPad, no one is the wiser. However, I stop reading and focus on the meeting once those preliminaries are completed.

So when you're deciding whether to multitask, think about the relative importance of each task and how much brainpower it requires. Don't try to do two important tasks simultaneously. Feel free to multitask if both tasks are low priority. If one task is important and the other isn't, I believe that multitasking is generally appropriate. But there is an exception to this general rule: if the important task is so critical—say, defusing a land mine—that you don't want to risk sparing any brainpower, don't distract yourself with a second task!

Understanding the Social Limitations of Multitasking

As I've learned the hard way, the social considerations of multitasking can be delicate if you are interacting with another person. Multitasking on a conference call is one thing; the other participants usually don't know what you're doing. But if you multitask at a face-to-face meeting, other attendees may be offended. As you might imagine, this has been brought to my attention several times. Over the years I've learned that by checking my email at meetings, I may unwittingly convey the impression that I'm not taking the meeting—or the attendees—seriously. So I've learned to accommodate their sensitivities in many situations. The appropriateness of multitasking depends on the context and people involved.

Some rules of thumb: you should generally not multitask when dealing with customers or potential customers. They will usually treat it as a sign of disrespect and you are likely to lose them to a competitor. Similarly, don't multitask when you are meeting with people who wield power over your business life, such as bosses and regulators. You cannot afford to risk offending them. Furthermore, don't multitask in any circumstance in which you want to convey your total commitment: for instance, when leading a motivational session for employees. In such a situation, multitasking will undermine the message you are trying to convey.

Although this advice would seem to be common sense, well-meaning people (aside from me) have made foolish mistakes in this area. In 2009, the billionaire businessman Tom Golisano paid a political call on Malcolm Smith, the Democratic leader of the New York State Senate. While Golisano tried to discuss state politics, Smith reportedly checked his email multiple times on his BlackBerry. Golisano was so incensed by this apparent disrespect that he convinced two Democratic senators to switch parties, giving Republicans control of the State Senate.[4]

In other situations, especially with colleagues, it is socially acceptable to multitask. In some cases, your colleagues are partners to your productivity: they want you to get a lot done because that will help *their* productivity. In others, they know the heavy volume of your workload and accept your need to multitask in order to get everything done. Indeed, some of your colleagues may be multitasking as they are working with *you*.

But then there are the ambiguous situations where you're not sure how your colleagues would react to multitasking. In that case, ask! When I'm unsure, I ask, "Do you mind if I multitask?" If people mind, they will say so. But most people don't mind because I've had the courtesy to ask.

There is an evolving etiquette that allows you to check emails discreetly and occasionally during internal meetings. In a poll in 2009,[5] one-third of workers said that they frequently checked emails during meetings. That percentage will surely rise as society becomes ever more connected. However, when "checking emails" turns into prolonged periods of inattention—not to mention checking Facebook or texting your friends—it's inappropriate and unprofessional.

If I ran the world, I would have no problem with emailing during meetings as long as it was done quickly and not distracting to others. But there is a generation gap on this issue. Roughly one-third of senior executives find emailing in meetings disrespectful.[6] I serve on one corporate board that bans emails at meetings but holds "email breaks" on a regular basis. However, I also serve as a strategic adviser to a group of young biotech executives, all of whom bring their smartphones to board meetings and check them periodically. There is no "right" answer on emailing; each group of colleagues has to develop an acceptable norm. Junior employees in particular would be wise to have an express discussion with their bosses about acceptable email behavior at meetings.

Accepting Imperfection

The OHIO principle and the strategy of multitasking should help you dispense with your small tasks as quickly as possible. But many professionals would question the wisdom of both of these strategies: "If I spend only a little time on each task, how can I ensure that everything gets done properly, without any mistakes?"

Unfortunately, this mind-set is counterproductive. Professionals who demand perfection out of every task—without regard to significance—will soon find themselves overwhelmed by the sheer volume of their low-priority tasks. As a result, they won't have time to accomplish their most important goals.

A colleague of mine used to spend days, and sometimes weeks, perfecting minor internal policies and procedures. He took care to address every conceivable contingency and cover every nuance, no matter how esoteric. By the end of the process, the policies were replete with footnotes and defined terms. Though completeness is a virtue, this level of depth was unnecessary because the particular risks involved were remote and inconsequential. But because he took so long on every minor project, his bosses were wary of handing him new or interesting assignments. He might have created the most comprehensive procedures, but at what cost?

This overemphasis on minor details leads some professionals to micromanage. In order to avoid even the slightest mistake, they feel the need to get overly involved in the projects of their subordinates, making every decision and directing every task. As a result, the manager spends far more time than is necessary to complete the project. I'll discuss in chapter 10, "Managing Your Team," how best to delegate functions more productively—but here's a key point: give your subordinates substantial freedom to accomplish noncritical projects, even if that means a greater risk of mistakes. In that way, you can have more time to focus on your highest priorities.

Overcoming perfectionism is critical to becoming more efficient at work. When you spend a lot of time on a specific task, you typically run into diminishing returns. It can take you a few hours to write a descriptive memo that covers the consensus view of a certain topic. But it could take you another week to write a memo that develops new approaches to the same subject. It makes sense for you to spend the extra time and effort in pursuing one of your highest-ranked Objectives or Targets. However, you would be wasting your time to devote that much attention to low-priority tasks.

It's true that having a keen eye for details may be a useful trait at the beginning of your career. Consider Marcus, a low-level employee in the human resources department. Marcus might rightfully spend hours going over the fine points of the firm's compensation plans for hourly workers, checking for inconsistencies or ambiguities. In other words, because his primary job is to look over the details, he should make sure they are right.

On the other hand, as you move up in your career, you will need to worry less about every little detail. If Marcus wants to advance within the department, he will need to become more skilled at handling delicate personnel disputes and advising senior managers. To be successful in those areas, he will have to spend less time worrying about the intricacies of the compensation plans for hourly workers. If Marcus continues to obsess over minor details, he will never have enough time to develop higher-level skills.

EVADING BUREAUCRATIC ROADBLOCKS

Even if you recognize the need to complete small tasks quickly, you may find yourself blocked by time-consuming bureaucratic rules. For instance, when I worked for the Commonwealth of Massachusetts, I had to fill out an elaborate form in order to be reimbursed for small expense items such as an official lunch. If a colleague wanted to move furniture from one office to another, she was forbidden to do so herself. Instead, she had to call the Department of Corrections and request that a team of prisoners— orange jumpsuits and all—be brought in to move the furniture. Silly rules aren't confined to government; some of the corporate email programs I've encountered filter out any email with even the mildest off-color word.

Don't get me wrong: some bureaucratic rules are very useful. Indeed, if there is a relatively high potential for serious harm, a standardized set of procedures can effectively reduce risk. For instance, safety regulations for nuclear power plants help nuclear technicians avoid meltdowns, and regimented checklists for airline pilots help them safely get from point A to point B.

But I'm not talking about rules like these. Rather, I'm talking about rules that force professionals to spend a lot of time on low-priority tasks. I'm talking about bureaucracy that requires employees to fill out long forms or get preapproval from different layers of management. In my experience, rules like these are based on *fear*—a fear that employees will make too many errors if they are given the slightest bit of freedom.

Here's an example from the U.S. Department of Defense. In the military, as in civilian life, officers often want to move people around to different units or different functions. However, as then secretary of defense Robert Gates observed, "A request for a dog-handling team in Afghanistan—or for any other unit—has to go through no fewer than five four-star headquarters in order to be processed, validated, and eventually dealt with."[7] Instead of planning operational details, officers were forced to spend too much time getting their reposition requests approved. Fortunately, Secretary Gates has worked to reduce some of those bureaucratic burdens by eliminating redundant headquarters[8] and streamlining acquisition procedures.

So what can you do when your employees are faced with burdensome and overly broad rules?[9] If you are in a position where you can change them, follow Gates's example: order a comprehensive review of all your organization's rules. Figure out what purpose each rule is trying to achieve, whether that purpose is important, and whether the rule actually works the way it's supposed to. Then weigh the benefits against the burden it causes to employees.

But you can't just talk to top executives and compliance officers; in a big bureaucracy, their image of a particular rule may be quite detached from reality. To get a better sense of how a rule works in practice, speak to the front-line employees (or customers!) who actually need to follow it. You'll likely discover that many rules waste too much time or impose too much control.

If you're not lucky enough to be in a position to eliminate those rules, learn how to deal with them—or get around them—as best as possible. Here are some specific suggestions:

- Learn the purpose of the relevant rule—there may be a legitimate reason that your proposed activity is restricted. If so, learn how to most efficiently deal with the rule; it is likely that it will come up repeatedly in your work, so you should be prepared to handle it with as little headache as possible.

- If the spirit of the rule is outdated or should not apply to your activity, try to figure out a creative way to interpret your proposed activity as outside the letter of the rule. For example, some companies quite reasonably prohibit flying first class in order to save money. But that prohibition should not apply to an employee who pays a low coach fare and gets a free upgrade.

- If a favorable interpretation is not feasible or too legally risky, ask for an exemption from the rule.

TAKEAWAYS

1. Discard most of the emails and letters you receive—80 percent of your inbox is crammed with low-priority items.

2. Respond immediately to important requests. Don't waste time by having to refind an email or think twice about an appointment.

3. Multitasking is a good way of accomplishing low-priority tasks efficiently. It's perfectly okay to skim a report while listening to a conference call.

4. Don't try to multitask if both activities are mentally demanding. The rapid switching between topics wastes your brain's energy.

5. Don't multitask in front of actual or potential customers; they expect your full attention.

6. Reach an express agreement with your colleagues on what are acceptable emailing practices at meetings.

7. Accept that you can't do every task perfectly. Turn in B+ work for your low-priority tasks so you can create A work where it matters more.

8. Avoid the tendency to micromanage. Give your subordinates significant freedom to complete projects, even if you think that could lead to a higher risk of mistakes.

9. If you have the power to do so, eliminate the bureaucratic rules that force your employees to fill out needless forms or get advance approval for trivial matters.

10. Learn how to deal with—or get around—bureaucratic impediments that force you to spend too much time on low-priority tasks.

Part II

PRODUCTIVITY EVERY DAY

Part I introduced my three big ideas for improving your productivity: articulating your goals in order of priority, always having the final product in mind, and getting your low-priority tasks done quickly. Part II is about implementing those big ideas on a daily basis.

Chapter 4 will help you develop productive habits in your daily routine. I'll show you how to manage your calendar so that you can link your daily appointments to your high-priority goals. I'll also explain why you should get eight hours of sleep every night and exercise nearly every day.

Chapter 5 will move from the office to the road. I'll show you how to maintain productive habits while flying on planes and sleeping in hotels. I will describe how to prepare for a trip, remain productive during the journey, and stay close to your family while you are away.

Chapter 6 deals with meetings at the office—a big drag on productivity in most organizations. Meetings are usually too long and unfocused to get much done. I'll show you how to avoid meetings when you can and run them efficiently if a meeting is unavoidable.

4

YOUR DAILY ROUTINE

Everyone has a daily routine, more or less. I maintain a highly regimented schedule in order to save energy for thinking and free up time for family. Though you may prefer a more flexible schedule, this chapter will suggest three general strategies to make your daily routine as productive as possible:

- Use your daily calendar proactively to manage your time and set your Targets.

- Follow standard routines to minimize the mundane aspects of life so you can concentrate on what's most important to you.

- Get eight hours of sleep each night and exercise regularly so you stay alert and sharp.

HOW TO MANAGE YOUR CALENDAR

In chapter 1, "Set and Prioritize Your Goals," I helped you create a to-do list that reflects your most important Objectives and Targets. But how can you make sure that you are accomplishing these highest goals every day? The key is to create a daily calendar that drives home your most critical Targets. That's why I use a two-column calendar. Take a look at the example on the next page; on the left are my meetings, conference calls, and other appointments that are scheduled for specific times. Also on the left-hand side (at the bottom) are some other Targets that I would like to get done today, at some point.

Many people fill in only the left-hand side when they compose their calendar. They collect all of their daily obligations and assigned tasks and consider their calendar complete. But that is only half the battle.

The right-hand side is where I finish the job. Here, I write notes about each item on the left side—what I want to achieve during each of my appointments and the importance of each unscheduled Target on the bottom of the page. This ensures that I am achieving my Targets through every meeting or phone call and that I am not wasting a lot of time on low-priority tasks.

I have seen many creative solutions for daily calendars; they all work effectively so long as they satisfy two conditions. First, your calendar must record all of your daily commitments in one place in a way that you can easily see the *purpose* of each appointment and the *importance* of each assigned task. Second, the calendar must be mobile: you must be able to carry—or have electronic access to—your calendar during the whole day, so you can easily add new items or revise your existing schedule.

Personally, I type the left-hand side of my calendar on Microsoft Outlook, then print out the pages and write the right-hand side in longhand. That way I can easily revise my goals throughout the day using a pen, instead of tapping on my BlackBerry's keyboard. Other people manage their calendar exclusively on their computer or smartphone, through Outlook or products such as Google Calendar. It doesn't matter—do whichever works best for you.

Exhibit #1: MY CALENDAR

	Appointments	Notes
8:00		
:15		
:30	**Weekly Meeting w/ Senior Staff**	**New compensation system**
:45		
9:00		
:15		
:30	**Global vid conference w/quality control**	**Quality metrics—lost revenue**
:45		
10:00		
:15		
:30		
:45	**Ride stationary bike**	
11:00		
:15		
:30		
:45		
12:00	**Lunch with potential CTO hire**	**Recruit Sally Smith**
:15		
:30		
:45		
1:00		
:15		
:30		
:45		
2:00	**Conference call with Wash. lobbyists**	**Speak with committee chair?**
:15		
:30		
:45		
3:00		
:15		
:30	**Site visit to see new product**	**Social media strategy?**
:45		
4:00		
:15		
:30		
:45		
5:00		
:15		
:30	**Meeting with _Times_ reporter**	**Improve internal controls**
:45		
6:00		
:15		
:30		
:45		
7:00	**Dinner at home**	**Lisa's field hockey practice**
:15		**Bart's history midterm**

Targets to be done today anytime:
*** Call Patty about next board meeting   High-priority
* Choose topic for next speech   Low-priority

The Left-Hand Side: Meetings, Phone
Calls, and Other Assignments

Take a look at my schedule for the day. Note that I have not filled up every hour—there are several blocks of "free time" in my schedule. Of course, I'll use some of that time to complete the two Targets at the bottom of the page, but I'll still end up with a good amount of unscheduled time throughout the day. Those gaps are crucial to a successful schedule: they give you time to make calls, write notes, or even think!

Many executives line up meetings and conference calls for every hour of the day. That is a big mistake—you need time to digest what has happened and develop strategies for the future. Jeff Weiner, the CEO of LinkedIn, put it succinctly: "Part of the key to time management is carving out time to think as opposed to constantly reacting."[1]

Google, the Internet giant, provides a great example of the benefits of unscheduled time. Through a policy called "Innovation Time Off," it allows its employees to spend 20 percent of their time working on whatever they want, even if it is unrelated to their current assignments. By fiddling around with their burning curiosities during their "free time," Google's engineers often figure out an idea for a new product—such as Google News and Gmail, both of which were dreamed up during their 20 percent time off.[2]

Google's experience with employees' free time matches my own experience. Some of my best ideas have come during unscheduled times when I am reading an article or calling a friend. For instance, when we were struggling with how to design the Fidelity Charitable Gift Fund, I decided to phone a former tax partner of mine at a Washington, D.C., law firm and casually mentioned the difficulties that we were having. He suggested that I look at a recent IRS letter ruling, which offered an imaginative solution to my design problem.

I find that periods of free time should each be at least thirty minutes long to allow adequate time for thinking. You should try to schedule these gaps at least twice a day. Their timing should depend on when you typically have your most fertile mental periods. Some executives are particularly creative in the early morning; others usually get their inspiration in the evenings.

Intentional gaps in your schedule also allow you more flexibility to deal with new opportunities or problems as they arise during the day. For example, suppose a local radio station asks me at 7:45 a.m. for a short comment about a current event. That can be squeezed into my schedule at 11:30 or 11:45 a.m. with minimal disruption to the rest of my schedule.

Or suppose that Sally Smith, the chief technology officer (CTO) candidate I'm recruiting, has called to say that she is stuck in traffic and will be thirty minutes late to lunch. If you give yourself some margin of error in your schedule, you can deal with the host of unforeseen situations that inevitably occur without wiping out your whole schedule.

There is a real danger, however, that "free" times can quietly be filled by assistants or coordinators. So it is crucial to make clear that this empty part of your schedule is as important as any other meeting or phone call. As the great Danish composer Carl Nielsen said about his music, "The rests . . . are just as important as the notes. Often, they are far more expressive and appealing to the imagination."[3]

The Right-Hand Side: Focusing on My Highest Targets

The left-hand side of the calendar is a fairly straightforward list of tasks to complete today; the real action is in the column on the right-hand side, which contains my handwritten notes about each event or obligation.

Next to a meeting or phone call, I write down my purpose for the event—what I want to get out of it. This ensures that I am focused on the purpose of each meeting or call while I am engaged in them. At the end of each appointment, I cross out the tasks I have accomplished and add "to dos" to my calendars for future dates, if necessary. That way I don't lose track of significant issues or projects.

Let's go back through my daily schedule to examine my notes in the right-hand column of my calendar.

- The weekly meeting of my senior staff at 8:30 a.m. will serve its usual functions, such as letting senior staff briefly share new information that needs to be discussed by the group. But I want to remind myself of my key Target for this meeting: discussing the deficiencies in the existing compensation system and building a consensus on what needs to change.

- During the global videoconference at 9:30 a.m., each region will report, as usual, on any activities requiring global coordination. But again I want to direct my attention to an additional Target: to expand the regional metrics to include rough estimates of lost revenues when quality problems temporarily close a plant or delay a product launch.

- Riding a stationary bike is a simple way to get in a quick workout (more on that in a bit). Other people like swimming or squash or running outside. It all depends on what you prefer and what equipment is readily available. If I were a serious athlete, I could use this space to write a specific goal I have for that workout (e.g., a running pace or a target heart rate). But I'm just trying to burn a few calories and work up a sweat, so I don't need to write anything down here.

- At the noontime lunch, I am trying to recruit an outstanding candidate to fill the vacant CTO position. Although she has been interviewed by my direct reports and the head of Human Resources, I know that my personal touch is needed to land such a talented person. Closing on senior appointments is one of the key functions that a senior executive—and only that executive—can perform (see chapter 10, "Managing Your Team").

- I want to remember that the 2 p.m. phone call with the Washington lobbyists is not just for updates. The House Ways and Means Committee is considering a technical provision that would impose a special tax on our industry. Collectively, we need to decide whether I should personally speak to the committee chair or whether that should be left to staff-to-staff negotiations.

- The review of a new product from 3:30 to 4:30 p.m. is partly a way to recognize the efforts of the development team. But I also want to make sure to ask the team whether they think the company should reevaluate how it uses social media to promote new products.

- The 5:30 p.m. meeting with a newspaper reporter involves a set of public relations issues where I as the CEO have to take the lead. There have been press allegations that an employee in one of our units has siphoned money out of a company account. Having read our internal analysis of these allegations, I have decided to announce decisive actions to strengthen the company's internal controls.

- As to the 7 p.m. dinner at home, I have reminders about events significant to members of my family—for example, the first practice of my daughter's field hockey team and my son's midterm exam in history.

- I'd like to call Patty at some point today to ask whether the board should discuss putting forward a new candidate for director at the next meeting. I really need to get this done soon—if it's being discussed, the board staff will need to write a fairly detailed memo due in a few days. So I write "high-priority" on the right-hand side.

- By contrast, there's no huge rush for me to finalize a topic for my next speech. It would be great to get it done today, but tomorrow will work just as well. So I write "low-priority" on the right-hand side.

After dinner, I will talk about the day with my wife and catch up on some reading. I will review my daily calendar—crossing out all the Targets that I have accomplished and moving others to future dates. I will also add notes to my appointments on tomorrow's calendar. In that manner, I try to keep focused on my key Targets, revise my schedule in light of recent experience, and avoid letting important items fall through the cracks. Once you get into the habit, as I have, such a schedule review should take no more than fifteen to twenty minutes each day.

As an exercise, create a daily calendar for your next workweek. For each day, take a sheet of paper and draw a line down the middle. On the left-hand side, list your phone calls, meetings, and other scheduled events, as well as all your unscheduled tasks that still need to get done. On the right-hand side, write down your purpose for each appointment—how each meeting or phone call will further your Targets. Then approach your meetings and phone calls over the next week with those purposes in mind. Also write down the level of importance for each of your unscheduled Targets. Then determine how much time you're really spending on your high-priority—and low-priority—unscheduled tasks.

ROUTINIZE YOUR DAILY ROUTINE

Try to keep as much of your daily routine as simple and automatic as possible. That allows you to spend more time on your work, family, and friends, and it helps you avoid fatigue. Over the past twenty years, various researchers have shown that making conscious decisions ("Which shirt do I want to wear?") as well as engaging in self-control ("I'd better eat the carrots instead of the cookies!") tire out your brain, much as a muscle fatigues from exercise.[4]

I like to keep my morning routine as simple as possible. Every day I wake up at 7:15 a.m. and leave the house between 7:50 and 7:55 a.m. During those thirty-five to forty minutes, I shower, dress, eat breakfast, and read a few newspapers. How? By preparing the night before and staying with the same routine. In the morning, I am very boring and proud of it.

Before I go to bed, I lay out my clothes for the next day. This is quite simple because I own five summer and five winter suits, all of which are gray or blue. I have shirts and ties that go with each suit (according to my wife). I also have two pairs of dark shoes to alternate. For me, dressing is a mechanical routine with little to think about.

I get dressed after shaving, showering, and brushing my teeth. Then I eat the same breakfast every day: a banana and a bowl of cold cereal with skim milk. The cereal is always Cheerios or Life—no complex choices. I started eating bananas at breakfast after a pro tennis player, Yevgeny Kafelnikov, stayed at our home during a Boston tournament. He ate a dozen bananas each day to keep his tennis muscles from cramping up. I hoped that eating bananas would improve my tennis game, but that has not actually happened.

For some people, my morning routine sounds incredibly unappealing or impossible, and that's fine! Indeed, professionals in certain industries, such as advertising or media, may devote more attention to dressing in style to be successful. Professionals who take care of younger children or older relatives may not be able to follow such a rigid routine in the morning. Others may simply enjoy having a greater variety of breakfast foods. I'm not suggesting that you need to follow my rigid routine to the letter; the point is for you to decide what you consider mundane in your own life and keep it as simple as possible.

Regardless of your menu preferences, having a healthy breakfast is important for your productivity. Several researchers have done experiments randomly dividing subjects into two main groups: those who are given breakfast and those who are made to fast. The results have been clear: skipping breakfast significantly diminishes cognitive performance.[5]

My recommendation about lunch is similar: keep it simple and routine. I don't eat lunch at restaurants unless I have a specific reason—for example, recruiting a new employee or networking with colleagues. Instead, I usually eat a simple lunch in my office—typically a chicken salad sandwich on whole wheat bread with a diet soda.

If I am eating lunch with a fellow employee, I offer him or her a sandwich or salad. Even when I have a lunch meeting with one or two outside visitors, they often prefer a simple sandwich or salad in my office because it is private, quiet, and quick—and they often are trying to keep their own weight down. Again, if this lack of culinary variety offends your nature, introduce more menu choices and think of other mundane aspects in your life that can be simplified.

TAKE A QUICK SNOOZE AFTER LUNCH

Soon after lunch, I always try to take a thirty-minute nap. That's enough to make me feel refreshed and more alert for the rest of the day. Without my nap, I get tired and less productive by late afternoon. Friends of mine like to nap later in the afternoon. The exact timing doesn't matter; take a short nap whenever is best for you.

WHY TAKE A NAP?

During the day, two biological forces fight each other. The "homeostatic propensity for sleep" encourages you to doze off based on how long you have been awake. Opposing that propensity is the circadian rhythm, which tries to keep you awake during daylight hours. However, the circadian push for wakefulness does not fully kick in until the late afternoon. Until then, your body naturally descends into a lethargic state of low energy.[6]

There have been many studies, with randomized controlled trials, on the efficacy of napping. Their conclusions are remarkably consistent: napping significantly increases alertness and productivity on a variety of measures. According to those studies, the first ten to twenty minutes of a nap are the most beneficial, suggesting that even very short naps can help you maintain energy into the afternoon.[7]

Some people claim that they just can't take a nap. Here's my secret formula: close your office door or find a quiet place, shut off your cell phone, take off your shoes, put your feet up on a desk or a chair, and cover your eyes with a blindfold. This formula is designed to create a feeling of being suspended in a sheltered cocoon—which helps me doze off.

Other people say that they are afraid to take an afternoon nap because they fear that they will sleep for several hours. This is an easily solved problem—set the alarm on your phone (or alarm clock) to ring thirty minutes into your nap. After a few weeks of these alarms, you will automatically start to wake up just before the alarm rings.

Unfortunately, many employees don't think they can take a short nap without attracting the ire of their superiors. But enlightened managers should allow short naps so that their workers will be more alert later in the day. In a poll, 40 percent of workers said that they would take a nap if they were allowed to do so and a space were set aside where they could doze off.[8] Letting subordinates nap would both endear the boss to the employees and increase their productivity in the late afternoon.

GOING HOME

A long commute can be a challenge at the end of the day. Currently, the average U.S. commute is roughly twenty-five minutes each way,[9] though the commute is longer for those who live in the suburbs and work in the city. A long commute is a perfect time to ruminate on new ideas or mentally review what you got done during the day. If you drive yourself to work, that's about all you can accomplish safely. For those of you who ride mass transit or carpool to work, you have a few more options: you can read, make phone calls in an appropriate place, or send emails on a smartphone.

As a regular habit, I leave work in time to get home by 7 p.m. and have dinner with my family. These dinners have greatly enhanced my family life. Before our children left for college, my wife and I enjoyed chatting with our children at dinner, reviewing their day's activities or discussing current events. And I believe that our family was much stronger for those dinners—even when our children inevitably replied that "nothing" had happened in school that day.

Try to go home for dinner nearly every day at a consistent, reasonable time. It is simply too easy to stay late at the office night after night to complete a few tasks, even though there is no real crisis. Over time those extra hours at work will really wear you down and irritate your family. If you need to finish work in the evening, you can do so after spending quality time with your spouse and children.

Luckily for me, my wife was able to provide me with extensive support throughout my career. She was also the primary caregiver for our children. Although men are taking on a greater role in household chores,[10] many women share Liz's experience: even today, women generally shoulder more child-rearing and household management responsibilities than their husbands.[11] I'm the first to admit that dual-career couples face a much tougher road than I did. It would be impossible for me to try to address the challenge of work-life conflict in just a few words. So for help managing the tension between the requirements of your work life and the demands of your life at home, turn to chapter 14, "Balancing Home and Work."

TAKING CARE OF YOUR BODY

A very important part of my daily routine involves getting enough sleep and exercise, both of which are easy to brush aside when work gets busy. But skimping on either of these key activities will seriously harm your productivity. In effect, sleep and exercise are investments of time that pay returns in the form of improved health and higher productivity throughout the day.

Get Enough Sleep

I've met a number of executives who claim that they can operate well on four or five hours of sleep a night. But I've noticed those same executives closing their eyes at afternoon meetings or losing the line of argument in debates. In my observation, it is a very rare person who maximizes his or her productivity by skimping on sleep. The vast majority of people need close to eight hours of sleep a night to do their best work.

My personal observations are confirmed by several types of scientific studies. For instance, one study led by Professor Hans Van Dongen at the University of Pennsylvania restricted subjects' sleep to six hours per night for several nights.[12] He and his colleagues found that those whose sleep had been restricted performed much worse on three tests of performance, relative to a control group that was allowed to sleep eight hours each night.[13] Furthermore, the gap between this "full-sleep" group and the restricted-sleep group grew larger every night.

Of particular interest, the "restricted sleepers" thought that they were adapting to cumulative sleep deprivation, yet their performance was actually suffering. Several times a day, researchers asked the subjects to rate their sleepiness using a well-known metric called the Stanford Sleepiness Scale. According to their self-assessments, their performance declined a little bit on the first day but then stabilized. However, their actual performance declined and did *not* stabilize; instead, their performance decreased quickly and continued to worsen after each night of restricted sleep.[14] This conclusion strongly suggests that most executives who swear "I need only five hours of sleep" are deluding themselves. Though they may think that their bodies have adapted to less sleep, they will probably be dragging their feet by the end of the week.

SLEEP DEPRIVATION CAN HURT CRITICAL THINKING

Some studies have used games to show that missing one night's sleep has a significant adverse effect on innovative decision making. One game provided players with new information and required them to make "business decisions" taking that new information into account. As the game progressed, the players received more complex information and faced decisions that required more flexible thinking. Those who missed a night of sleep did a much worse job of adapting their business strategies than the control group did; the sleep-deprived stuck to their existing strategies despite learning new information. At the end of the game, most of the players who had missed a night of sleep went "bankrupt," while the control group managed to stay profitable.[15]

A second game involved a gambling scenario in which subjects drew a card from one of four different decks of playing cards. Each deck had a unique distribution of risks and rewards: some held out the potential for high payoffs with low chances of success, while others offered relatively low risks and low rewards. Players who were sleep-deprived were more likely to choose a card from the riskier decks, even after they were shown to be profit losers.[16]

All these studies point to the same conclusion: try to get around eight hours sleep each night. How can you make that happen on a regular basis? Try to sleep during the same hours each night (e.g., 11 p.m. to 7 a.m.); this routine will help you develop a sleep rhythm. Don't have dinner after 8 p.m., or you may have digestive problems when you get into bed for the night. Install effective window coverings to keep your bedroom very dark. Take extra care to eliminate blue light coming from cell phones, clocks, and so forth, as blue light is especially disruptive to the hormones that make you feel sleepy. Last, keep a pad of paper on the nightstand next to your bed. I sometimes cannot fall asleep until I have cleared my mind by jotting down reminders of things to do or ideas to explore.

Even if you follow all these strategies, there will be nights when you get little sleep—because of work, family, sickness, or simple insomnia. After a poor night of sleep, do your best to recover as soon as possible by taking long naps or sleeping more than eight hours the next night. However, a single full night of sleep is usually not enough to completely recover.[17]

Exercise Regularly

Like a good night's sleep, physical exercise is essential to your personal productivity. Many studies find that regular exercise improves productivity as well as health. For instance, one study found that midday exercise enhanced the mood and efficiency of employees and also reduced their health care costs through fewer sick days and lower medical expenses.[18] These benefits only require a modest amount of low-intensity daily exercise.[19]

Researchers from the London School of Economics used a cutting-edge experiment to offer new evidence that exercise makes people happy. In that experiment, volunteers downloaded an app to their smartphone. At least once a day, their phone would beep, and they would report their level of happiness along with whom they were with and what they were doing. After aggregating the data, the researchers were able to determine when the volunteers were happiest— what times of day, in what activities, and with which people. Exercise ranked number two on the list of happiness-inducing activities—just behind sex.[20]

Your employer can encourage daily workout regimes by offering access to gym facilities and allowing employees to exercise during the day. Ultimately, however, it is up to you to make time for a regular workout. So figure out what type of exercise appeals to you—say, running, swimming, or Pilates. And choose a time of day that makes sense for you, such as early in the morning, around lunchtime, or after work. Being busy or lacking equipment is no excuse for missing exercise: a friend of mine blocks off forty-five minutes in the middle of the day to walk up and down the stairs of our office building. However, if you follow this particular workout regimen, lobby for the installation of showers. Or at the very least do your coworkers a favor by buying and using an air freshener.

Some take a different approach to exercise: they go out and purchase a fancy piece of home equipment or an expensive gym membership. Though such purchases do work for some people, they will not magically lead to an exercise regime. In many homes, unused stationary bikes and NordicTracks stand as proud monuments to lofty goals long ago set aside. Regardless of your equipment, exercising on a regular basis requires great discipline that you must teach yourself.

One helpful approach is to get support for regular exercise from other people: for instance, a running group, a yoga class, or a personal coach. Such support puts peer pressure on you and makes exercise more fun.[21] That is why I am so enthusiastic about playing in a regular game of doubles tennis. It provides a both vigorous exercise and warm camaraderie, though it is hard to organize more than twice a week.

TAKEAWAYS

1. Use a daily calendar with notes on your Targets to remind you of the purpose of every appointment.

2. Do not schedule every hour in the day; you need time to react to the unexpected and to think strategically.

3. Prepare for the next day every night: review your schedule and lay out your wardrobe.

4. Maintain a simple and repetitious routine for mundane daily tasks.

5. Take a short nap in the afternoon to raise your effectiveness later in the day.

6. Have dinner regularly with your family, unless you are traveling or facing a crisis.

7. Get eight hours of sleep each night on a regular basis.

8. Recover from a poor night's sleep by sleeping longer than eight hours the next night.

9. Exercise regularly, preferably doing a modest amount of exercise nearly every day.

10. Find a group of people, such as those on a sports team or in a workout class, that can offer support for your exercise routine.

5

TRAVELING
LIGHTLY

E ven if you have a productive daily routine when living at home, you
will have a harder challenge when you travel across the country or
around the world. Although improved telecommunication has somewhat
reduced the need to travel, there will never be a substitute for face-to-face
interaction in certain situations.[1] Business travel is not going away, so professionals should learn how to remain productive when on the road for
business.

HOW TO PLAN THE DETAILS OF A TRIP

The key to a productive trip lies in good advance planning. There are
hundreds of i's to be dotted and t's to be crossed; forgetting a single step
can lead to major headaches later. For those like me who are lucky enough
to have an executive assistant, you should delegate many of those tasks to

him or her. If you don't have an assistant, create a comprehensive list of all the logistical steps so that you do not overlook any critical detail.

For relatively short trips within the country, you can get away with booking flights and a hotel online. But for complicated overseas trips, it's worthwhile to use a travel agent to sort through the hundreds of flight options, find the best deals, and get you upgrades. Only a travel agent will know the peculiarities of international destinations (e.g., is sixty minutes long enough to change planes in Delhi?). Likewise, agents are a good resource for finding a nice but reasonably priced hotel near to the places you'll be visiting.

After you book your flights and hotel, plan your local transportation. In some countries, it is a little risky to take a city cab from the airport to the hotel. As a well-dressed foreigner, you are an easy target for a scam, despite the best efforts of local police. I find it well worth the money to be taken straight to my hotel from the airport by a driver who waits for me at the airport holding my name up on a placard. Get the name and cell phone number of the driver in case of unexpected problems. For transportation from the hotel to a meeting site or other destination, ask a local contact to give you an idea of how long it actually takes to get from one place to another; many cities are plagued by severe traffic congestion.

If you need a visa for the trip, promptly get the paperwork you need to apply for it. Obtaining a visa can be a time-consuming process; a travel agent might have to hire a service company to quickly process a visa application. The application must often include your actual passport, which you might need in the meantime for other trips.

If you are traveling to a country where English is not widely spoken, have your business card translated into the local language. Then print a large number of copies of your card, keeping in mind that *everyone* will want one from *everyone* else at *every* meeting. Employees at all levels in a delegation traveling to foreign countries should bring along a generous supply of business cards.

Finally, compile a detailed daily schedule for your trip with the addresses, phone numbers, and emails for all of your appointments. Attach to this schedule relevant backup documents such as airline schedules, hotel confirmations, and maps of your destination. It's a good idea to give your spouse a copy of this itinerary so that he or she can contact you easily.

HOW TO GET THE MOST OUT OF YOUR TRIP

Aside from these logistical details, you will still need to do considerable advance work to make your trip productive. Specifically, you have to think clearly about your goals for the trip and make sure that your schedule reflects those goals. To get started in this process if you are traveling internationally, do some background reading about the country's history and its cultural mores. Then talk to local contacts to understand the background of the people you will be meeting and the restrictions under which they are operating.

Making a Sales Pitch

Sometimes you will travel to make a sales pitch to potential clients. Throughout my career, I've traveled all over the world to try to convince institutional investors to hire our firm to manage their money. Before I leave home, I make sure to prepare a persuasive presentation about my company: its history, its investment record, its risk controls, and the biographies of the relevant portfolio managers.

As part of this preparation, I need to learn a great deal about my potential clients—their motivations and their constraints. Are they willing to bear a lot of risk in order to try to make money quickly? Or would they rather invest more conservatively in order to protect their nest egg? I tailor my presentations very differently depending on their preferences. (For more on understanding your audience when giving presentations, see chapter 9, "Speaking Effectively.")

Making presentations in foreign countries can pose some difficult challenges. Though you may have a decent understanding of the country's culture, you may need to delve more deeply into the technical standards applicable to your potential client. In my case, pension funds (investment pools to pay for retirement benefits) operate very differently in certain countries. In Australia, for instance, many of the largest pension funds are run by labor unions rather than companies. In order to make a sales pitch to those potential clients, I need to be highly aware of this dynamic and think carefully about how it might affect the preferences of the pension trustees.

To get all the information that you need, you should get in touch with a local contact. If you're lucky, your firm will have a representative in that country whose job entails understanding all of the relevant details about potential clients. Failing that, you might call a local consultant to get the latest information about the company and its workforce. To find out more about the applicable regulations, you might ask a local law firm or a government agency.

Visiting Your Own Company

On other occasions, you may travel in order to meet colleagues at a distant office of your own company or a related venture. I recently visited the Shanghai offices of Nielsen, Inc., of which I am an outside director. Nielsen is doing some fascinating work on social media in China, which is especially relevant to me because my most recent two books have been translated into Mandarin.

In visiting the Nielsen office, I had pretty simple goals: to learn more about Nielsen's Chinese business, rally the troops, and offer any useful ideas I might have. After an introduction from U.S. headquarters, I emailed back and forth with a Shanghai executive on what type of activities would be mutually beneficial. We agreed that I should see two presentations reflecting each of Nielsen's business segments in China. We also agreed that I should attend an informal coffee to meet and greet senior members of the local office.

One executive at Nielsen's U.S. headquarters offered to provide me with an extensive background paper on Nielsen's business in China. But I knew how much extra work that would entail. Instead, I suggested that he write a one-page cover note, attached to already existing documents describing Nielsen's Chinese operations. He quickly put together that small package, which was quite helpful to me. It struck the proper balance between getting me the necessary background, while not creating a lot of extra work for others.

In short, you must diligently prepare for your trip *before* going on the road. Carefully think through your goals and discuss with local contacts how best to accomplish them.

HOW TO GLIDE THROUGH THE AIRPORT

Airports are hectic places. There are long lines, frazzled passengers, and a general sense of hurriedness. The best way to avoid some of this stress is to pack lightly enough to avoid having to check luggage. Checking luggage is a disaster from a productivity standpoint. It takes time to check in and much more time to wait for your bags after the flight.[2] If you have one bulky item that is too big to carry on, consider sending it well in advance via a parcel service.

If you are checking a bag on a short trip, you have probably packed poorly. Recall the scene from the film *Up in the Air* where George Clooney's character shows his young colleague how to pack more effectively. He discards a pillow that she brought along, saying, "They have nicer ones where we're going." Hair dryers are also standard equipment in hotel bathrooms. If you think through what you actually need to take, you can avoid wasting time checking a bag.

I have seen many professionals make the mistake of taking a bulky overcoat on a business trip in the fall or spring months. On many trips, you spend nearly all of your time indoors and take taxis between the office, the hotel, and the airport. A sweater or jacket (as part of a suit) is usually warm enough for you to survive the few steps you actually take outside—unless you are traveling to Anchorage or Moscow. If you're traveling to a rainy destination such as Seattle, it is more important to bring along a small fold-up umbrella than a heavy overcoat.

After deciding what can be left at home, pack clothing that is easy to mix and match. I take two dark blue suits and two pairs of black shoes, which can be alternated each day. A female colleague of mine told me, "My outfits are neutral colors (black or gray) so I can mix and match skirts, pants, and shirts and layer since I travel not just within different time zones but also different climates quite frequently on a trip. I buy only noniron shirts and fabrics that don't wrinkle easily."

If you pack smartly, you can fit everything into a roll-aboard suitcase and another small bag. You should choose your roll-aboard carefully to get the maximum size that fits into overhead bins. Although the dimensions vary by airline, that generally means around 24 by 15 by 10 inches; you can easily find models that are just small enough to fit. Most roll-aboard suitcases have several compartments besides the main holding space. Use those compartments to segregate items such as plastic bags for your standard toiletries and needed medications, since you usually have to process them separately through security.

Instead of a briefcase, I carry a large canvas bag, like one you might take to the beach. Such a bag can hold a lot more than a traditional leather briefcase with its thick outer walls and internal dividers. A canvas bag is also much lighter than a leather briefcase.

My canvas bag holds the tools I need to sleep when I travel: eyeshades and earplugs. If I want to sleep on a plane or a train, I get a window seat, insert the earplugs, and put on the eyeshades. Then I feel as though I am in a cocoon and can easily wander off into my own dream world. Though many people prefer aisle seats, they make me feel too exposed to the external world when the flight attendant serves drinks or other passengers go to the bathroom. But this is just my own personal experience; taller individuals may have a stronger preference for the extra legroom of an aisle seat.

Although I use a BlackBerry, I still carry hard copies of reading material, enough to occupy the several hours of downtime that inevitably arise when traveling. I also carry a small flashlight in the event that I wind up in a taxi or other place where it is too dark to read. The more computer-savvy can use the canvas bag to carry an iPad or computer—or a flashlight app on a smartphone instead of a traditional flashlight. In whatever way suits your style, be prepared to take advantage of expected or unexpected periods of downtime.

If I have a long layover or my flight is delayed, I slip into the business lounge of my favorite airline. Clubs like these are worth the price if you travel a lot for business. They offer quiet, cool, well-lit places to work, as well as food, drinks, and clean bathrooms. Figure out the airline you use the most, and join the club. Many clubs offer special deals from time to time, and some firms will pick up the membership tab for their employees. Moreover, certain credit cards give you free access to airline lounges—albeit in exchange for an annual fee on the credit card.

Make sure to sign up for the frequent-flyer program for all the airlines you fly. Even if you travel only a few times per year, the miles can add up: most airlines award "entry-level" elite status to customers with only 25,000 miles each year—less than five round-trip coast-to-coast trips. Airlines also coddle their elite customers by offering them shorter lines at security and early-boarding perks.

You should print out your boarding pass *before* you get to the airport. If you don't have access to a printer, many airlines let you download your boarding pass to your smartphone. In either case, you can skip the check-in lines and head straight for the security checkpoint.

To get through security quickly, try to take advantage of the Transportation Security Administration's new PreCheck program. The program allows you to go through a separate line—and you can usually keep your shoes on and leave your laptop in your bag. Unfortunately, the program is still in its infancy; it's available only on a handful of airlines at thirty-five airports across the country.

Those of us with metal implants can't make full use of PreCheck. Because I have a knee replacement that triggers the metal detector, I am often forced to undergo an embarrassing pat down if I go through the regular line. If you, too, have some sort of metal implant, you can often choose a line leading to the new full-body scanners rather than to the normal metal detector. The scanner sees the implants and lets you pass without the hand search. Although you sometimes have to wait a few minutes for the full-body scanner to be activated, that's a minor inconvenience when compared with the invasive pat down.

HOW TO REST ON AIRPLANES

I'm not the sort of person who buys a fancy car or flashy jewelry, but I do believe that you should fly business class if the trip entails an overnight on the plane. I'm not buying a business-class ticket to get a better meal; I'm buying it so that I can get a good night's sleep. If you're too tired to work effectively in the morning, what is the point of making the trip in the first place?

WHY IS IT EASIER TO SLEEP IN BUSINESS CLASS?

There are several reasons. First, there are fewer passengers near you—fewer people are getting up, using the restroom, or otherwise making noise. Furthermore, the seat is wider and allows more legroom. Most important, business-class seats recline to become flat or nearly flat, depending on the airline. It is this last feature of business-class seats that is most relevant for its effect on sleep.

Researchers from the Royal Air Force in Britain have examined how the recline angle of a seat affects the quality of sleep. Their subjects slept several nights in chairs of various recline angles—an armchair (17.5° from vertical), a reclining chair (37°), a "sleeperette" (49.5°), and an old-fashioned bed (90°). They examined the quality of sleep and found that all of their subjects slept reasonably well except for those who slept in the armchair. When sleeping in the armchair, subjects took longer to fall asleep, engaged in shallower sleep, and ended up sleeping for less total time. The researchers concluded that the "magic number" for recline angle was roughly 40°—it is hard to get a good night's sleep with any less of a recline.[3] Unfortunately, the 17.5° recline of an armchair is roughly equal to the typical recline angle of a coach-class seat.[4]

Even in business class, a red-eye flight from the West Coast to the East Coast or from the East Coast to Europe can be a challenge. The flights are typically in the air for less than six or seven hours—not enough time to get a decent night's sleep. So I wake up early on the day of travel and eat dinner before I get on the plane. I immediately take my window seat and go into my cocoon trance with earplugs and eyeshades. Because I have woken up early, I am tired, even if takeoff is only at 6:00 p.m. local time. If I do everything right, I can usually get in five or six hours of sleep on those shorter flights. On longer flights to Asia or from the West Coast to Europe, there is plenty of time to eat and sleep on the plane. However, I admit to taking a sleeping pill if I wake up after an hour or two.

I take care to avoid drinking alcohol while traveling because it interferes with my sleep. Though alcohol may help you fall asleep, it prevents many of the restorative features of sleep; even with only a few drinks, you're more likely to have a shallower night's sleep and wake up several times in the middle of the night.[5] The end result is that you feel less refreshed in the morning. Given the difficulties of getting a good night's sleep at 35,000 feet, avoid the additional challenge of alcohol.

Though I don't drink alcohol when I fly, I do drink lots of water. Cabin air typically has a very low relative humidity—around 10 to 20 percent—causing you to lose moisture through your skin and through your breath. This dehydration makes you feel physically weaker and impairs your mental functions.

Beverage services aboard the airplane are not frequent enough to provide adequate rehydration. So take your own water bottle(s) on board.

Although you can't take filled water bottles through security, you can buy them (or fill them up) on the other side. My personal rule of thumb is one quart of water for every four hours on a plane, though this varies tremendously by person. Also keep in mind that alcohol and caffeine can aggravate dehydration, so stick to water or juice.

STICK TO YOUR ROUTINE ON THE ROAD

During your stay away from home, keep to your established daily routine as much as possible. Prepare your calendar before going to bed, get eight hours of sleep each night, eat a light breakfast, and exercise daily if you can (see chapter 4, "Your Daily Routine").[6] But traveling can make it harder to keep to this routine. For instance, you may have to attend lunches and dinners with a large number of sumptuous courses. To be polite, eat a little of each course and try to turn down heavy desserts at the end. They feel like dead weights in your stomach when you later retire for a night's sleep.

I am also not very enthusiastic about the late-night clubbing that is part of the business cultures in many countries. I am always amazed to see a straitlaced foreign bureaucrat say very little during a day of meetings and then turn into an energetic Elvis impersonator after a few drinks at a karaoke club. If that's your idea of a good night, then have at it. But those long nights use up a lot of my energy, and I can't say that I have much fun at them. So I typically bow out early by claiming a bad case of jet lag or an early-morning conference call. Without fail, the party goes on without me. Meanwhile, I get more sleep, and I'm more alert the next day.

Nevertheless, I am still often overcome by jet lag in the afternoon. Jet lag is the invisible enemy of every traveler, business or pleasure, so it is important to learn how to overcome it. Unfortunately, jet lag cannot be conquered simply by flying often. Studies have shown that airline pilots also suffer from the effects of jet lag despite their years of flying.[7] But jet lag can be managed to some extent.

How to Reduce Jet Lag

Here's how jet lag works.[8] Roughly speaking, your circadian rhythm (or "body clock") regulates when you feel sleepy (at night) and when you feel alert (during the day). Your body clock responds heavily to light cues, but not instantly. This is a good thing, or else it would be impossible to fall back asleep after, say, turning on a light to check on a crying baby in the middle of the night. But this resistance is what causes jet lag: even though the sun is rising, your body might still think it's 3 a.m. Without any proactive steps, it takes approximately one day per time zone for your body clock to adjust. So if you're traveling from New York to San Francisco (three time zones), you should expect three days of jet lag.

One well-studied element of your body clock is melatonin—at night, glands in your brain release more of this hormone into your body, helping you fall asleep. Some people believe that taking a melatonin supplement at a strategic time (say, a few hours before sunset if you are about to travel eastward) can help your body adjust quickly. But the research on the effect of melatonin on jet lag is inconclusive at this point—although it will help you get to sleep, it is unclear whether it actually "advances" your body clock.[9]

If you don't want to take a pill, you can still adjust more quickly by getting into the time zone of your destination on the day of travel. For example, if I am flying from Los Angeles to Boston in the morning, I go to bed early and wake up at 4:30 a.m. L.A. time since that is 7:30 a.m. Boston time—and turn on all the lights in my hotel room to simulate daytime. After eating lunch on Boston time and taking a short nap on the plane, I will be closer to being in sync when my plane touches down in Boston that evening.

Even if you follow these rules to manage your jet lag, it can be difficult to stay awake during a full day of work following a red-eye flight. Nevertheless, you should be careful to avoid falling back asleep. A short nap is okay—great, in fact!—during the late afternoon, but you need to set an alarm for thirty minutes and actually wake up when it rings. If you end up sleeping during the day and staying awake at night, you will have a harder time adjusting to the new time zone.

When I get to my destination, I go for a quick swim in the hotel's pool, if it has one. This moderate exercise leaves me refreshed and awake. Other people take a quick jog or hit the stationary bike in the hotel gym. Indeed, athletes often use this strategy when traveling to competitions. In high school, my research assistant was a member of a rowing team in Seattle; every October, his team flew to Boston for a big race, taking a red-eye (in coach, of course) to save money. With only a few days to get adjusted to the new time zone, his coach immediately took the team from the airport to the river for a quick, easy row—despite the complaints from the cranky team.

If the hotel does not have a pool or workout facilities, you can take a warm shower. A warm shower can raise your body temperature and get your blood flowing, waking you up. Drinking coffee is also a good strategy, so long as it fits with your typical routine. The key is simply to stay awake throughout the day—aside from a quick nap (thirty minutes or less), which can give you an extra kick if you need it.

HOW TO STAY CLOSE TO YOUR FAMILY

For me and many other professionals, the biggest challenge of travel is not the hassle of security, the jet lag, or the prep work but rather the separation from our family. Like jet lag, this cannot be completely overcome: there is no substitute for the daily face-to-face interactions between you and your spouse and children. Nevertheless, there are ways to lessen the impact on yourself and your family.

The negative effects of long travel on your spouse and children have been well documented. The World Bank is an organization that works closely with governmental bodies around the world, so its expert staff members spend a lot of time away from home. The World Bank decided to study how this difficult travel schedule affected its staff and their families.[10] To get a complete picture, researchers surveyed certain members of the staff—who were away from home ninety days per year, on average— as well as their families. They found solid agreement from all parties that travel caused stress in the traveler and the spouse and had deleterious effects on children.

For children, the biggest challenge is simply the lack of daily contact between the absent parent and the child. Small children especially have the potential to be confused as to why their parents are leaving so frequently. The World Bank study reported on one particular three-year-old child who innocently asked his mother, "Does Dad have another family and house in another country?"

Other young children may fear that the traveling parent will not return. To help alleviate this worry, the remaining spouse should make the traveler part of the conversation at home—by discussing with the child where the traveler is today and what he or she is doing. If your family is religious, including the traveler in your children's daily prayers can help calm their fears.

Spouses are often further stressed by their extra household responsibilities when their spouse is away—they can't off-load the laundry, cooking, cleaning, and child-rearing duties. To reduce this burden, travelers should take care of as many practical chores as possible before leaving on the trip: take the clothes to the dry cleaner, make a run to the family's favorite grocery store to stock up on supplies, and deal with the monthly bills. You need to do some advance planning in order to get those tasks done in the hectic days before a long trip.

After a long trip away, the World Bank's staff reported difficulty readjusting to life at home—for a few days, they felt like an outsider in their own house. They wanted to spend quality time with their spouse or children after being gone for so long, but they found themselves too exhausted to do so. Personally, I address these concerns by returning at the beginning of the weekend whenever possible. That means that I have a day or two to recover and focus on my family instead of being consumed by the backlog of work.

When my children were small, I liked to buy them a local gift to show that I had been thinking about them throughout the trip. A piece of local craftwork is easy to buy and light to carry. If you have no time to buy anything before you get to the airport, there are always the duty-free shops. But those gifts are usually less authentic and more expensive.

Most important, phone your family every day if you are away for an extended period. Even if you are busy on the road, you can take ten minutes out of your day to chat with your spouse and children on the telephone. Video chats are more feasible than ever before; Skype is a free service requiring only a good Internet connection, and many smartphones have video chat features as well.

Of course, video chatting cannot replace the daily interactions among you, your spouse, and your children. If your job consistently requires more than a hundred days per year away from your family, I believe that it's not sustainable over the long term. After a few years, you may come to realize that you do not want to continue in the job as currently structured.

TAKEAWAYS

1. Make a to-do list—one you can use every time you travel—that includes the dozens of small tasks involved in preparing for a trip.

2. Line up a driver from the airport and check out local transportation when you plan your itinerary.

3. Be clear about your goals for the trip, and make sure your schedule reflects those goals.

4. *Never* check luggage on a trip lasting less than a week. Instead, take a large carry-on roll-aboard with the items you really need to bring.

5. Carry a canvas bag on the airplane with tools for sleeping (eyeshades, earplugs) and reading materials (hard copies and flashlight or computer/iPad).

6. Buy a business-class ticket for overnight flights. A good night's sleep is worth the extra price.

7. Drink lots of water on the airplane—roughly one quart per four hours.

8. Maintain your daily routine on the road: review your calendar each night, get eight hours of sleep, and exercise daily.

9. Get into your destination time zone as soon as possible to mitigate jet lag. Exercise as soon as you land so that you can stay awake during the day.

10. Talk to your spouse and children every day while on the road. The phone is okay, but video chatting (such as Skype) is better.

6

EFFICIENT MEETINGS

I f run correctly, meetings can be quite productive. They can help formulate and implement an organization's policy, and they can provide forums to discuss and resolve issues. Unfortunately, too many meetings lack focus and fail to achieve any meaningful purpose. And in most organizations, there are simply too many meetings, and they last too long. As a result, there's less time to get work done. Meetings reportedly take up approximately 35 percent of the workday for middle managers[1] and up to 60 percent of the day for top executives.[2]

HOW TO AVOID MEETINGS

When I was president of Fidelity Investments, I could easily have spent every hour of every day at meetings. Everyone wanted to talk to me about their problems and plans. They included the members of my management team, the top executives from the various marketing divisions, the risk and compliance functions, and the system development units, as well as outside officials from government bodies and service providers. At the same time, I wanted to meet regularly with the significant players in our investment group and our key institutional clients.

In order to satisfy the demand for meetings within my available hours, I refused many meetings and dealt with certain matters through emails, memos, or phone chats. Today, before I call any meeting, I carefully think about what I want to get out of it. If I'm not satisfied with my answer, I don't go forward with the meeting.

There are two main reasons to have a meeting. First, you should call a meeting if you need to establish a personal relationship with someone outside your organization, such as an elected official or new customer. Second, meetings are often necessary if you want to engage people in a debate; face-to-face dialogue cannot be replaced by email or phone calls.

SHOULD YOU HOLD A BRAINSTORMING MEETING?

When managers face a tough challenge, they often call a "brainstorming" meeting. They bring in a broad swath of employees and solicit ideas on how to resolve the problem, without worrying for the moment whether ideas are good or bad. According to the theory, one person's suggestion may inspire someone else to put forward another idea, so it's useful to bring people together for this purpose. However, research has found that simply shouting out the first thing that comes to mind is *not* an effective way of generating ideas. To have an effective brainstorming session, this research concluded that you must be willing to criticize the suggestions put forward.[3] This helps shape the discussion and turn raw ideas into workable proposals.

By contrast, many meetings are called simply to share information, rather than debate or discuss it. Such meetings tend to be unnecessary; usually you can accomplish this just as well via email in a fraction of the time. For example, the group at Fidelity responsible for preparing board materials wanted me to meet with it for two hours each month to review the materials. Instead, I asked them to email me the materials, along with a cover email highlighting the key issues. I then sent my comments by email to the board group. Although reviewing the material and writing the email took some time, it invariably took less than the two hours or more that I (and they) would have spent at the meeting.

Similarly, you should not call a meeting simply because "it has always been there." At the beginning of the year, the boss may schedule a meeting every Monday to go over plans for the next week. Some weeks, the meetings may be necessary—but the boss should decide every week whether the meeting is actually needed.

Last, many in-person meetings are unnecessary in light of recent developments in videoconferencing. I used to be very put off by the regular delays in transmitting speech over video. But last year, when my two-hour flight to Minneapolis was canceled at the last minute, I was forced to hold a videoconference instead of an in-person meeting. Wow! The picture was vivid, and the voices transmitted instantaneously. My colleagues in Minneapolis agreed that I had no reason to make similar trips in the future. It's unproductive to spend hours on air travel to meet in person when you already know the other attendees and have access to top-quality videoconferencing.

For meetings that are necessary, try to limit invitations to those who truly need to attend, thus allowing as many people as possible to *avoid* the meeting. In the past, I have participated in many meetings of fifteen or twenty people. That number is far too big to get anything done. Various researchers have arrived at different conclusions as to the optimal meeting size,[4] but they would all agree that a meeting of seven or eight people is better than a meeting of fifteen or twenty.

Another technique for reducing the number of meetings is to ban meetings one day each month. This allows you (and any employees you manage) to catch up on work that you have been putting off in order to attend meetings. It also shows you and your employees how much work they can get accomplished without meetings. At MFS Investment Management, we instituted a policy that meetings were forbidden on the first Friday of every month.

Nevertheless, despite all attempts to reduce the number of meetings, you will be invited to meetings that seem likely to be unproductive. How can you avoid those meetings? Just say no! You can politely explain that you are too busy, have deadlines to meet, or have too much scheduled on that day.

As a busy executive, I decline many external requests by directing them to more appropriate employees in my organization. A lot of external firms want to meet with me to discuss supplying services to my firm. I refer them to the appropriate division, such as an advertising firm to the marketing division and a software firm to the systems unit. Many charities request meetings with me to request a donation. Although they may be pursuing worthwhile goals, I politely refer them to an employee responsible for vetting corporate contributions.

Declining invitations for internal meetings may require a little more tact. Politely emphasize to your colleague that the reason for saying no has nothing to do with the content of the event—or the person making the request—and everything to do with your crammed schedule. Be clear that you would like to attend such a meeting, and express regret about the conflict. For example, if a response by email is appropriate, you can reply as follows: "I am pleased that you invited me to the meeting on developing best practices for internal audits. I am a huge believer in improving the risk management of our firm. However, I must be preparing for client presentations the next day, so I will unfortunately be unable to attend. Thanks again for the invitation."

What if the meeting is being hosted by your boss? Those requests are harder to avoid. However, if you and your boss trust each other, you should describe your situation and ask for a reprieve from your boss. In other words, negotiate! You might explain that you have several deadlines to meet and ask which items should be delayed or deleted due to attending the meetings—for instance, "I can attend this meeting, but is it okay if I complete my assigned report on Wednesday instead of tomorrow?" Either your boss will get the point and allow you to skip the meeting (or leave after the first hour), or he or she will reschedule your other work commitments.

HOW LONG IS TOO LONG?

As any professional can tell you, many meetings run too long. For instance, a colleague told me of a four-hour meeting that was dominated by two employees arguing about what section should appear first in an internal planning document! The discussion probably cost their firm several thousand dollars: their employees were getting paid, but little work was getting done. Most meetings can be completed effectively within sixty minutes, and meetings really should never run longer than ninety minutes. After meeting for an hour and a half, most participants become too tired, bored, or impatient to engage productively.

HOW PEOPLE PAY ATTENTION

No matter how worthwhile the topic may be, lengthy meetings are unproductive because of how people pay attention—and how they don't. Back in the 1970s, two researchers attended more than ninety college lectures and observed when students were focusing and when they had lapses.[5] They noticed that students paid attention to the professor and studiously took notes for the first ten to eighteen minutes of lecture. At that point, the students' attention would lapse: they would look at the clock, stare blankly into space, or even doze off briefly. After a brief lapse, they would refocus on the lecture. However, as the lecture continued, the lapses occurred more frequently as the students found it harder and harder to pay attention. By the end of the fifty-minute lecture, they were paying attention for only three to four minutes at a time before their attention wandered.

Given their maturity and training, I'd like to think that professionals are better able than college students to maintain focus. But the basic principle holds: attention is most concentrated at the beginning of a meeting and then gradually declines.

One way to keep a meeting to ninety minutes is simple: schedule it for ninety minutes. If you schedule a meeting for two or three hours, that is how long it will take. If you schedule a meeting for one hour on the same subject, it will still finish on schedule. As Saul Kaplan, the founder of the Business Innovation Factory, put it, "Meetings are like a gas expanding to fill all available space." Cabletron, a cable TV company in New Hampshire, takes a more radical approach: it bans chairs in its meeting room. With everyone standing, it's easy to enforce the company's thirty-minute limit on meetings.[6]

Off-site meetings for all employees in a division or department tend to have a similar problem: although they may build team spirit and allow for in-depth discussion, they often last too long. In my experience, an off-site meeting can be done well in one day at a local hotel or college. If participants come from across the country, two days may be needed for an effective off-site because of travel logistics. Moreover, if employees travel from around the world, it is useful to surround a two-day off-site with other meetings involving those travelers. But an off-site of three or four days usually involves a significant waste of time.

HOW TO RUN AN EFFECTIVE MEETING

After working hard to shorten, eliminate, or avoid meetings, you should then maximize the productivity of the few meetings that you *do* need to attend. Take a look at figure 5 below to learn about the five main elements of an effective meeting, along with what can go wrong when these elements are absent.

Figure 5: KEY ELEMENTS OF AN EFFECTIVE MEETING

Good	Bad
The meeting has a clear agenda based on a well-developed set of goals. The day before the meeting, the convener sends out the agenda as well as any background materials. Participants can read them in advance and prepare to discuss the issues at the meeting.	The discussion does not follow a logical progression to specific ends. No one has had a chance to read the advance materials, since they were distributed 15 minutes before the meeting. As a result, the first part of the meeting is consumed by going over the materials.
The convener of the meeting starts off with a 10-to-15-minute presentation to put the meeting into context, highlight the key issues, and outline what needs to be decided at the meeting.	The convener of the meeting makes a presentation with too many PowerPoint slides cluttered with dense information. The presentation takes so long that there is almost no time for discussion.
After the brief introduction by the convener, the meeting participants vigorously debate the key issues. As a result of the collective interaction, they come up with a new solution to a tough problem.	The most senior executive so dominates the meeting that other participants are afraid to ask probing questions or advocate opposing views. The discussion rehashes conventional approaches.
During this vigorous debate, people use clear language and plain English. By the end of the meeting, everyone knows where everyone else stands.	Because no one wants to stick his or her neck out, participants fall back on vague language, jargon, and acronyms, speaking up without actually saying anything. As a result, conclusions are muddled.
Near the end of the meeting, the convener summarizes the group's conclusions and the next steps to be taken. The participants collectively assign responsibility and deadlines for each step.	At the end of the meeting, the most senior executive orders other participants to take specific steps by a specific date. The participants drag their feet since they have not bought into this plan.

Agenda and Advance Materials

How can you have meetings with more good than bad features? To begin with, every meeting needs an agenda, preferably one that spells out its purpose. Most meetings also need some background materials so everyone has a common information base. If the meeting is being run by your boss—and he or she tends to forget this step—you could volunteer to draft the advance materials yourself. This will make the meeting run more smoothly, and you will ingratiate yourself to your boss at the same time.

If the meeting is being run by a peer, you should make your attendance of the meeting conditional on receiving the agenda and the advance materials at least a day before the meeting. If the agenda and materials do not arrive or show up at the last minute, don't go to the meeting.

Introductory Presentations

If there are no advance materials—or if participants do not have the time to read them—the convener will have to make extensive opening remarks describing the issues in detail. I have often been in meetings where the presenter starts to go through a large number of PowerPoint slides, literally reading every word on every slide. This reflects intellectual laziness—the presenter is passively transferring information from his research to his audience without distilling it. Making complicated information more concise is part of the presenter's job.

Even useful presentations become boring if they last too long. Just like students at a college lecture, employees won't be able to pay attention for more than twenty minutes. In order to hold their attention beyond that point, the mode of the meeting should change from a presentation to a discussion. Such a change in the middle of the meeting effectively "resets" people's attention clock, helping them refocus on the subject under discussion.[7]

What should you do, then, when the leader of the meeting ignores this advice and keeps plowing through PowerPoint slides, even when the group has a solid understanding of the issues at hand? This requires some diplomacy. As the leader of the meeting, I usually make a polite remark after the initial fifteen to twenty minutes, such as "You've made some really interesting points, so please make sure that we all have enough time to discuss them." If the presenter does not get the hint, I might become more pointed: "Perhaps you could finish up in a few minutes, so we could begin the discussion." If the presenter still persists with a robotic march through PowerPoints, I often find myself tempted to take a cue from an old movie and start yelling, "I'm mad as hell and I'm not going to take this anymore!"[8]

A VERY COMPLEX POWERPOINT SLIDE

In April 2010, newspapers such as the *New York Times*, the *Daily Mail*, and the *Guardian* reported on a particularly complicated Power-Point slide. The slide, presented to U.S. generals in Afghanistan, depicted a dense flowchart tracing how each of 119 factors, such as "Perception of Coalition Intent & Commitment" and "Ins. Provision Of Gov't & Services," affected one another. At the time, General Stanley McChrystal, then the commander of U.S. forces in Afghanistan, quipped, "When we understand that slide, we'll have won the war."[9]

I had intended to include a copy of the slide in this book. However, its creators, a consulting firm, declined to give me the rights to reprint it. Although the slide has been widely published, their email claimed that "client confidentiality agreements" prevented them from letting me reprint the image. So if you want to take a look at the slide, you'll have to find it yourself. That shouldn't be too hard—you might type "Afghanistan PowerPoint" into a search engine.

Sometimes, however, long-winded presentations are *not* the leader's fault. The leader of the meeting may have done everything right—he or she sent out advanced materials and is prepared to enter into vigorous debate. But everyone else in the room hasn't fulfilled their end of the bargain by reading the advance materials. So the leader finds it necessary to make a longer opening presentation than he or she had planned.

If this happens to you when you're leading a meeting, strategically call your colleagues' bluff. Proceed on the assumption that the advance materials have been read, and begin a debate after a few introductory remarks. This will doom the present meeting to failure (so maybe you should pick a meeting that's not crucial). But you can bet that before the next meeting, the other participants will do their homework.

Promoting Vigorous Debate

The potential domination of a meeting by the most senior executive is a complex problem. Most bosses underestimate the huge impact of any opinion they express to their employees. I was at a meeting with Ned Johnson, the chairman of Fidelity, when he made an offhand remark about the location of a large tree near a company office. Within three days, the tree was moved several hundred yards at a cost of more than $200,000. When Ned heard the cost, he was dumbfounded that his remark had been interpreted as a command.

On the other hand, a boss has to keep the meeting on track. An unstructured and leaderless meeting is likely to be chaotic and unproductive. In leading a meeting, you should follow the agenda and encourage everyone to talk.

That's why again I use the rebuttable hypothesis (see chapter 2, "Focus on the Final Product") to reach a proper balance: it allows the boss to focus the meeting without dominating it. I might say, "Here is the area where we need to do something. But it is a difficult area, and there are several ways to address this problem. Now, this is my tentative view on the approach we should take, but I could be wrong. I want you to feel free to disagree and offer alternatives." Then I have to hold up my end of the bargain: I have to be willing to discard or modify my hypothesis if someone comes up with a better idea.

In certain cultures, however, you should recognize that subordinates will be extremely reluctant to disagree with any proposal made by a senior official. To get the discussion started, you could arrange in advance for someone to lead off the debate. Or you could go around the table and ask everyone to question one aspect of the proposal.

Even in the United States, I recommend that you appoint someone in every meeting to play devil's advocate. That person's job is to argue against what is being proposed by emphasizing the negatives, such as tough competitors or regulatory hurdles. In that manner, the meeting avoids the problem of "in-house baseball," where everyone agrees on a proposal without careful analyses of the counterarguments. I've attended too many meetings that proceeded as if the firm faced no serious competitors or resource constraints.[10]

AVOIDING DISTRACTIONS

We've all been to meetings where two chatterers distract everyone else by having an annoying side conversation. As the leader of a meeting, don't be afraid to call out your colleagues. In most cases, it's enough to shoot the offenders a quick glare—knowing that they've been caught, they usually end their side conversation. If you can't catch their attention, discreetly pass them a short written note: "Your conversation is distracting everyone else." If they still don't get the message, stop the meeting and politely ask that everyone give the meeting their full attention.

Similarly, I consider a ringing cell phone to be a serious offense. It is disruptive, not to mention quite embarrassing to the owner—

especially if the ringtone is a lively Top 40 hit. So before starting every meeting, ask people to put their phone on vibrate. If someone is expecting a really important call that truly can't be missed, he or she can leave the meeting room when the phone vibrates.

Using Plain Language

Many meetings are unproductive because participants use a lot of jargon that obscures the real issues. Quite often, people use buzzwords as fallbacks—making it sound as though they have something substantive to say when they actually don't.

For instance, consider the word "synergy." In making presentations to investors, many CEOs try to justify a proposed merger or acquisition by saying it is "synergistic" or that the combination will result in "synergies." When professional investors hear any version of this magic word, they usually sell the stock. Why? Because if the CEO had a good reason for the merger, such as reducing costs or acquiring patents, he or she would have said so. By invoking "synergies," the CEO is signaling that he or she does not have a clear reason for doing the deal and is just trying to put a positive spin on a poorly understood transaction.

Another vacuous phrase that I try to eliminate is "think outside the box." Roughly speaking, this phrase is a general exhortation for you to dream up a totally new and creative approach to a problem—a quite reasonable concept. However, it has evolved into such a cliché that it has lost all meaning. Today, it is a fallback phrase that merely means thinking beyond the tried and true. In my experience, if a manager keeps asking his colleagues to "think outside the box," you can be quite sure that he or she is thinking firmly *inside* the box.

Similarly, don't get bogged down by using obscure acronyms. There are some common acronyms such as ASAP (as soon as possible) and NYSE (New York Stock Exchange) that are generally understood. And every organization has its well-known shorthands for departments and procedures. It's perfectly okay to use the acronyms that everyone knows by heart. But when the penchant for acronyms goes too far, it effectively excludes newcomers from the conversation.

I recently attended a meeting in Washington, D.C., where several people referred to the EGTRRA. Later I found out that "EGTRRA" stood for the Economic Growth and Tax Relief and Reconciliation Act of 2001, better known as one of the "Bush tax cuts." I later went to an initial meeting at a company where the conversation revolved around OEMs (original equipment manufacturers) for ICDs (implantable cardioverter-defibrillators). Since those acronyms were not intuitively obvious to me, I had a hard time following the discussion. To help newcomers get up to speed, every organization should compile a list of acronyms that are peculiar to that industry or company and make that list freely available.

Getting Buy-In from Everyone

A meeting needs a proper ending: an agreement on actions to be done by certain people at certain times. That follow-up should be recorded in a list and distributed to all participants. But the list will be effective only if it reflects the collective consensus of the meeting, rather than the "word from on high" handed down by the boss.

At the end of a meeting, I always ask, "What are the action items, who's going to do them, and when will they be delivered?" I want the participants to agree on the action items and set their own timetable for the deliverables. At most, I gently suggest that their timetables include a margin of error to allow for the possibility of unforeseen delays or problems.

By letting the participants create their own follow-ups and time schedule, I'm trying to create a sense of ownership in them. This principle is known as the "IKEA Effect," named for the home furnishings retailer whose products are notoriously difficult to assemble. The IKEA Effect states that by forcing consumers to play an active role in the assembly of their dresser or bookshelf, they will value the product more highly than if it were assembled in store.[11] In a similar fashion, by creating their own deadlines, employees will be more motivated to meet them. Indeed, I find that meeting participants often set more aggressive deadlines for meeting follow-ups than I would have requested.

TAKEAWAYS

1. Think hard about whether you really need to call a meeting. You can share information just as effectively via email or a phone call.

2. Politely decline meetings that will not advance your priorities or seem as though they will be unproductive.

3. Try to limit your attendance at your boss's unproductive meetings by diplomatically explaining your workload.

4. Keep meetings as short as possible—schedule no more than ninety minutes at the maximum.

5. Hand out materials to be read one day before the meeting so that people have a chance to actually read the material.

6. Limit your opening remarks at meetings to fifteen to twenty minutes. Do not bore your audience to death with too many PowerPoint slides.

7. After the introduction, organize vigorous debate on the key points. The most powerful executive in the room must be willing to be challenged.

8. Keep jargon to a minimum at meetings—don't use the word "synergy"!

9. Develop a list of commonly used acronyms so that new-comers can easily participate in the discussion.

10. At the end of the meeting, ask participants to collectively decide who should do each task and when each task should be completed.

Part III

DEVELOPING
PERSONAL SKILLS

There are three key personal skills you need in order to be a productive professional: reading, writing, and speaking. In this part, I'll help you sharpen those skills. Since this book is focused on your professional career, I won't address reading novels for pleasure, writing works of fiction, or giving speeches at weddings.

My advice will be similar in each chapter: begin by thinking carefully about your goals, and then apply specific techniques to improve your effectiveness. Although I hope these techniques will increase your speed in all three areas, they are primarily aimed at increasing your productivity—the quantity and quality of your results for the time spent.

7

READING EFFECTIVELY

O nce when I was trying to help two young science students improve their reading skills, I looked at what they had underlined in a twenty-page chapter from their chemistry textbook. One student had underlined every other sentence on every page. The other student had underlined only three sentences in the whole chapter. Both of those approaches reflect poor reading skills; it is impossible that so much of the chapter—or so little—was important enough to be underlined.

These two students were not unique. In 2003, a large study tested the reading skills of thousands of American adults; it found that only 31 percent of U.S. college graduates could be considered "proficient" readers.[1]

READING THE NEWS

If you want to be an effective reader, you have to know your purpose for reading and stick to it. By adhering to this principle, I can read four newspapers each morning in less than one hour. Here is my specific approach.

- *Boston Globe*: I read the *Globe* to keep current on Massachusetts politics and follow the Boston sports teams. That means taking a quick look at the front pages and the first page of the Metro section, plus briefly reviewing its excellent sports section. And that's it. National politics are covered better by the *New York Times*, and business stories are handled better by the *Wall Street Journal*.

- *New York Times*: I read the *Times* mainly to learn about national politics. I look at the front page, skim through the rest of the A section for stories that interest me, and review the editorial page to get liberal perspectives on current issues. I resolutely ignore the other sections despite their tempting headlines or save them for when I have time for pleasure reading.

- *Wall Street Journal*: I spend the most time reading the *Journal* because its reporting on business issues is deep and comprehensive. I read the summary blurbs on the front page and then the whole article on subjects important to me. I also read the editorial page to stay abreast of conservative perspectives on current issues.

- *Financial Times* (*FT*) of London: I finish by reading the *FT* for its coverage of international issues. It often carries articles on foreign economics and politics that the U.S. papers don't address in depth. I skip the articles on the United States, and read the editorial page of the *FT* for its diverse perspectives on international topics.

Personally, I prefer to read physical copies of the newspapers instead of their online equivalents; this is a personal preference developed long before the Internet era. But younger professionals often choose to get their news from reputable online sources, and that may work for you as well.[2]

My research assistant typically starts his day by scanning the headlines of an authoritative source such as the website of the *New York Times*. If there's an article on a topic relevant to our research, he will read the whole article. For deeper analysis, he usually goes to the pages of his favorite bloggers across the political spectrum. Those bloggers—and the pages they link to—often provide more insight than a typical news article. But just as with physical newspapers, the blogosphere can overwhelm you with the amount of material available, so you still need to stay focused on your purpose for reading.

> *List all the news sources, virtual and physical, that you read regularly for reasons other than amusement. Next to each source, jot down your rationale for reading it—politics, sports, business news, and so on. Next ask yourself how you're reading each source: are you concentrating on your goal for that publication, or does your attention wander every time you see an entertaining headline? Now, next to each publication, jot down an estimate of how much time you spend each week reading it. Does your allocation of time make sense, given your professional Objectives? If not, read only those sections that are relevant to your purpose, or stop reading that publication altogether.*

KNOW YOUR PURPOSE

This exercise in reading newspapers should help you adopt the general principle of reading with a particular purpose in mind. Let's consider a few typical purposes for reading and what each means for my method of reading.

1. *Understanding key ideas.* I recently read an article in the *Economist* on declining marriage rates among women in Asia. I had no immediate use for the detailed statistics in that article, but I thought I might use them in the future to

describe how demographic trends affect public retirement plans. So I skimmed it to learn the general trends.

2. *Finding specific facts.* At the opposite pole is reading closely for facts. When I'm preparing for a board meeting, I carefully look over the memos and reports related to the company's quarterly performance. I want to be able to remember certain key statistics and substantive points to discuss with the board.

3. *Discovering new sources of information.* I often read an article purely to find other sources of information on the same or related subject. In that case, I skim the article until I find a reference to a relevant source. Similarly, my research assistant might skim a blog post looking for a link to a report or a data source.

4. *Evaluating an analysis.* I sometimes receive business plans for launching a new product with an assessment of the competitive landscape and financial projections for the product's initial years. In reading those proposals, I home in on the key assumptions in the analysis. The projections are worthless unless the underlying assumptions are well supported.

5. *Supporting my job.* When I was a lawyer advising a publicly traded company, I would review its financial reports before they were distributed to investors. That was part of my job to reduce the company's legal exposure by insisting that it make sufficient disclosures about potential problems. If part of your job requires this sort of specialized reading, keep this goal in mind when you're deciding what to read and how long to spend reading it.

ACTIVE READING: DOING THE THREE-STEP

To implement the general principle of active reading, you should follow a three-step process:

1. Grasp the *structure* of the reading.

2. Read the *introduction* and *conclusion*.

3. Skim the *tops of the paragraphs*.

SPEED-READING VERSUS EFFECTIVE READING

I'm not trying to teach you speed-reading in this chapter. Speed-reading is a technique to increase the number of words you read per minute. Evelyn Wood, the pioneer of speed-reading, advocated using a finger or a pen to move quickly underneath each line of text. However, that procedure runs into a biological roadblock: the human eye can recognize only eight to ten letters at a time (try it for yourself) and can move only four to five times in one second.[3] That implies a maximum reading speed of about five words per second, or three hundred words per minute.

By contrast, one of my key techniques for active reading is to skip over certain words or sentences. This allows you to concentrate on the content that you want to remember. Thus, active reading increases your speed not by *maximizing the number* of words you read per minute but by *covering fewer* words per minute.

1. Grasp the Structure of the Reading

Most people read by just jumping in and starting at the first sentence. That is the wrong way to read when you're trying to extract information quickly. Before you start to read a document, take a few moments to understand its *structure*—how it begins and ends, and how it divides the major topics in between. In books and longer works, look at the table of contents. In shorter works, glance at the headings throughout the piece. This will help you both read faster and understand more, because you'll already know how the author plans to move from one idea to the next.

Professors Jukka Hyönä and Robert Lorch performed several experiments exploring how readers interact with the structure of a text. One experiment, using a system that tracked subjects' eye movements, showed that many readers fail to take advantage of titles and headings.[4] Their eye-tracking system showed that only seven of their forty subjects read "strategically" by focusing attention on key structural elements such as topic sentences and headings. Most everyone else read linearly, from one word to the next.[5]

Linear readers fail to take advantage of an easy, basic strategy to become more efficient readers. As Hyönä and Lorch found in a later study, headings are critical for understanding a document.[6] The researchers randomly presented adult subjects with one of two informational texts. The texts were identical in every way except that one had clearly marked headings at the beginnings of new sections, while the other text did not. Hyönä and Lorch found that subjects who read the text with headings were able to read the text faster and were able to retain more information. By being able to understand the structure more easily, those subjects had become much more efficient readers.

To show you the importance of reading headings (and to illustrate other suggestions for reading effectively), I've included a short excerpt in appendix 1. It is adapted from an article I wrote for the *Harvard Business Review* called "The Case for Professional Boards."[7] Just like most of what you read at work, the piece is dense and somewhat technical. But then again, if all your professional reading assignments were as gripping as a Tom Clancy novel, you would have little need for this chapter.

The excerpt provides a good example of why you should read the headings first. Take a look at the excerpt—specifically, the headings from the first half of the article. Without reading anything except the headings, how much could you learn about my proposal for professional boards? All three of my main recommendations! The headings indicate that better boards require "smaller size," "greater expertise," and "increased time commitment." With those headings firmly in mind, you can then read to find the supporting points on each of the three recommendations.

2. Read the Introduction and Conclusion

Most people read in a linear fashion: first the introduction, next the body of the piece, then the conclusion. Although this sequence appears logical, it's not the best order for you to follow. After grasping the structure of the reading, here's how you should proceed.

First, read the introduction carefully, looking for the theme sentence or paragraph that will unlock the whole article or chapter. The theme sentence or paragraph often encapsulates the ideas and structure of the piece. Then skip directly to the conclusion. Why? Because the conclusion tells you where the writer is going to end up. It usually summarizes his or her main points and, if it's well done, suggests what the writer thinks are the key takeaways. Only when you know where the writer is aiming should you read the body of the text. (I'll have more to say on how to read the body of text shortly.)

To illustrate the benefits of reading the introduction and conclusion before the main body of text, take another look at the excerpt. Start with the introduction: you learn about how the Sarbanes-Oxley Act works and why I believe that it is insufficient. The introduction also provides a road map to the article—how it will be organized.

To find the solution to the problem of ineffective boards, you need to go to the conclusion, which does an excellent job of recapping the article. Specifically, look at the conclusion's first paragraph. Each of its final three sentences captures one of the three main pillars of my proposal: smaller boards, directors with more industry knowledge, and a greater time commitment from board members. You'll also see how the conclusion goes further than a summary. It offers an additional insight: the different mechanisms that may be utilized to implement my proposal.

3. Skim the Tops of the Paragraphs

If the introduction and conclusion have given you a good idea of the main points, you can safely skim the body of a piece. That's because you have already narrowed your purpose in reading the body: to expand your understanding of the key points or clarify complex concepts. As a general rule, skimming allows you to zero in on what's most important to you—and skip the rest.

SKIMMING TO INCREASE COMPREHENSION

Researchers from the University of Utah performed an experiment[8] to see how college students studied for exams. They presented students with a long text and told them that they would be tested on the material after reading. At various points in the text, readers were instructed to talk to the researchers to explain what exactly their study habits had been in that section of text (for example: underlining, skimming, paraphrasing, writing an outline, doing nothing). On the basis of the results, the researchers organized their subjects into six groups based on their study habits and examined how each of these six groups did on the recall test.

They described one group, containing only six of their sixty-seven participants, as the "Good Strategy Users." This group adapted their study styles depending on whether the section of text was dense or light and on the extent of their background knowledge on a given subject. Notably, the Good Strategy Users were far more likely to report that they frequently skimmed text when it appeared trivial and unimportant. Skimming did not force those students to miss out on valuable information in the text; rather, it allowed them to devote more attention and brain space to parts of the text deemed more important. After reading the section, that group did better on a recall test than the other groups did.[9]

Unfortunately, skimming has gotten a bad rap in the academic community. In the minds of many educators and observers, a reader who skims is simply being lazy—and in many cases, they're correct. For instance, two professors from the University of Saskatchewan examined how college students read a particular textbook.[10] Not surprisingly, they noticed that those who actually read the textbook (in depth) ended up with a better grade in the course than students who merely "skimmed" it. But the skimmers were simply moving their eyes across the page. As the researchers stated, "Some students acted as if learning would miraculously occur just because their eyes had scanned all the assigned lines of the textbook."[11] Others skimmed a chapter quickly, telling themselves that they would come back to it and read it in depth later—which was an overly optimistic prediction for most of them.

But I'm not talking about that kind of passive skimming. To *actively* skim the body of an article or chapter, you should read the top of each paragraph. A good writer starts each paragraph with a topic sentence, followed by supporting facts or arguments. Once you've read the first sentence, you can decide whether it's worth reading the rest of the paragraph.

To figure out whether you should read the rest of the paragraph, you should answer this critical question: will the rest of the paragraph help you achieve one of the reading purposes that I mentioned earlier? If you're reading for specific facts or to discover new sources, the question is easy to answer: read the rest of the paragraph only if it includes such a fact or source.

If you're reading to grasp the main ideas, it's more complex. For this purpose, decide if the topic sentence provides enough information on the main ideas or if you need to delve further into the paragraph to grasp them. Take extra time if the content is new to you; research consistently shows that readers comprehend less when they do not have the relevant background knowledge.[12]

Skimming to evaluate the author's analysis requires even more judgment. After reading the topic sentence, determine whether the rest of the paragraph will advance a new argument or merely parrot the conventional wisdom. If the paragraph challenges the commonly accepted worldview, read it closely, as such paragraphs often form the crux of the author's argument. Take special care to have an open mind if you have a strong opinion on a subject; people often fall into a trap of overemphasizing evidence that supports their intuitive position at the expense of equally compelling evidence to the contrary.[13]

Look again at the excerpt in appendix 1. Imagine that you're reading to try to pick up its main ideas. If you haven't done so already, review the headings and then read the introduction and conclusion. Next read just the topic sentence in the paragraphs from part A of the article, "Smaller size." After reading each topic sentence, glance at the rest of the paragraph and decide if it's worth reading. If not, go on to the topic sentence in the next paragraph.

Here is where I came out.

First paragraph (starting "Many of the financial institutions"): I read only the topic sentence because I could immediately tell that the remainder of the paragraph was just providing details supporting the topic sentence—that many failed institutions had large boards. (If I were reading to learn some specific facts, I would read the entire para-

graph closely, as it describes one particular example of a failed board.)

Second paragraph (starting "But even eleven directors"): I read the entire paragraph because it explained why boards should be smaller— the central idea of this section.

Third paragraph (starting "Research on group dynamics"): I read the topic sentence and then skimmed the rest. The rest detailed a research project supporting the topic sentence's suggestion of a six- to seven-person board. (If I were reading to evaluate the argument, I'd want to take a closer look at the research, so I'd read the whole paragraph carefully.)

Fourth paragraph (starting "The six independent directors"): I read only the topic sentence, which indicated that the paragraph described some technical aspects of boards with a level of detail that I didn't particularly need to know.

As you can see, reading off the tops of the paragraphs is an active, not passive process. After reading every topic sentence, you have to decide whether it is worth your time to read the rest of the paragraph. If you read the rest, will you learn significantly more than you already know by then? Quite often, the answer is no.

ACTIVELY REMEMBERING

As you read an article or memo, constantly ask yourself what you want to remember from it. Although this is closely related to the earlier discussion of reading purposes, it has a different time dimension. Think about your purpose for reading *before* and *during* your review of the material. Think about what you want to remember *during* and *after* you review the material.

When my nephews were in high school, I devised an exercise to help them focus on what they should remember. After they read a chapter in a history or science book, I asked them to write out the handful of key points that they wanted to remember for the test a month later. After they did that a few times, I urged them to read with an eye to finding those two or three key paragraphs while they were reading. Before long, they were able to read chapters much more quickly while still doing well on tests.

You should follow a similar practice: distill what you want to remember into a few key points relevant to your purpose for reading this particular piece. If you're reading to learn specific facts or discover new sources, you should simply write down a list of those specific facts or new sources. If you're reading to understand the key ideas, capture those ideas in the form of a short summary.[14]

> *Let's use the excerpt in appendix 1 to explore how to write a good summary: as you read it, write down five to eight key points that you want to remember about the main ideas of the piece. Could you have read the excerpt more quickly if you had been focused on finding those key points?*
>
> *Below, I've provided a sample of seven points that summarize this excerpt. Did your summary cover all the points that I included? If not, were the points you omitted worthy of remembering? Did your summary include additional points? Were your additional points important to remember?*
>
> 1. *The new procedures of Sarbanes-Oxley were insufficient to ensure proper corporate governance. To improve governance, corporations must make fundamental changes to their boards of directors.*
>
> 2. *Large boards are ineffective because they lead to social loafing and inhibit bold actions; a better board would have only six independent directors.*
>
> 3. *It is more important for directors to have industry-specific expertise than diverse general knowledge, so boards should try to recruit directors with extensive industry experience.*

4.   *The average director spends roughly two hundred hours per year in activities related to the company. This is insufficient to fully understand a large company's business. To compensate directors for increasing their time commitment, their pay should be increased.*

5.   *The new class of professional directors will come largely from the pool of retired executives.*

6.   *Professional directors would not be subject to significant legal risk, so long as they act diligently and in good faith.*

7.   *Though some power would shift from management to directors, board members would not be involved in the day-to-day operations of a company.*

Evaluating my argument is even more difficult. To organize what you want to remember for this purpose, write down the key steps of my argument: the research and examples that I cite, the logic that I use to support them, and the counterarguments that I address. Here are the key steps in the article's argument, which:

- cites research on group dynamics and statistics about the average board size to claim that the typical board of directors is too large;

- utilizes three examples—Citigroup, a temporary CEO, and Merck—as evidence that many directors have insufficient industry expertise;

- performs some back-of-the-envelope calculations to estimate that most directors spend only two hundred hours per year on the business, which, it asserts, is not enough;

- suggests that professional directors could come from the
  ranks of retired executives—so long as the mandatory
  retirement age for boards is relaxed;

- estimates that, even if professional board members
  were paid more, the total compensation cost would be
  roughly the same, since boards would be much smaller;

- cites legal precedent to argue that diligent professional
  directors would not be subject to significant increases in
  legal liability.

Once you create this list, you'll still have to do the heavy lifting of *evaluating* each of these steps—which means delving into the research cited and thinking critically about the strength of my logic. Moreover, you would have to decide if these steps together support my thesis that corporate boards need more "professional" directors. Though this evaluation process is not easy, you can concentrate more on the key steps of the argument if you write them down as you read.

TAKEAWAYS

1. Don't try to read more words per minute; increase your
   speed by reading fewer words—the ones most relevant
   to your goals.

2. Before you pick up a text, think carefully about why
   you are reading. Are you looking to learn the author's
   general thesis? Are you looking for specific facts?

3. Have a clear rationale for reading a particular newspaper or other news source. What are you getting from
   this newspaper or source that you can't get from others?

4. Look at the structure, especially headings, before you start to read. These will show how the piece is organized and give you an idea what topics will be covered.

5. Read the introduction in depth, looking for a thesis or theme sentence and a paragraph showing the organization of the piece.

6. Read the conclusion *before* you read the body. Often, the conclusion shows where the author is going and reviews the author's main points.

7. Read the tops of body paragraphs. This will allow you to actively decide whether each paragraph is worth reading, in light of your reading purpose.

8. Don't go further if the paragraph just repeats points that are already familiar to you, or if its content is not central to your purpose.

9. Focus constantly on finding what you want to remember from an article or memo.

10. If you are reading for the document's main ideas, write a short summary of the ideas you want to remember when you finish the document.

11. If you are reading to evaluate the author's analysis, write down each of the main steps in his or her argument. This will allow you to focus on these key steps as you delve further into the argument.

8

WRITING EFFECTIVELY

Writing is an essential skill for knowledge-based workers. They must compose documents to inform, lead, and persuade others both inside and outside their organization.

Unfortunately, good writing is hard to find. As a professor, I have often encountered MBA students who are very articulate when they participate in class, but when they hand in exams, their writing is disjointed. In the business world, I have met very smart people who have a great idea for a new product but cannot compose a good memo about that product. And in government agencies, I've dealt with officials who can brilliantly defend a position in a debate but whose briefs on the same subject are turgid and wandering.

As emails increasingly take the place of phone calls, writing skills are becoming even more critical to personal productivity, but many professionals have been poorly trained. The Business Roundtable, which represents the largest corporations in the United States, estimates that its members spend $3 billion per year to send their workers to remedial writing classes.[1] Poor writing undermines professional productivity in many ways, frustrating customers with unreadable product manuals, baffling employees with unclear documents, and creating office tension due to miscommunication among employees.

PLANNING THROUGH OUTLINES

George, a friend of mine, is an expert in the field of medieval history. But he takes more than a year to write an article after he has completed his research. Why? Because he keeps getting "stuck" during the writing process. He stops writing when he becomes uncertain where the article is going.

Diane, a clinical psychologist, complains that she can't figure out what she wants to say until she writes the conclusion of a lengthy paper. Unfortunately, the rest of the paper then doesn't fit well with the conclusion, so she is forced to revise and rewrite the body of the paper.

Both of those writers would be better off if they started with an outline. George wouldn't get stuck because he'd know where the article was going, and Diane wouldn't have to rewrite her paper to fit a conclusion that somehow takes her by surprise.

As these cases illustrate, you should think of writing as having several distinct phases, including an initial phase of mapping the terrain and a second phase of translating that map into actual prose. Remember the principle of focusing quickly on the final product, which I discussed in chapter 2? This is a similar idea: formulate a rough plan for the entire piece *before* you put pencil to paper. If you try to write without a plan, you will face an enormous challenge.

WHY OUTLINING MATTERS

It is very difficult to plan and write at the same time, because the task of writing is very demanding of what's called your "working memory." Working memory is the mental space where information is held and processed in your brain, allowing you to perform higher-order tasks such as reasoning and learning. In the context of writing, it is this process that allows you to manipulate words into sentences and paragraphs. But your working memory has limited resources: it can only hold and process so much information.

Psychology professor Ronald Kellogg demonstrated experimentally that the different components of writing—planning, translating, and revising—all compete for the same resources in your brain.[2] Thus, if you can do most of your planning by creating an outline first, you can devote more effort to translating your ideas into text when you compose an actual draft.

Professor Kellogg also performed a controlled experiment to explicitly test the hypothesis that outlines improve the writing process.[3] He randomly assigned students into two groups: one that was required to spend five to ten minutes outlining their written work and another that was forbidden to outline. He found that those in the "outline" group wrote better papers—because they were able to focus more on the "translation" process while actually writing the paper. In sum, the "outline" group wrote just as quickly as the "no outline" group, even taking into account the extra time they spent outlining. All of this means that writing an outline allowed those individuals to write better papers in the same amount of time.

My approach to creating an outline is completely systematic: first I brainstorm, next I categorize, and then I outline the final product.

- *Brainstorm*: I take a blank piece of paper and jot down all my thoughts on the relevant subject. My goal is to get down as many ideas as possible, not to put them into any particular order.

- *Categorize*: Next I put the ideas into various categories and subcategories. This process helps me organize my ideas into groupings, which will become the building blocks of an outline.

- *Outline*: Then I arrange and rearrange the groupings in various combinations. In the end, I try to find a logical order for the groupings, which can serve as a writing outline.

Now it's your turn to practice this three-step process. Suppose your boss asks you to write a short memo to persuade your organization's top executives to undertake a "greening" initiative to become more environmentally friendly.

I'm going to work with this example a few times in this chapter, but feel free to choose one of the two options below if you prefer:

- *Imagine that you're an employee at a theme park. Write a memo to convince the head of Human Resources to hire ten more actors to walk around the park in animal costumes.*

- *Imagine that you are in the research department of a large food company. Write a memo asking the department's head to fund your development of an antiobesity cereal or drink.*

Start by brainstorming on a sheet of paper.[4] Jot down all your ideas for this memo, without worrying too much about how they fit

*together. How broad is your list of ideas? Here is my nonexhaustive
list of ideas for what may be relevant to the executive committee:*

<u>*Step 1: Brainstorm*</u>
> *Company image*
> *More recycling*
> *Renovate windows*
> *Lower/raise thermostat*
> *Energy costs*
> *Tax considerations*
> *Public transit passes*
> *Cost of renovation*
> *Carbon offsets*
> *Ban Styrofoam cups*
> *Redesign product packaging*
> *New lightbulbs*
> *Hybrid company vehicles*
> *Work from home*
> *Right thing to do*

*Next, take your list of factors (plus any of mine) and organize
them into relevant categories. Below are the categories that I used to
group my list of potentially relevant factors. I have begun to put the
categories into a logical order, in preparation for writing an outline.
Note that some ideas from my brainstorming list didn't make it into
these categories—indeed, discarding less important ideas is a critical
component of the writing process.*

<u>*Step 2: Categorize*</u>
Energy
> *Renovate windows*
> *Lower/raise thermostat*
> *New lightbulbs*

Garbage
  More recycling
  Redesign product packaging

Profits and Losses
  Energy costs
  Tax considerations
  Cost of renovation

Transportation
  Public transit passes
  Work from home

Intangible Benefits
  Right thing to do
  Company image

Now for the final step: turning your categories into a writing outline. In taking this step, think about your audience: your organization's top executives. What do they care about most? What will be the most persuasive and logical sequence for this audience?

Here is my writing outline for this memo. Note that I have added an introduction at the top of the outline and a conclusion at the end. I've grouped the two categories into two overarching themes—how the organization could become "greener" and why that might be a good idea. Finally, I've moved up the section about profits and losses so that it comes before the section about intangible benefits. The organization's executives probably care most about the concrete financial impact.

Step 3: Outline
Introduction
How
   Energy
      Lower/raise thermostat
      Renovate windows
      New lightbulbs

   Garbage
      More recycling
      Redesign product packaging

   Transportation
      Public transit passes
      Work from home

Why
   Profits and Losses
      Energy costs
      Tax considerations
      Cost of renovation

   Intangible Benefits
      Right thing to do
      Company image

Conclusion

HOW TO STRUCTURE YOUR WRITING

With your outline in hand, you are ready to start writing. The three key elements of any essay are the introduction, the conclusion and the body. These are the same three elements we discussed in the prior chapter on effective reading. This is not a coincidence; you should write in a way that makes it easy for others to follow you.

Start with an Introduction

In my view, a good introduction must fulfill three objectives:

- Provide the reader with context

- State the main theme of the author

- Explain the organization of the writing

At the start, the reader needs background facts to understand why he or she is spending time on the piece. In the memo discussed above, you could state the context as follows:

> The executive committee is considering a broad range of reforms to make our organization more environmentally friendly. This memo explains what steps the committee could take to "green" our organization and why taking those steps makes good business sense.

Next, the introduction should summarize the main theme of your memo. In other words, tell the reader the core of your argument. Here is one illustration of a thematic summary for such a memo:

> This memo will argue that a "greening" initiative would improve the company's bottom line. The costs of this initiative would be more than offset by reduced energy expenses, potential tax savings, and long-term improvements to our company's image.

The final portion of the introduction should lay out a road map for the rest of the memo, explaining the structure in a way that's consistent with any headings or subtitles. This will help your readers follow your reasoning.

A good road map should be just one paragraph with a clear sequence. Here is an example of a good road map for our memo:

> First, this memo will describe how our organization could become more environmentally friendly, by reducing energy consumption, transportation, and garbage. Second, it will argue that these changes will benefit the organization by generating tax credits and reducing energy costs over the short term, while providing marketing opportunities over the long term.

Use Summaries and Conclusions

There is a lot of confusion about what constitutes a summary and what makes for a good conclusion. A summary is simply a condensed repetition of the main points of an article or memo. A conclusion should go beyond a summary in various ways: it may draw out lessons for other subjects, suggest larger implications for public policy, or recommend further research in specific areas.

I'm not disparaging summaries; they're often essential—especially "executive summaries," which are so named because executives don't have time to read long or complex documents. If a memo or article is lengthy or dense, it should have an executive summary before the introduction so readers can grasp the main points in a few minutes. This part of a document is crucial, largely because it has the greatest number of readers! In practice, readers at all levels of an organization often choose to read only the executive summary.

Executive summaries aside, all articles and memos need a conclusion that goes beyond a mere summary. Any intelligent reader who has gotten that far already knows the main points; he or she is looking for something more in the conclusion. I get really irritated when I read a "conclusion" that simply regurgitates the points already made. That is lazy. I've already seen those points twice before, once in the executive summary (or introduction) and once in the body of the article or memo.

Here are two paragraphs based on the same article about a certain type of medical research. One is a summary and the other is a conclusion.

(Peek at this endnote[5] to learn which is which.) What does the conclusion add for the reader that is not in the summary?

Paragraph 1

As discussed above, charities should use a seven-dimensional performance framework to analyze the success of translational medical research (TMR). They should measure the amount and diversity of funding, the level of talent attraction, the progress that has been made on key drug pipelines, the number of publications and citations in peer-reviewed journals, the extent to which they share information with other organizations, the amount of third-party uptake of their ideas, and the willingness to collaborate with other firms. These seven dimensions are key to understanding how well TMR is performing.

Paragraph 2

As charities and governments increase their funding of translational medical research (TMR), it is critical that they work with researchers to establish an effective system for performance assessment. Officials at funders should collaborate with active participants in TMR to articulate the objectives for their programs and the metrics to gauge progress in the seven dimensions discussed above. In this way, both funders and recipients will better understand their priorities and will generate the information needed to evaluate the extent to which these programs are delivering on their objectives.

Body Paragraphs

Now that we understand the design of the introduction and conclusion, let's turn to the body of the article or memo. Again, we want our writing to support effective reading. That means doing two things:

1. Dividing the body with headings or subtitles to show the structure of the document.

2. Starting each paragraph with a topic sentence so readers can easily read off the tops of the paragraphs. Readers should be able to follow the progression of your argument by reading only these topic sentences; the rest of each paragraph should provide factual or analytic support for the topic sentence.

Here are two paragraphs about the British television show *Downton Abbey*. One of the paragraphs is well structured with a strong topic sentence, but the other needs improvement.

Paragraph 1

Downton Abbey, a TV show about an aristocratic British family, has become a surprising hit among middle-class Americans. The lavish lifestyle of the Crawley family, who live on a sprawling Yorkshire estate during the early twentieth century, fascinates American viewers. The audience also loves to watch the complex relationships within the Crawley family and among their many servants. However, the family faced a crisis because the three Crawley daughters may not inherit the estate under British law. Fortunately, a male cousin inherited the estate and married the eldest Crawley daughter.

The topic sentence describes the main idea of the paragraph—that *Downton Abbey* is a hit among American viewers. The rest of the paragraph then describes why the audience has been tuning in. This is an example of a very well-structured paragraph: the topic sentence articulates the main idea, which is then clarified by the rest of the paragraph.

Paragraph 2

The TV show *Downton Abbey* is about an aristocratic family living in England during the early twentieth century. The Crawley family is encamped in a large Yorkshire estate with lots of servants, who are often at odds with each other. The family is also facing a major crisis since the three daughters may not inherit the estate under British law. Fortunately, a male cousin becomes the heir to the estate and becomes the husband of the eldest Crawley daughter. These dramatic events, together with the family's lavish lifestyle, have made the show a surprising hit among American middle-class viewers.

This paragraph has a weaker structure. Although its topic sentence introduces *Downton Abbey*, it does not indicate why the author is writing about it. A reader would have to read the entire paragraph up to the final sentence, which finally expresses the main idea—that *Downton Abbey* is a surprise hit. This final sentence would be a better topic sentence, and the other sentences could be modified to provide better support for that topic.

After reading these examples, try your hand at writing effective paragraphs. Turn back to your outline from earlier in this chapter describing a possible "greening" initiative for your organization (or whichever other option you chose). Then try to write two body paragraphs in the body of the memo under whichever category you feel most interesting. Use strong topic sentences, supported by the other sentences in the paragraph.

In reviewing your two paragraphs, answer these three questions:

- *Do both of your paragraphs begin with a topic sentence that conveys the main point of the paragraph to the reader?*

- *How, by marshaling facts or otherwise, do the other sentences in each paragraph support the topic sentence?*

- *Can the reader move easily from the topic sentence of the first paragraph to the topic sentence of the second paragraph without reading anything else?*

If you want more practice, try to compose the entire memo on the "greening" initiative, including an effective introduction and a conclusion that does more than summarize the main points.

WRITING GOOD SENTENCES

Now that you understand the role of the introduction, conclusion, and body paragraphs in between, let's quickly review how to actually write those paragraphs—with effective sentences, concise language, the active voice, accurate words, and flawless spelling and grammar.[6]

Write Short Sentences

When I was in high school, I became enamored of Ernest Hemingway's style—short, simple sentences. Using short sentences is the best way to express thoughts clearly. By contrast, run-on sentences are hard to follow; they suggest that the author is not sure where he or she is going.

Example: Run-on Sentence

After several hours at the beach, I had not caught any fish so I walked into town and found a bar that served tasty sandwiches and good beer, where I met an attractive woman named Maria who had a conversation with me about how the town was changing.

Example: Short Sentences

After several hours at the beach, I had not caught any fish. I walked into the town to find lunch. I ate at a bar that served tasty sandwiches and good beer. At the next table was an attractive woman named Maria. She struck up a conversation with me about how the town was changing.

Show Clear Relationships

When you are trying to connect more than one clause, sentence, or paragraph, make sure to express the relationship between them clearly. This means using words such as "since," "because," "after," "before," "however," or "nevertheless," which show the reader why, when, where, or how the new idea relates to the prior one. By contrast, additive words such as "and," "in addition," and "besides" fail to show how the ideas are related.

Example: Additive Connections—Weak Relationships

She hurt her knee and went to the hospital. In addition, she had an X-ray of her knee at the hospital.

Example: Adverb Connections—Strong Relationships

She went to the hospital because she hurt her knee. Soon after she arrived, the doctors ordered an X-ray of her knee.

Use the Active Voice

By using the active voice, a writer tells the reader exactly who is doing or saying what. When a writer uses the passive voice, it is often unclear who is doing or saying what. The two sentences below illustrate this contrast.

Active:

Sally provided the money for the down payment to buy a house for her brother.

Passive:

The down payment was provided to buy a house for Sally's brother.

Use Precise Language

Business writing should favor clarity and accuracy at the expense of creative wordplay. Here is one example: writers frequently try to introduce new words with similar meanings in order to create variety. But clarity is more important than variety in business writing. Consider these two sentences.

The company president was obsessed with following the priorities included in its five-year plan. While the other officers of the company supported the requirements, they were willing to consider modifications if
needed.

Are the "requirements" in the second sentence the same as the "priorities" in the first sentence? That is probably what the writer intended, but
the choice of different words for variety's sake creates confusion.

Specify Antecedents

Though pronouns are useful shorthand, it can be unclear what a particular pronoun is referring to. Consider the two sentences below.

Brady, his father, and the bunch all played in the football game, but only
he got hurt.

Does "he" refer to Brady or his father?

Brady, his father, and the bunch all played in the football game, and they
got hurt.

Who exactly is covered by "they"—Brady and his father, or the bunch?

Get the Spelling Right

It is simply unacceptable to have spelling errors in your written work. Although your work may still be understandable, spelling errors convey the
message that you are lazy and/or sloppy—a really bad message to any current
or potential employer. In a 2006 poll, 47 percent of hiring executives said they
would toss the résumé of a job applicant into the garbage if it had one spelling
error—if it had two spelling errors, 84 percent would toss it.[7]

One common error is an overreliance on spell-check programs. Although spell-checks will catch most errors, they cannot distinguish ho-
mophones ("heel" and "heal") and won't catch a typo if you accidentally

write another word (e.g., "the lad of paper," instead of "the pad of paper"). The only solution is to take the time to carefully review your written work to look for spelling errors.

Get the Grammar Right

The intricacies of language make it even more difficult to create a computer program that accurately checks for grammar usage. This means that grammar-checking software tends to be unreliable: the program will often identify an error even if your grammar is correct, and vice versa. For instance, take a look at the two sentences below, both with egregious grammar errors. Yet both "passed" the grammar check on Microsoft Word.

John looked right at me and he says, "What do you mean by that?" (change of tense)

The market has responding favorably to the surprisingly strong earnings that the high-tech sector reports yesterday. (improper verb use)

FREQUENTLY ASKED QUESTIONS ABOUT THE WRITING PROCESS

Now that you understand the basics of how to outline your ideas, structure your writing, and use effective language, let me answer some questions that I've often been asked about the writing process.

Q: I have a hard time writing because I have so much going on around me. How can I clear my mind to get down to writing?

Writing requires a high degree of concentration. You should try to find a place that is a little out of the flow and clear your plate of possible distractions such as computer games and ringing cell phones. Personally, I like to write early in the morning before the buzz of the day begins. I have a friend who can write only in the evening after everyone has left the office and it is very quiet. Both of us like to write on long plane or train rides, where we can get a several-hour block of undisturbed time. You should write regularly at the time of day that works best for you.

Q: *I take forever to write. I compose a sentence and then rewrite it over and over and over because I'm not satisfied with how it reads. Can you help me make my sentences better?*

If this question applies to you, your problem is not that you write poor sentences—it's that you are a perfectionist. To put it bluntly, this is not an effective way to write. Just as you cannot plan and write at the same time, you cannot write and revise at the same time. Don't try to spew forth a final product at your first sitting. Writing is an iterative process, which takes place in multiple steps over time.

You might worry that creating a less-than-perfect first draft would harm the quality of your writing; that couldn't be further from the truth. Try to write a first draft, go on to another project, and revise the first draft the next day. With a little time for reflection and editing, your revised draft will be much improved.

One way to get a simple draft out is to use speech recognition software, such as Dragon. Though they aren't perfect (and will produce many errors), they can help you create a first draft, since many people feel that talking is mentally easier than writing.

Q: *How long should my article be?*

This is a common question with a short answer. Your article should be as long as necessary to cover the topic well for the relevant audience—*and no longer*. Don't equate the length of a paper with the value of its content; conciseness can be hugely valuable.

Q: *Since I hate the idea of procrastination, I try to compose my entire article all at once. But after a few hours, I get stuck. Should I try to break it up into smaller pieces?*

Yes, you should divide a long document into smaller pieces, writing for several hours each day for several days with regular breaks. Professor Bob

Boice of SUNY at Stony Brook came to that conclusion when he studied the way his colleagues wrote lengthy research articles.[8] Some colleagues were "binge" writers, working many hours at a time in a small number of sessions. He found that binge writers were particularly likely to become frustrated and stuck in the middle of those long sessions. By contrast, colleagues who wrote on a more regular schedule tended to write with fresh ideas in mind and were more able to reflect effectively upon their work. In the end, regular writers composed as much as binge writers during each session—despite spending only one-third as much time.

Taking breaks can help you come up with new ideas. At the end of the day, I often find myself stuck on a conceptual or translational problem in my writing. Sometimes I wake up the next morning with a new approach to yesterday's problems. The creative process works in fits and starts, not in a straight line.

TAKEAWAYS

1. Before you start writing, create an outline that shows the logical progression of your piece. Start by brainstorming ideas; then put them into relevant categories, and finally organize them into a logical order.

2. Use the introduction of a piece to provide context, establish the theme of the piece, and indicate how it will be organized.

3. Create an executive summary for long or dense documents that describes the big picture so that readers short on time can understand the main points.

4. Start each paragraph with a topic sentence presenting its main idea. You want your reader to be able to read off the tops of the paragraphs if he or she is skimming.

5. Don't use your conclusion to merely summarize the piece; provide the reader with additional insight, such as broader implications or suggestions for future actions.

6. Use effective language. This means short sentences, clear relationships between clauses, and proper use of antecedents for pronouns.

7. Proofread your paper for grammar and spelling mistakes. When you've finished, proofread again. One error is one too many.

8. Accept that your first draft won't be perfect. Don't try to write and revise at the same time, or you'll get hung up on every sentence.

9. Use as many words as you need to cover your topic to your audience's satisfaction, but don't add length for length's sake.

10. Don't try to write a long piece in one sitting; write regularly every day for an hour or two in an environment that best suits you.

9

SPEAKING EFFECTIVELY

The thought of speaking in front of an audience terrifies most
people. Jerry Seinfeld once quipped that "to the average person, if
you have to go to a funeral, you're better off in the casket than doing the
eulogy."[1] Indeed, a Gallup poll found that 40 percent of Americans claim
a fear of public speaking—second only to a fear of snakes.[2]

But public speaking is an important skill for most professionals. They
often need to make oral presentations to groups within their own organization and sometimes are asked to deliver speeches to public audiences.
Because most professionals have not been trained in this area, they make
predictable mistakes. Fortunately, you can become an effective public
speaker with a little guidance and planning.

Start by recognizing the fundamental differences between speaking
and writing. On the plus side, speakers can immediately sense the audience's reactions to what they're saying and quickly shift gears if needed.
And unlike writers, speakers can use gestures, intonation, and other rhetorical devices to convey emotions.

On the other hand, speaking has two inherent *disadvantages* relative to writing. If you give a speech you don't like, you can't throw it away and start again, the way you can with a piece of writing. And you have to work much harder in a speech to convey a clear line of argument to your audience; you can't place headings throughout the speech or divide it into paragraphs.

In this chapter, I will teach you how to become a more effective speaker in several chronological steps, before, during, and after a speech. Though I have written much of this chapter from my perspective as an executive who frequently gives speeches to external audiences, many of the tips will also help employees at any level give presentations at internal meetings.

PREPARING FOR A SPEECH

The key to effective speaking is preparing well before the event. Preparatory activities can be divided into three main areas: knowing your audience, structuring your speech, and practicing your delivery.

Knowing Your Audience

When you prepare your speech, start by figuring out the three Ws of your audience—*who* they are, *why* they are attending, and *what* they care about. For an internal audience, you likely know a lot about the attendees. Are they your bosses, your peers, or your staff? For a public speech, you may not personally know your audience, but you can easily find out who they are. The convener of any meeting, internal or external, will have a preliminary list of attendees—and you'd better pay attention to it! By looking at such lists, I have avoided making jokes that would have offended particular people in the audience.

Similarly, you should think hard about why your audience will be attending your speech. Start by reviewing the agenda for the meeting or conference so that you clearly understand the main topics to be discussed. For an internal meeting, you should also determine whether your colleagues are attending out of their own free will or whether the event is mandatory—in which case you will have to do more work to hold their attention. For a public speech, ask the conveners about the attendees' expectations. Do they want to learn something or be inspired? Is your speech intended to be an entertaining break between networking events at a beachside resort?

It is more difficult to predict what your audience will really care about. For internal meetings, make sure you clearly understand the priorities of your boss and your colleagues. Is your boss most concerned about minimizing cost, or does he or she have a more ambitious vision for the unit? For an external speech, think about the "bread-and-butter" issues that will affect the livelihood of your audience. For instance, if you are addressing a group of biotech executives, they will be very keen to learn about any developments related to drug approvals by the federal government.

Once you understand the three Ws of your audience, you can more effectively tailor your speech to their interests by modifying an assigned topic or choosing your own topic from scratch. In making this choice, you should obviously favor topics that you know a lot about. Within that range, however, the desires of the audience should trump your personal preferences. Although you may be the world's expert on Russian-American relations, the audience may be more interested in Chinese-American relations. Or another speaker on the schedule may be slated to give a talk on Russian-American relations; you want your speech to be appropriate without directly overlapping the topic of another speaker.

Structuring Your Speech

Once you've settled on a topic, write an outline of your presentation. In doing so, make sure that your line of argument is crystal clear. As I've mentioned, a speech has no headings or subtitles to provide directions to the audience. That makes it crucial for you to divide your speech into its introduction, body, and conclusion.

An introduction to a speech should have four components. First, you should introduce yourself. If you're speaking to a large external audience, provide one paragraph about yourself for someone else to read as an introduction. Résumés are too long and detailed; select the specific facts to be included in a one-paragraph introduction. If you're speaking to an internal meeting, make sure that everyone knows who you are—your formal position as well as your role in whatever endeavor you will be discussing.

Second, you need an effective opening. That means thanking the group that invited you to speak and expressing appreciation if someone gives you a nice introduction. Next, you should tell a joke or story to loosen up the crowd and show your human side. For example, after expressing appreciation for an effusive introduction, I might say, "But you forgot my basketball career!" I would then briefly recount my teenage efforts to guard Calvin Murphy, who went on to be a high scorer at college and an All-Star player for the Houston Rockets. I was determined to guard Calvin closely—if he went to the water cooler during time-outs, I went, too. By guarding Calvin really closely for the whole game, I held him to 56 points—only 6 above his season's average. At that point I decided to give up my basketball ambitions and concentrate on finance.

Humor works well even at internal meetings—as long as it's short, clean, and generally related to the situation. Nevertheless, many audiences are uncertain about whether they are "allowed" to laugh; they may feel that the subject of the speech is too heavy or the speaker is too serious (this is especially true if a boss is presenting to his or her subordinates). So you may have to give your audience "permission" to laugh. I sometimes remark that I wanted to be a stand-up comedian when I was in college, so I would appreciate it if the audience would laugh at all my jokes. That remark usually elicits chuckles and relaxes the audience.

Third, after getting your audience into the proper mood, you should explain why the topic of the speech is relevant to them—why they should want to listen to you. This might mean tying the speech to a recent headline in the news or a current event in the organization or unit. Or it might mean relating the topic to a problem of special interest to the audience—for example, increases in the crime rate to community groups.

Fourth, you should lay out a road map for the rest of the speech: "I will begin by describing X, next I will argue Y, and finally I will propose Z."

This is not a time for subtlety; be direct and explicit. If you are going to use visuals to support your speech, you should spell out these three steps in an "agenda" slide. Such an explicit road map helps your audience see how the different components of your argument fit together in a logical fashion.

The body of your speech should have a clear structure with a logical progression. One possible structure is:

- Here's the problem.

- Here's my analysis.

- Here's how we could solve this problem.

Another possible structure might be:

- Here's an issue of current interest.

- Here's my take on this issue.

- Here's how we might rethink this issue in the future.

In putting together the body of a speech, remember that you are trying to persuade your audience to accept your viewpoint. Even if you're just giving a status report, you're trying to convince your colleagues that the project is going well—or maybe that it isn't. In any case, it is easy enough to be applauded by people who already agree with you. It is more difficult to win over people who were previously neutral or against your position. How can you win them over?

Occasionally you can rely on the strength of your analysis and supporting information, especially if they are little known to your audience or run counter to the conventional wisdom. But speaking is more of an emotional than an intellectual experience, and I don't recommend relying only on logic. If you want to persuade people, present examples or anecdotes as well as arguments. Your audience is more likely to be moved by vivid stories about a few individuals addicted to alcohol than a chart showing abstract statistics on alcohol abuse.[3]

Similarly, your audience will be more receptive to your ideas if they can tell that you really care about the subject. To convey emotion, use dramatic gestures and vary your tone of voice. Repeat the same phrase several times, add some strategic pauses to underscore key ideas, and put multiple ideas into a parallel structure to stress how they connect to each other.

If feasible, reach an emotional crescendo near the end of your speech. I know the typical advice to speakers goes like this: "Tell them what you're going to say, then say it, and then conclude by telling them what you've just said." I strongly disagree—it's boring for an audience to hear again the points you've just told them. Instead, use your conclusion to leave your audience in a certain frame of mind—say, inspired to donate to your cause or curious to learn more about your company.

In your conclusion, offer your audience a few takeaways—key points you want them to remember. One takeaway could be a call to action, such as taking market share away from your main competitor. Another takeaway could be to adopt a different perspective on a subject: "The next time you see a critical article on U.S. foreign aid, I want you to think about how little the United States actually spends on aid relative to the entire budget." Or a takeaway could be a plea to change the personal behavior of your audience, such as Steve Jobs's appeal from his highly praised Stanford commencement address: "Stay hungry, stay foolish."[4]

Finally, you should close by thanking your host for giving you the opportunity to speak at their meeting or conference.

Rehearsing the Speech

After you've outlined your speech, rehearse it out loud, several times. Although this is hard work, there is no other way to get comfortable with your speech so you can appear confident and natural. At the same time, rehearsing will show you the weak spots in your speech. After rehearsing, I often change the order of presentation or replace an example with a better one.

A good way to rehearse is to present your speech to someone—a colleague or friend—who is willing to provide honest and constructive comments. If that is not feasible, rehearse your speech in front of a mirror. That will give you a feel for how you come across visually. In any event, don't just read your speech silently to yourself. Speaking is a performance art, so you need to practice by talking out loud.

Some people insist on writing out the full text of their speeches before giving them. That's a very dangerous habit. Once you have written out a full text, you will be inclined to read your speech word for word. Follow that approach, and you'll lose your audience.

Soon after the financial crisis of 2008, I was the third speaker at a global conference on financial services in Europe, so I had a chance to observe the two speakers before me. Their styles couldn't have been more different, and they had strikingly different effects on the audience. The first speaker, a distinguished expert on financial accounting, read a lengthy speech word for word. The audience members were bored and distant; they responded with polite applause. Next up was Bob Benmosche, the CEO leading the rehabilitation of the insurance firm AIG. A tall man with an imposing stage presence, Benmosche spoke enthusiastically without any text. Captivated by his candor and humor, the audience gave him a rousing ovation.

I like to speak from a one-page outline. The outline might include an actual sentence to get started and another sentence as a closer. But the rest would be a brief sketch of the main steps in the speech, with a few supporting points for each step. This helps me keep the line of argument foremost in my mind and convey it clearly to my audience. It also allows me to adapt my speech to the audience easily as I sense the mood in the room.

As a compromise, you could write out a longer outline of your speech in two or three pages if you feel you want more detailed notes. That would give you the comfort of more guidance without losing the spontaneity of talking informally from a series of points. In any event, do *not* read the full text of your speech; that is a surefire way to put your audience to sleep.

Now let's see how much you've learned about preparing speeches. In appendix 2, I've included the full text of a speech that I gave in Boston, which was a big success with the audience. It was well organized from a technical perspective and passionate in a personal way. The speech begins by complimenting the audience and laying out a road map for the speech. It tells a vivid story, moving chronologically through the life of my older brother Michael, ending with his tragic death. Then it draws out a few implications of Michael's struggle for needy children. And it ends with a strong call to action, with an emotional reference to "our children."

I actually spoke from one page of notes and later wrote out the text to send to friends. I want you to proceed in the opposite direction: read this speech and then compose a short speaking outline based on the text. In the process, you should identify the key steps and rhetorical devices of this speech.

After you do that, try to start from scratch. Compose a one-page outline for a talk that you might be invited to give—either to your colleagues or to a public audience. Feel free to choose your own topic, but here are three ideas if you get stuck:

1. *How did your organization manage through the financial crisis of 2008–2009?*

2. *How are recent changes in government policy affecting your organization?*

3. *Why is it important for your organization to expand its reach?*

Write out one sentence to start and another sentence to conclude, with the rest in outline form. Is your line of argument clear? Could you actually speak from only this outline?

THE DAY OF THE SPEECH

Now we come to the day you're slated to speak. The day can be divided into three time periods: before, during, and immediately after the speech.

Getting Ready for the Speech

Here are some of the steps you should take in the hours before you speak:

- Review the agenda and list of attendees. This is to make sure you understand the composition of the audience and where your talk fits into the flow of the program.

- Practice your speech one last time by going over your outline. This should be done out loud—in the shower, at the office, or in a hotel room or taxi if necessary.

- Read the headlines in today's newspapers, and search the Internet for any late-breaking news relevant to the audience or topic. You may want to revise your outline or be ready to respond to a question based on a very recent event.

When it is time to head over to your speaking venue, get there well in advance. If the speech is not taking place within your own building, plan on arriving thirty to sixty minutes early. This allows you to check out the room, the equipment, and the audience.

When checking out the room, remember that the organizers of meetings and conferences typically overestimate the number of attendees. Perhaps they want to promote the significance of the event, or maybe they neglect to consider the inevitable falloff at the last minute. Whatever the advance estimate of the audience, I assume that only 60 percent will actually attend. That assumption helps me avoid being disappointed when I arrive at an event to find an audience of thirty instead of fifty.

If you can choose your venue, select the smallest room possible that can seat 60 percent of the projected audience. If more actually show up, that's great. People sitting in the aisles and standing in the back increase the buzz. If you discover that the room is much too big, you should ask for curtains or other dividers to make the room smaller. If that is not feasible, politely ask the audience to move to the front and center of the room.

I believe in the energy theory of public speaking: to be an effective speaker, you have to increase the energy in the room. One way to do this is to wander around the room instead of staying tied to the podium. The audience will be more engaged if you walk through the aisles to address remarks or direct questions to specific individuals sitting in the room. If you need a microphone, you should ask for a lavalier microphone that can be pinned on your suit jacket, shirt, or blouse. If you are using slides, you should have a clicker that will work away from the podium.

When you arrive early for your speech, make sure that you have all the necessary equipment and that it actually works. Check that your microphone is set to the right volume. If you are using visuals, make sure that you have the right file for your slides and double-check that they are in the correct order. I have encountered problems with the slides in about 20 percent of my speaking engagements.

Most important, arrive early to get a feel for your audience. If another speaker is at the podium, listen carefully to what he or she is saying. That will allow you to grasp the mood of the audience and possibly provide you with tie-ins to what has previously been covered.

If there is a break before you speak, use that opportunity to ask questions of attendees, both strangers and colleagues. What have they liked most about the conference or meeting so far? What areas are they looking for you to address? That way, you can start to build a rapport with audience members.

Furthermore, in light of their answers, you can revise your speaking outline. For example, if someone says that another speaker has talked in depth about recently passed legislation, reduce the time you spend talking about a new law. Conversely, if they are particularly interested in a new breakthrough from the research department, give a more detailed account of this development.

Arriving early allows you to match the tone of previous speakers. I once spoke between James Carville and lunch—a terrible speaking slot. James is a Democratic political consultant with a wicked set of jokes about growing up in Louisiana. After listening for forty-five minutes to his high-energy performance filled with hilarious anecdotes, the crowd was in a boisterous mood. So I introduced myself as "Billy Bob" Pozen, and the audience responded with enthusiastic laughter.

As one final step of preparation, go to the restroom so that you can check your appearance. Nothing is more embarrassing than spinach stuck in your teeth or a "wardrobe malfunction." Once you make this last check, you are ready for prime time.

Dealing with Nerves

As you walk up to the podium, you are likely to feel jittery and nervous about your upcoming appearance. So does everyone else. As Mark Twain said, "There are two types of speakers: those that are nervous and those that are liars."[5]

Your feelings of anxiety are the result of a small dose of adrenaline that has been released into your bloodstream. Some of the effects of adrenaline, such as an elevated heart rate, are not helpful for giving a talk. But adrenaline also makes your senses a bit more acute and your mental processing a bit quicker. In other words, when you feel nervous, your body is giving you a little bit of extra energy and focus to help you perform your speech.

Nevertheless, you need to be able to manage your nerves. As a practical step, this means being well prepared and having a well-rehearsed speech. Early arrival can also help with nerves. It is hard to be relaxed when you arrive two minutes before your speaking time, unsure of your appearance or the audience's mood.

DON'T LET YOUR NERVES MAKE YOU NERVOUS

For most speakers, fear peaks in the moment before the speech and declines once the speech gets going. Unfortunately, researchers estimate that roughly 25 percent of people get *more* nervous as the speech goes on. They tend to fixate on the signs of their own nervousness—their sweaty palms or quavering voice. As a result, they get more worried, and then have more issues to worry about.[6]

If you notice yourself becoming anxious about your own anxiety, take a step back and concentrate on what you need to say next. Deal with any symptoms as they occur—if your voice is trembling, take a deep breath; if your mouth is dry, take a sip of water. But whatever you do, don't exacerbate the problem by focusing on your own nerves. In more extreme cases, consider seeing a psychotherapist or speech coach to help you work through your issues.

Giving the Speech

Your opening sets the tone for your whole speech. Put on a bright smile and start with a funny joke or an amusing story. Next, introduce your audience to your thesis and show how the speech will be organized, as I have discussed.

At that point, your challenge is to turn the audience into active listeners. We have all been passive listeners, barely hearing the words of the speaker as our minds stray to other people and other issues. By contrast, active listeners are focused on what the speaker is saying, evaluating his or her arguments and feeling his or her emotional intensity.

How can you transform your audience from passive attendees to active listeners? I sometimes ask the audience to vote on questions of relevance to your speech. For example, suppose you are giving a presentation on your division's new streamlined procedures for project approvals. You could begin by asking: How many hours do you think you spend each month filling out paperwork? How could all this paperwork possibly be useful? By forcing the audience to consider their own personal stake in these issues, you will get them more interested in hearing your presentation.

Asking questions of the audience goes along with wandering around the room. If you walk down the aisle next to the seats of meeting participants, it becomes very difficult for them to remain passive—you are standing only two feet away from them! Similarly, try to make eye contact regularly with all parts of the audience, especially those sitting in the far right and left wings as well as the back rows. Otherwise, you may lose their attention quickly.

Though good visuals can stimulate active listening, bad visuals have the opposite effect. Here are my basic rules for using slides with speeches:

- Include an agenda slide near the beginning with a road map for the speech.

- End with a conclusion slide listing the key takeaways for the audience.

- Use the slides particularly for charts, diagrams, and data displays.

- Never, *never* read the bullet points in a textual slide; use them as takeoffs for your remarks.

- Limit the total number of slides—no more than fifteen slides for a thirty-minute speech.

The last bullet leads to a more general point: keep your speeches as short as feasible. Audiences generally stop paying attention after thirty minutes, so that is a good guideline for a keynote address to a conference. In other contexts, your talk should be even shorter. In a one-hour meeting, for instance, the opening presentation should be limited to ten to fifteen minutes. In any case, don't go over your allotted time; that is a sure way to annoy participants and organizers.

After the Presentation

At the end of all presentations, you should plan on a question-and-answer (Q&A) session. In a speech to an external audience, you should expressly plan on your Q&A session taking the last fifteen minutes of a forty-five-minute speech. In an internal meeting, you should invite questions at any time, especially if your remarks are intended to lead into vigorous debate, as I advocated in chapter 6, "Efficient Meetings." In whatever form, a Q&A session is critical to the audience: it gives the listeners a chance to find out more about their own concerns.

From the speaker's perspective, however, a Q&A session is much more challenging than giving a speech. You never know what you will be asked, so it is impossible to formulate complete responses in advance. Moreover, the scope of the inquiries is likely to be broader than the subject of the speech.

Nevertheless, you should try to prepare for your Q&A session by thinking about probable questions and sketching out answers. One strategy is to ask your colleagues and friends to generate questions about the speech. In addition, you can "plant" questions from colleagues in the audience that you want to answer. Planted questions not only give you a few "softballs" to hit but also get the Q&A session going if nobody else is brave enough to ask the first question.

Once the Q&A session begins, you should abide by the following ground rules:

- When someone asks a question, make sure it is heard by everyone. Repeat the question if necessary.

- To encourage more questions from the audience, respond to initial volunteers by saying, "That is an excellent question."

- Don't let one person dominate the Q&A session; if no one else volunteers, call on one of your "planted" questioners.

- Don't let anyone give a speech instead of posing a question; if someone starts down that road, ask him or her politely to get to a question.

- If you are asked an unexpectedly tough question, repeat the question to give yourself time to think of a good answer.

- Give a thoughtful answer to each question, but don't go on too long. An in-depth answer might be of interest only to the person who asked.

When you see the number of hands decreasing, say that there is time for one last question. But don't wait until there is only one hand left in the air. It's very awkward to end when no one else wants to ask a question. Instead, prepare a closing sentence or two to end the Q&A session.

After a speech, try to get constructive feedback. That will help you improve your general public speaking skills and can also help you revise a particular presentation that you may give again. Although conferences usually ask participants to fill out evaluations, they tend not to be very useful. The people who actually fill out the forms are not usually a representative sample and the results are often expressed as numerical scores without any reference point (say, the median ranking for all speakers).

The best type of feedback is a video of your actual speech, or at least a video of a practice session. You don't need a studio or fancy equipment; a colleague or a friend with a smartphone will do just fine. I guarantee that you will be shocked the first time you see yourself on video; we all have speaking faults that we do not recognize. Personally, seeing myself on video greatly improved my speaking. I previously had an image of myself as an engaging and poised speaker. But when I watched myself on video, there were so many awkward pauses, jerky movements, and mumbled phrases! Starting with my next speech, I was more cognizant of those faults and tried to correct them.

If the sponsor or convener is not willing to record your speech on film, you should ask a colleague or friend to sit in the audience. They can provide you with helpful information about how the audience reacted to what you said—if you encourage them to be brutally frank. You have to be receptive to constructive criticism if you want to improve as a public speaker.

TAKEAWAYS

1. After introducing yourself to your audience, tell a joke and let your audience know that it is okay to laugh. A more relaxed audience makes for a more effective speech.

2. Next, use your introduction to explain why your topic is relevant. Then provide an explicit road map so that the audience can easily follow your line of argument.

3. End your presentation with a few takeaways and, if possible, an emotional crescendo.

4. Don't write out the full text of your speech; use a one-page outline instead. This makes your speech more vibrant and allows more improvisation.

5. Arrive early so that you can scope out the venue, the at-
    tendees, and any speakers slated before you. You want to
    gauge the mood of the crowd and the tone of the other
    speakers.

6. It's normal to get nervous before speaking in front of
    others. But don't fall into a downward spiral by worry-
    ing about your own anxiety.

7. Engage with your audience: wander around the room;
    ask questions of your audience and make them take a
    stand, or offer suggestions.

8. Keep your speech as short as feasible—thirty minutes is
    usually as long as you want to go.

9. Allow time at the end for a Q&A session. Be prepared
    for what types of questions may be asked.

10. Get feedback—a video recording is best, but a frank
    colleague can also be helpful.

Part IV

MANAGING UP AND DOWN

So far, I've been focused on increasing your productivity as an individual. Now, switching gears, I'm going to help you manage the relationships between you and others in your organization.

To be productive within an organization, you should not leave your relationships with your coworkers to chance. Instead, you should proactively manage your relationships with employees above and below you.[1] Chapter 10 will discuss how to manage your team and maximize their productivity. Chapter 11 will discuss the art of "managing up"—creating a mutually beneficial relationship with your boss. If you're not at the top or the bottom of the totem pole, think about these two chapters as part of one overall idea: how to manage the relationships with your colleagues to achieve your goals—and those of your organization.

10

MANAGING YOUR TEAM

A few years ago, a colleague at Harvard, Professor Teresa Amabile, started an ambitious three-year study of American professionals at work. She tracked 238 subjects, each of whom was engaged in a project with a definite start and end date. Every day, Amabile sent her subjects an email asking them to describe their mood, their motivation, and the quality of their work. She also asked them to identify one event that stood out to them each day. By the end of her study, Amabile had collected nearly 12,000 individual responses.

When Amabile analyzed the data, she came to a clear conclusion about one key factor: workers are happiest—and most motivated—when they feel that they accomplish something meaningful at work. These accomplishments do not need to be major breakthroughs: incremental but noticeable progress toward a goal was enough to make her subjects feel good. As one programmer described it, "I smashed that [computer] bug that's been frustrating me for almost a calendar week. That may not be an event to you, but I live a very drab life, so I'm all hyped."[1]

The lesson here is that managers can get the most out of their employees by helping them achieve meaningful progress every day. Sadly, most managers don't seem to be aware of this. In a related study, Amabile asked 669 managers to rank five different factors affecting employee morale: support for making progress, recognition for good work, monetary incentives, interpersonal support, and clear goals. Only 5 percent ranked support for making progress first, and most ranked it *dead last*.[2]

To be an effective boss, you don't have to give rousing speeches like a football coach at halftime; you just have to set up a system that enables both you and your employees to get meaningful work done. The heart of that system, in my view, is delegation.

DELEGATING FUNCTIONS

If you're following my advice from previous chapters, you're spending most of your time on Objectives and Targets that rank highest for you and your organization. But your lower-ranking goals still need to get done. Here is where delegation comes into play: it allows you to focus on your top priorities while other people complete or assist with your lower-ranking goals.

Effective delegation expands the output of the whole organization. Without delegation, one executive can lead only one large group of employees on one large project. With delegation, one executive can guide multiple small teams in multiple large projects. In other words, effective delegation leverages the skills of the top managers across the organization.

When I became the chairman of MFS Investment Management in 2004, it was recovering from an SEC enforcement case. With many fronts to cover, Rob Manning, the talented CEO, had to decide where the organization needed him most. Though both of us had managed investment teams, Rob had relatively little experience with boards and regulators. So we reached an explicit agreement: Rob would focus on improving the investment performance—the most critical priority for the firm—as well as other internal functions such as the back office and budgeting. He delegated to me the external functions: negotiating with the regulators, meeting with large clients, and calming down board members. By allowing each of us to concentrate on areas where we were most useful, this agreement quickly enabled MFS to achieve a successful turnaround.

OWNING YOUR OWN SPACE

So what's the key to effective delegation? You and your lieutenants need to embrace the principle of "Owning Your Own Space." Under this principle, all employees in a large company view themselves as the owners of a small business. I'll show you later exactly how to implement this principle, but here's the gist of it: *after setting clear goals for a project, give your employees broad discretion to decide how best to achieve these goals—and then get out of their way.* This creates the right environment for your employees to do their best work, and it frees up time for you to focus on your highest Objectives and Targets.

Embracing the principle of Owning Your Own Space builds the entrepreneurial spirit of your employees. Lynn Blodgett, the former head of ACS, a unit of Xerox, agrees: he wants his business to "look like a whole bunch of sole proprietorships," where employees make choices as if they were spending their own money. He wants his employees to ask, "Do I have to buy that computer right now or can I get by with one that's two years old?"[3]

By contrast, if your employees don't feel that they own their own spaces, they will constantly wait for your day-to-day directions and expect you to solve every problem. That wastes everyone's time. One CEO told me, "If employees are looking for prescriptions from the boss, this will never work. There are just too many different issues and situations for the boss to provide detailed instructions."

There are two key advantages to managing by this principle:

Adapting on the Fly

If you allow your workers to own their own spaces, they can adapt quickly to changing conditions rather than waiting for your approval. That advantage was exploited brilliantly by Marine Corps lieutenant general Paul Van Riper, a "commander" participating in war games in the early 2000s. Ostensibly commanding the army of a rogue Middle East dictator, his job was to "wage war" against the United States. Despite the United States' overwhelming advantage in simulated firepower, Van Riper "defeated" the United States by allowing his subordinates to make judgments on their feet instead of requiring them to come back to him for orders. His officers could see the evolving situation on the ground, while the Americans' traditional military hierarchy became bogged down in the fog of war.[4]

Although your employees probably won't be asked to react quickly to bullets whizzing overhead, they will need to adjust to rapidly moving markets or unexpected technical problems. Here's one story where implementing Owning Your Own Space resulted in firm-wide productivity gains. For many years, a consumer electronics factory in the United Kingdom had given strict orders to its operators of robotic machinery: when their equipment broke down, the operators were to contact a specialist and not attempt to fix the malfunction. Then researchers conducted an experiment: they taught the operators how to make small repairs themselves and encouraged them to do so whenever possible. After this intervention, the most trouble-prone machinery spent 39 percent less time out of order, making the factory much more efficient.[5]

Making Work Feel Meaningful

When you give your workers broad discretion to carry out projects, they feel responsible for the outcome and become much more invested in its success. They're energized because they know that their daily actions have a direct impact on their unit and their organization.

This effect was firmly established by Richard Hackman and Greg Oldham, professors of psychology. They visited seven organizations, studying 658 employees who performed sixty-two different jobs. They asked the workers about the nature of their job and how they felt about it. They also asked managers to evaluate the output of their workers in terms of effort, quality, and quantity. Oldham and Hackman found that those who were given more autonomy felt more responsible for the outcomes of projects. They further found that this state of mind—which they called "experienced responsibility" because it described the workers' subjective "experience" rather than their position in a hierarchy—increased their motivation to work harder and achieve better results.[6]

EXECUTIVE ASSISTANTS

The principle of Owning Your Own Space applies to employees at all levels, including executive assistants. Every executive knows that there is a huge difference between executive assistants who await instructions and passively follow orders as compared with those who own their own spaces. I have been lucky enough to have an assistant, Courtney, who enthusiastically owns her own space. She controls my daily schedule, works out travel arrangements, and tries to prevent conflicts from arising. She also identifies and corrects my many errors—in a polite manner.

Behind many effective executives are executive assistants who take the initiative. Jack Welch, the former CEO of GE, worked with his assistant Rosanne Badowski for more than fourteen years. She describes an example of how she owned her own space:

By studying the calendar on any given day, I could translate the straightforward list of appointments, meetings, and events outside the office into a tip sheet on the kinds of questions he would want answered over the next eight to ten hours. If he was due to be visited by an important customer, chances were good he would want to know something [about him or her]. . . . At least one day before, I would have been in contact with the key GE executives who dealt with that customer to ask for a summary of the relationship, including all the current pluses and minuses.[7]

By owning their own spaces, executive assistants such as Rosanne and Courtney contribute substantially to the productivity of their organizations. By relieving their boss of administrative distractions and conducting essential fact finding, they leave the boss free to concentrate on where his or her work is particularly needed, such as formulating company strategy.

GAINING CONFIDENCE IN YOUR LIEUTENANTS

For the strategy of Owning Your Own Space to be successful, you must surround yourself with talented people you trust. Managers are more willing to delegate when they have subordinates with strong skills and sound judgment. If you trust your lieutenants, you will feel comfortable letting them run at their own speed. By contrast, if you have doubts about their ability to do the job, you will be tempted to micromanage them—or do their tasks yourself.

Hiring Right

Trust in your employees begins with hiring the right people—talented professionals with high energy and sound ethics. If you have the power to hire people, take advantage of it! I consider the recruitment of lieutenants to be a nondelegable function for any executive. It is always tempting to save time by letting your colleagues in the human resources department do the hiring for you. But this is penny-wise and pound-foolish. If you select the right lieutenants, you will save thousands of hours through effective delegation. If you make the wrong choice, you will spend a lot of time closely supervising your team and resolving disputes instead of concentrating on your higher Objectives and Targets.

What can you do to increase your chances of hiring the right lieutenant? While there are many extensive checklists for conducting interviews available,[8] here are the lessons that I consider most essential to the recruitment process:

- In the interview, ask candidates to talk about their personal history, starting with where they went to high school. The answer will help you understand their character and motivation; we are all heavily influenced by our roots.

- Ask candidates how they made the biggest contribution in their prior jobs. Don't be satisfied with an answer about "working hard"—you want to hear specifically how they came up with a different approach or solved a difficult problem.

- Engage candidates in intellectual debate about a subject of their choosing that they know well. That way, you can judge the caliber of their thinking. How well can they make their argument? How do they deal with possible inconsistencies and counterpoints?

- Try to gauge the creativity of the candidate. Ask a question such as "What are all the possible uses of a brick for our business?" One future employee of Microsoft came up with thirty-five uses.

- Choose the candidate with the most potential, not the person with the most experience in the industry. Just as a good overall athlete will develop skills specific to a sport, a smart, hardworking individual will learn the intricacies of a new field.

- Make the reference calls yourself and press hard for honest evaluations, rather than the usual platitudes. Owing to legal and social pressures, many employers are reluctant to say anything negative about a former employee. So make it easy for the reference to subtly provide negative inputs about the candidate. Ask questions such as: Was this candidate the best you've worked with? Why not? Are there any potential downsides to hiring this candidate? Would you hire him or her back?

Fostering Trust

After you hire or select good people, work hard to build relationships of trust in both directions. The more you trust your lieutenants, the more you will be willing to delegate to them.[9] Similarly, the more your lieutenants trust you, the more motivated they'll be to put forward their best work. Unfortunately, the corporate scandals of the 2000s have eroded employees' trust in management. A 2011 poll by Maritz Research found that only one in ten employees believe that the senior management of their organization is ethical and honest.[10]

How can you earn the trust of your team? First, you must perform your job with the utmost integrity; that means being honest and ethical and keeping your promises. If your employees believe that you are not telling the truth, they will not want to work for you. Similarly, you must be consistently courteous and polite; your employees will not be supportive if they think that you are nasty or rude.

Second, keep open lines of communication with your employees. It's not enough to *speak* to your employees; you should be willing to *listen* as well. In fact, you should listen more than you talk. Keep an open mind for suggestions coming from your employees, and convey this openness in face-to-face interaction; employees need to trust that you care about what they think.

Third, employees must trust that you are working toward shared goals and not your own personal agenda. If they think that all you care about is your own glory, they won't be motivated to help you. By contrast, if they know that you're all pulling toward the same goals, they'll be more willing to put in extra effort.

Fourth, employees must feel that you trust them to get the job done— which you can demonstrate by allowing them to own their own spaces. When you provide your employees leeway to accomplish a goal as they best see fit, you are showing that you trust their judgment. By contrast, a micromanaging, controlling style of management shows that you fear that your employees will make mistakes if you give them any freedom.

IMPLEMENTING OWNERSHIP: SETTING YOUR TEAM UP TO SUCCEED

After building a good team with a trusting relationship, here are the five main steps to implementing the principle of Owning Your Own Space on a project basis:

1. Set Project Goals

At the start of a new project, you must communicate clearly your goals and constraints for it. Suppose, for example, that you want your operations manager to choose a new manufacturing site in the United States. Instead of designating a specific city, you might indicate that the site should:

- Be within quick shipping distance of customers;

- Be cost-effective to operate;

- Have access to a skilled supply of labor.

You should also give your lieutenants considerable leeway in establishing the time frame for those goals. If your lieutenants choose the project's deadlines, they will be more committed to meeting them. Nevertheless, you can help your team think through what needs to be done first in order to achieve the goals—what I call "gating" issues. For instance, you might suggest that they first determine which cities offer an attractive tax structure for this type of factory.

2. Establish Accurate Metrics

After broadly defining the goals for a delegated project, you and your lieutenants should reach an explicit agreement on the metrics for the project. They should include both quantitative and qualitative criteria—for instance, reducing the processing time for Internet transactions and improving customer satisfaction. Such metrics can then guide your team's work—and allow them to focus their attention where it is most critical.

Choosing the right metrics can be an enlightening exercise; it will often force you to have a deeper discussion with your team about what you really consider important about the project. Although you should lead this discussion, it is best if your lieutenants make the final decision on the metrics to be used. Again, your team will be more committed to achieving metrics that they themselves formulate.

Consider the example of selecting the site for a new factory. Metrics for each goal, respectively, could be:

- The percentage of customers within a one-day shipping distance of the factory.

- A small number of cost measures, such as the price of land, the local tax rate, and the prevailing wages.

- With respect to a skilled labor supply, one simple metric could be the time it takes to hire the first ten specialists (say, chemical engineers) with appropriate skills. If you have access to more data, you could measure skilled labor more directly—e.g., by the number of chemical engineers in the region.

Not all metrics are equal. You should make it clear if you consider one metric to be more important than another. That will help your team consider trade-offs—moving the facility from one city to another could improve one metric and hurt another.

Carefully design each metric, especially the highly weighted ones, to capture the project's goals. If you establish bad metrics, your project will be doomed from the start. Though there is a well-developed academic literature on good and bad metrics,[11] here's the main idea: make sure that your metric measures what you think it does—and that it won't motivate your employees to make the wrong decisions.

Some metrics create perverse incentives to *select* instead of *affect*. Imagine that you are the mayor of your city. In order to reduce crime, you decide to pay the city prosecutors based on the percentage of their trials that end in conviction. In your mind, that will incentivize prosecutors to work harder to dig up evidence and make stronger cases. However, over the next few months, you see more and more defendants being released before ever getting to trial. Instead of putting more criminals behind bars, you have only incentivized your prosecutors to avoid the hard cases.

Many "pure volume" metrics, such as calls made and repairs completed, are susceptible to cherry-picking concerns. In such cases, use multiple indicators that are adjusted for the risks involved—metrics that take into account the difficulty of cases taken instead of encouraging your employees to take only the easy ones.

Other metrics are so badly designed that they produce misinformation. For instance, online marketing typically tries to maximize the number of eyeballs on a given website. But simply measuring page views is problematic; maybe your website is so poorly designed that a visitor has to surf through eight pages to find what he or she wants. That will show up as eight page views—great job!—but you really only created one frustrated customer.

3. Supply Needed Resources

After setting project goals and metrics, the next step is to make sure that your employees have access to the resources required to complete the project. These resources include the dollars, head count, and equipment needed to get the project done. In many companies, unfortunately, lieutenants are not given those resources because of budget constraints. If this is the reality at your organization, you as a manager should try to reduce the parameters of a project or reconsider whether the project is feasible at all. Setting tough goals without providing adequate resources is a recipe for a failed project and unhappy employees.

You should also supply your lieutenants with less tangible forms of support. Stand ready to act as a consultant to help them resolve tough issues. For instance, when I was president of Fidelity Investments, a chief investment officer (CIO) asked me for advice on how to give feedback to a portfolio manager with weak performance over the last year. I helped the CIO think through the sensitive issues and pointed out that even excellent portfolio managers can experience an occasional down period. That helped the CIO engage in a long dialogue with the portfolio manager in a constructive manner—and meant that I did not have to be part of that dialogue.

Similarly, be ready to help your lieutenants win battles with other parts of the organization. Because of your relative seniority, you are in a stronger position to influence significant decisions by your organization's centralized functions. Suppose the human resources department has a general limit for how much it can spend to offset a new employee's moving expenses. Meanwhile, your lieutenant wants to hire a talented professional who was unlucky enough to buy a house in California early in 2008—when prices were sky-high. Now housing prices are lower in California than Boston, to which the prospective employee will have to move. To persuade that professional to move to Boston, the boss will have to help secure an exception to the usual relocation limits.

4. Monitor Without Suffocating

This component of Owning Your Own Space is the most difficult for most managers: giving your subordinates freedom to complete their tasks as they see fit. Most bosses think that they have mastered this principle if they don't demand that subordinates use a specific format in an Excel spreadsheet or if they don't hover over their subordinates' desks giving ongoing directions. If they don't fit this stereotypical image of a micromanager, they dismiss the idea that they could be one themselves.

In reality, micromanagement is a lot more subtle. It often takes the form of taking back authority over previously delegated projects or having an overly critical eye for details. So consider the following questions. If you answer yes to any of them, you may be an inadvertent micromanager.

- If there is a problem with a project, do you take it over and issue detailed orders?

- Do you tend to object if your team takes an unorthodox approach to a project?

- Do your subordinates always seem to follow your "suggestions" to the letter?

- When you're looking at a finished project, do you search for every small mistake?

To avoid micromanaging, you don't have to give up all control of a project; you should not assign a project and then withdraw completely. Instead, actively monitor the project in a supportive manner.

Many managers try to stay in touch with their lieutenants by asking for occasional status reports. But that's not enough for large delegated projects; as much as I hate meetings, this is one of those times when a meeting is actually necessary. Around the halfway point of a project, meet with your direct reports so that you can have a conversation about how it is progressing. Go over the status of the project, and discuss any unforeseen areas of difficulty. In light of this discussion, you together may decide to revise the goals and metrics of the project. (This is a perfect example of the strategy of the midflight check, which I talked about back in chapter 2.) But make sure that your team knows that you're only offering suggestions; be clear that they are free to achieve the revised goals in the way they think is best.

5. Tolerate Mistakes

Since the principle of Owning Your Own Space gives your employees leeway to try out different strategies, they will occasionally assess a situation incorrectly or launch a product that fizzles out. However, if you really want your employees to take chances with new ideas, you have to accept the inevitable failures.

Of course, you should not ignore illegal or unethical actions or failures caused by sloppiness or laziness. Nor should you tolerate a failure to learn from a previous error. For example, in trying to improve customer service, a systems team revised the main computer's code and inadvertently triggered an unintended effect due to a quirk in an old layer of that code. Their mistake was understandable, but it would have been unacceptable if the same type of problem arose the next time the team revised the main computer's code. One of my favorite sayings is "Let's make a new mistake!"

Though you shouldn't accept errors arising from a failure to learn or a lack of integrity, be quick to forgive your employees if they make a well-intentioned mistake. Indeed, smart bosses understand the value of tolerating, and even celebrating, failures. For instance, a payroll services company in Illinois offers the "Best New Mistake" award—an annual cash payment of $400 given to an employee who tried something new, made a mistake, and learned from it. Similarly, Grey Advertising in New York hands out a "Heroic Failure" award each quarter for ideas that are edgier, riskier, or totally unproven.[12] The prizes encourage employees to talk openly about their mistakes—so that others do not become scared to try out new strategies. As Gary Shapiro, the CEO of the Consumer Electronics Association, wrote, "Mistakes are okay—hiding them is not."[13]

When you learn of a project failure, you should calmly provide honest and constructive feedback; such situations have the potential to teach your employees a great deal. But no matter how spectacularly the project flopped, don't attack the person. Instead, point out the mistakes that contributed to this particular failure. Make it a "teachable moment" for the individual and preferably the whole team. You can ask employees to change specific actions and behaviors, not to alter their personalities. To obtain this balance, talk about what went right before you discuss what went wrong.

Giving your employees effective feedback helps them do a better job next time; humiliating them works against that goal. Although this would seem to be common sense, two business professors recently discovered that many workers felt humiliated by their bosses. For instance, one manager in their study had been verbally rebuked—in front of his twelve subordinates—for being wasteful. His sin? Dropping a paper clip into the trash can. According to this research, *half* of all humiliated employees *intentionally* decreased their productivity in response to their boss's actions.[14] How can you avoid humiliating your subordinates? Deliver critiques in private, not in front of others—and keep the dialogue respectful.

Whereas tactful negative feedback is vital to learning, praise is critical to employee motivation. Lavish your employees with praise whenever possible, and let them know how their contributions are meaningful. In my experience, it is virtually impossible for a boss to give too much positive feedback to his or her troops. Bosses usually think that they are bending over backward to express praise for the hard work of their subordinates. However, I rarely meet a team that believes their work is well enough appreciated by their boss; from their perspective, expressions of gratitude are few and far between.

THE HEAVY WEIGHT OF CRITICISM

Research consistently shows that people react more strongly to negative events—such as criticism from one's boss—than positive events.[15] One group of researchers, led by University of Minnesota professor Theresa Glomb, gave forty workers at a light manufacturing company a handheld device that beeped roughly once every two hours. At each beep, workers briefly reported their mood, as well as any positive or negative events that had occurred since the previous beep. The researchers found that employees' negative reaction to criticism was, on average, *ten times* as strong as their positive reaction to praise.[16] The lesson is clear: Be generous with praise, but use criticism sparingly.

Unlike criticism, praise should be bestowed in public. Give lots of credit for the contributions of your team—before the organization's top brass, if possible. Few things build more trust with employees than a feeling that their boss is behind them and trumpeting their achievements to others in the organization. Conversely, nothing destroys trust more quickly than a boss who takes credit for his employees' achievements while publicly marginalizing their contributions.

Indra Nooyi, the CEO of PepsiCo, dreamed up a particularly creative way to deliver praise in public. During a visit to her home in India, she was inspired by how happy her mother was at her success. So she began sending letters to the *parents* of her top reports, expressing gratitude for their having raised such a helpful and successful child. Glowing with pride, the parents reinforced the executives' loyalty to their CEO. To follow Nooyi's example, you should try to develop your own unique way of thanking your reports for their hard work.

TAKEAWAYS

1. Delegate your low-priority goals so that you can spend most of your time on your top Objectives and Targets.

2. Set broad goals for your subordinates, but allow them to decide how best to meet those goals.

3. Let your employees suggest metrics that will judge their success in achieving the broad goals that you have set.

4. Personally recruit or select your top reports. If you delegate this vital task, you might not be able to delegate anything else.

5. Carefully build trust between you and your employees. Have integrity, be courteous, and communicate openly and frankly. Provide your employees with support and resources to complete tasks that they have been assigned. Be their advocate elsewhere in the organization.

6. During the course of a delegated project, discuss its status with your team and revise the project's goals and metrics if needed.

7. But let your employees decide how to implement those revised goals and metrics; don't take control of the project.

8. Tolerate and celebrate well-intentioned mistakes, but don't condone repeated errors or ethical lapses.

9. If you need to criticize your employees, do so in private. Address their specific behaviors; don't attack their personalities.

10. Be effusive with praise of your subordinates. It's very hard to give them too much positive feedback.

11

MANAGING YOUR BOSS

J ust as your productivity depends on how you manage your team, it depends at least as much on how you deal with your boss by "managing up."[1]

"Managing up" does not mean manipulating your boss or apple-polishing; it means establishing a mutually beneficial partnership. But this is not a partnership of equals; your boss has the upper hand. So you can't let your relationship depend on how well you and your boss happen to get along. As the management expert Peter Drucker wrote, "You don't have to like or admire your boss, nor do you have to hate him. You do have to manage him, however, so that he becomes your resource for achievement, accomplishment, and personal success."[2]

WHAT TO COMMUNICATE ABOUT

Communications with your boss—both content and style—are critical to developing a productive relationship. Start by agreeing with your boss on what you should be doing. If you have done the goal-setting exercise in chapter 1, "Set and Prioritize Your Goals," you have already carefully considered what your boss wants from you. But don't assume you know all the nuances of your boss's thinking, especially since that can change rapidly with events. Get your Targets on the same page as your boss's by giving him or her a list of your assignments, ranked in order of importance from your perspective. Your boss can then amend the list if there are any misunderstandings. Discuss the list every week with your boss so you can make sure that your Targets are correct.

During periods of intense deadline work, you may be tempted to skip this step. My advice is, don't. A lot can change in a week, especially at your boss's level, and in the crush of events your boss may forget to fill you in on details that could affect your work. He or she will appreciate the chance to say, "Oh, that reminds me . . ." And you won't waste time on tasks that have suddenly dropped in priority.

After agreeing on your assignments and their relative priority, figure out how your boss wants you to carry them out. Some bosses like to approve in advance a detailed budget for any project, with a staffing plan for each step. Other bosses are content to let you do whatever you think is necessary to get a good result at reasonable cost. And there are lots of bosses in between these polar extremes. To figure out where your boss fits on this spectrum, have an explicit discussion with your boss on his or her preferred level of involvement.

To make sure you're on the same wavelength as your boss, don't be afraid to solicit feedback. In my experience, many bosses are hesitant to give constructive criticism. Some bosses expect you to read subtle cues, and others simply prefer to avoid conflict. In either case, take the initiative to ask for the feedback explicitly. After a meeting or at the end of a project, ask casually, "How do you think that went?" If your boss responds with mere platitudes, be more specific: "Is there an area where I could have done better?"

This sort of informal feedback is critical. You need to know how your boss really feels about your work. If your boss is quietly unhappy with your performance, he or she might fire you instead of giving you a chance to improve. In any case, have this discussion with your boss *before* a formal performance evaluation; many bosses consider such performance reviews to be a bureaucratic formality.

MATCH THE MODE OF COMMUNICATION TO THE BOSS

On a daily basis, adjust your method of communication to reflect the preferences of your boss. Take notice of the types of interactions that he or she initiates. Does your boss call you to ask for information on a current project? Does he or she tend to stop by your office for a chat? Or does he or she simply send you an email asking you for information? Most likely, the form of outgoing communication reflects his or her desired form of incoming communication. So you should generally respond to your boss using whatever medium your boss typically uses.

As an example, I personally have a strong preference for reading printed documents rather than electronic pages. If one of my assistants or associates sends me an email longer than a page, I print it out. After a short while, my colleagues realize my preference and automatically print anything they want me to read, making my life easier and making me appreciate their contributions more.

In most work environments, emails are the most common form of communication. But different bosses use email in different ways. Personally, I use very brief emails with a few bullet points, without adding many words for niceties. Others craft more detailed emails and use complete sentences. In either case, you should respond in kind: if your boss uses bullets, reply with bullets. If your manager prefers longer thoughts and complete sentences, provide more analysis and use better grammar in your emails.

However, be aware that email is notoriously susceptible to misinterpretation. People often write emails in a rush, use ambiguous wording, and assume that others can read their minds. Don't be one of those careless writers. Whether your emails are short or long, convey your message as precisely as possible—and read it over before you hit "send."

Many bosses have different expectations regarding the urgency of their emails. Some managers check their email only a few times a day. If they send an email, they don't necessarily need a reply for an hour or more—if they require immediate action, they'll make a phone call or pay a brief face-to-face visit. By contrast, other bosses seemingly walk around with their BlackBerrys permanently held six inches in front of their faces. If they send an email, they assume that you will see it immediately and begin to craft a reply. If your boss fits this description, try to persuade him or her that it is more productive for you to check your emails once an hour. But if your boss insists on immediate email replies, you should obviously cooperate.

Similarly, follow a reporting regime that works best for your boss—submitting hard-copy, email, or oral reports. Highlight the key points in your submissions in a useful format. For example, I like my direct reports to provide status reports that are divided into separate sections: significant existing projects, new assignments, and other issues. In any event, keep your reports down to a page, if possible, with only as much detail as your boss wants. If your boss likes to receive updates face-to-face, keep the meetings short and to the point. You won't impress your boss by talking too much. He or she will be far more impressed if you make your points succinctly and move on.

ADAPT TO THE MANAGEMENT STYLE OF YOUR BOSS

Beyond communication preferences, you should generally adapt to your boss's managerial style. Take a close look at your boss's habits by hearing what he or she is saying (or not saying) between the lines, and adjust your own habits accordingly. You don't need to match your personality perfectly with your boss's; you just need to make sure that your actions and habits are compatible with your boss's management style.

Here's an exercise to help you think about the management style of your boss. Respond to the multiple-choice questions on the next page and choose one answer to each question.

My boss prefers the role of:
   a. The one in charge
   b. Coordinator
   c. Problem solver
   d. Analyst

My boss values most in other people:
   a. Practicality
   b. Teamwork
   c. Innovation
   d. Perfectionism

My boss's decision-making style is:
   a. Consensus—seeks agreement from all
   b. Dictatorial—it's my way or the highway
   c. Debater—has an idea, but is willing to listen to others
   d. Risk-averse—sticks to what has been done before

My boss responds to problems by:
   a. Blaming subordinates for making mistakes
   b. Looking to external actors as causing the problems
   c. Asking for detailed information to analyze the situation
   d. Trying to prevent similar problems from recurring

When thinking about your boss's management style, it is useful to categorize him or her as belonging to one of several "personality types." Though there are many elaborate frameworks for organizing people into various personality types, I prefer to keep it simple. I have observed four main types of managerial styles in the working world: Inventive, Empathetic, Cautious, and Obsessive.[3] Although most bosses do not neatly fall into a single type, this framework can help you think about how to recognize your boss's weaknesses and compensate for them.

An Inventive boss is eager to take risks and perform experiments—to try something new. As a result, this sort of boss typically leads a dynamic and stimulating work environment. Unfortunately, such managers can create an air of chaos. They have a "vision" and don't wish to be pestered with the details of implementation. If you work for an Inventive boss, recognize that your organization probably hired your boss precisely because of this love of experimentation, so don't get in the way of his or her major initiatives. Instead, quietly fill in the details behind the scenes. To communicate with an Inventive manager, use brief bullet points and leave out the details—unless these details would significantly revamp the bigger picture.

An Empathetic manager pays a lot of attention to the feelings of his or her employees. This sort of boss goes to great pains to make sure that all of his or her employees feel appreciated. If done properly, this approach fosters trust and can be very productive. Unfortunately, some Empathetic managers spend too much time talking about feelings instead of getting things done. To work for such a boss, try to adopt some of the warmth of his or her style: be friendly, listen to what your boss is saying, and be sensitive to how your peers are feeling. At the same time, you still have to get your own work done. So be prepared to cautiously enforce time limits and project deadlines—for instance, by politely mentioning that you will have to leave a meeting after ninety minutes so that you can make a client call.

A Cautious boss values his or her established routine and works hard to minimize risk. He or she is organized and performs tasks slowly but steadily. In some ways, a Cautious boss is the easiest to emulate: just adopt his or her routine. Organize your time well, and show up to meetings prepared (say, by reading advance materials). However, a Cautious boss will often perform poorly when the situation calls for drastic change. If you feel the need to propose a more radical shift than your Cautious boss can handle, provide details, emphasize risk management, and allow your boss time to think over the issues. You must be patient when asking Cautious managers to do something new.

Obsessive bosses are very demanding of themselves and their employees. They get mired down in minor points and get upset about any oversight. Their abrasive style is often the result of a high level of anxiety about their own performance, and they tend to be unaware of how their behavior is affecting others. Admittedly, it is quite difficult to work for such a manager. You must make an extra effort to research the details of a project and collect appropriate data. Unfortunately, even if you produce high-quality work, your Obsessive boss might still offer a sharp critique. If so, one way to protect your sanity is to shrug your shoulders and accept that it will never be "good enough" for your boss. But if such critiques occur repeatedly, you've got to talk to your boss. (For advice on initiating this type of conversation, see "How to Deal with a Bad Boss" later in this chapter.) If this behavior still continues, look for another position where your boss will be more supportive.

HOW TO MAKE THE PARTNERSHIP WORK

Whatever the management style of your boss, he or she will become your biggest fan if you consistently deliver high-quality projects on time and within budget. When you do good work, your boss will be more receptive to your ideas and give you more discretion to run your own show. Your boss will try to keep you happy through salary increases, job promotions, and better assignments.

You should also be a team player. Willingly perform whatever tasks need to be done for your boss, even if they involve grunt work. For instance, when I was working at the SEC, we had many emergency deadlines for filing briefs with courts and agencies. Everyone was appreciative when the young lawyers pitched in to copy, staple, and mail those briefs. If a lawyer shied away from those mundane tasks, he or she quickly gained a bad reputation around the office as a prima donna.

When you do succeed, make sure that your boss knows it: make your boss aware of your accomplishments, especially before performance reviews or bonus decisions. As a boss, I would always ask my direct reports for an email that listed their accomplishments during the relevant period. With that list in hand, I could avoid overlooking something important when reviewing their performance or setting their bonus. Even if your boss does not ask, you should submit a list of accomplishments at appropriate times. This is not a time to be modest: without your list, there is simply no way for your boss to know the full range of your achievements.

On the other hand, your boss will turn against you if you do not produce results as expected. Here, the key word is "expected." If your boss has high expectations about what you will produce, he or she is more likely to be disappointed. So try to underpromise and overdeliver; bosses don't generally complain if you exceed expectations!

If a project looks as though it may fail, make sure to give your boss plenty of advance warning. Bosses don't want to be surprised by long delays or major blowups. It is bad enough if they occur; it's even worse if they occur without prior warning to the boss. With advance notice of a serious problem, your boss may be able to revise the project goals, reshuffle its resources, or come up with a brilliant solution. At the very least, your boss won't make promises to his or her superiors that cannot be kept.

When you warn your boss of a serious problem, you should simultaneously offer possible ways to mitigate its negative effects. I like to say that it's a "cheap date" to identify a problem without suggesting a solution. Try to come up with a creative solution to whatever internal or external constraints are standing in your way. If you truly understand a project's goals, you may be able to figure out how to achieve them through indirect means—such as by gaining practical control of a joint venture through clever contracts and executive appointments, even if your company is legally prohibited from holding a voting majority.

You should also accept responsibility for a problem that has arisen under your watch. I always found it irritating when one of my reports blamed problems within his or her unit on other people or external events. There is a huge difference between an explanation and an excuse. An explanation may correctly list a number of factors leading to a serious problem. But those factors don't excuse you from responsibility for the delay or blowup. It is your job to anticipate and plan for a wide range of adverse contingencies.

Stay Loyal to Your Boss

Though you can build a solid relationship over time by producing high-quality work, you can destroy the relationship in an instant by being disloyal. To be loyal to your boss, be his or her ally. This means that you can't publicly air negative opinions about your boss. If you have a personal beef with your boss, discuss it privately with him or her. That also means thinking twice before you make a joke at the water cooler at your boss's expense. Although it may seem funny at the time, disparaging remarks have a way of getting back to the boss—without the relevant context.

Another way to display your loyalty is to look for opportunities to make your boss look good to his or her superiors. For instance, if you see a blog post praising a speech or decision by your boss, bring it to your boss's attention. Better yet, circulate the blog post to other employees, including the boss's superiors.

As a general principle, be quick to give your colleagues credit, regardless of whether they are your bosses or your subordinates. Though giving your boss credit for your own hard work may make you feel slighted in the short term, your boss's goodwill will help you down the road.

Take particular care not to jump the chain of command by going over your boss's head to his or her superiors. If you cannot resolve an issue with your boss and plan to take it up the line, ask permission from your boss—or at least give your boss advance notice of your plan. This is an essential courtesy to your boss—unless he or she is engaging in unlawful activity, in which case you should blow the whistle to the compliance department.

Similarly, if you receive a request from your boss's superiors, keep your boss in the loop. Show your loyalty by checking with your boss before you carry out that request—or, alternatively, ask the superiors to give your boss a heads-up about the request. If you don't, your boss will likely resent your direct relationship with someone higher up on the totem pole.

If you're a junior manager, you may feel uneasy when your own boss talks directly to members of your team. Although this can be disruptive to you, it is an effective way for your boss to quickly obtain information and get a practical feel for a situation. I suggest an intermediate approach: request that your boss and your subordinates let you know about any conversations they have.

HOW TO DISAGREE WITH YOUR BOSS

Even if you generally have a trusting relationship with your boss, there will inevitably be times when you and your boss disagree. This is perfectly legitimate—a boss does not want subordinates who are total sycophants. He or she wants to hear if a lieutenant believes a strategy does not make sense or an execution plan is not realistic. Napoléon Bonaparte once said, "The people to fear are not those who disagree with you, but those who disagree with you and are too cowardly to let you know."[4]

Nevertheless, you can avoid some types of conflicts with a bit of planning. One way to head off disagreement is to talk to your boss in advance about how you intend to implement a project, even if your boss claims to provide you with total discretion. For example, before you take a bold step such as inviting in another business unit, approaching a government agency, or retaining an outside consultant, give your boss a heads-up on what you intend to do. Once you've done that, you don't need to wait for formal approval before proceeding with your plan. But you've given the boss a chance to object if he or she has serious concerns about how you are implementing an assignment.

For conflicts that do arise, how should you pick your battles? Consider the following questions when deciding whether to discuss a disagreement with your boss: How big are the stakes involved? Do you think you can prevail in this argument? What will happen if you don't fight at all? If the stakes are modest or your chances of prevailing are low, grit your teeth and go along with your boss's position. Remember the lyrics from the Kenny Rogers song: "You gotta know when to hold 'em, know when to fold 'em."[5]

When you do decide to stand your ground, you have to do it in a problem-solving way. I give a few examples below. The key things to remember are: do your research and keep the tone collaborative. That means marshaling objective facts to support your argument and not making the disagreement personal between you and your boss. Instead, present it as a discussion about how best to achieve your organization's goals.

Let's review a few situations where disagreements with your boss are likely to arise, and how you might respond constructively.

- You've been assigned a project but not given enough resources to carry it out successfully. In such a situation, carefully document the staff and budget you need to complete each component of the project. Then try to offer alternative approaches, such as narrowing the scope of the project—perhaps by deleting a secondary portion—or shifting a staffer temporarily to your unit.

- You've been given another big project on top of your already crushing burden. In such a situation, review your current workload with your boss and ask for his or her ranking of projects. That can provide the basis for a request to delay or drop a low-ranked project.

- You've been asked to develop a new product or service that you view as a clear loser. In such a situation, provide objective data on why this product or service would be inferior to those of the firm's competitors or why customers wouldn't be receptive to this new idea. If possible, try to suggest a modified version of the boss's proposal that will have a higher probability of success.

In sum, when disagreeing with your boss, recognize his or her authority to make the decision, provide detailed research to support your concerns, and suggest alternative approaches to resolving the problem. Don't get angry or confrontational, and don't attack your boss's intelligence or integrity. Present objective facts to support your position, and propose ways to work together to settle the disagreement.

HOW TO DEAL WITH A BAD BOSS

The strategies I've just described work well when you and your boss disagree over a course of action but share a solid working relationship. However, what if your problem with your boss is more serious, resulting from repeated clashes rather than a onetime disagreement? In other words, what if you work for a "bad boss"?

The answer is that it's even *more* important for you to take the initiative in problem solving, because your boss almost certainly won't. Here are a few types of bad bosses and suggestions on how to react to each of them.

Micromanaging Boss

As I discussed in the last chapter, I strongly disapprove of micromanaging. A micromanager plays an overly large role in the projects of his or her subordinates. Instead of letting them use their own judgment, the boss makes every decision or dictates every step to take. This can be especially frustrating to capable workers, turning an interesting task into boring grunt work.

If you think your boss is a micromanager, first make sure that he or she isn't merely responding to your own poor performance. If you have shown that you cannot perform good work without heavy-handed supervision, your boss may feel that he or she has to constantly look over your shoulder. In that event, try to regain your boss's confidence through a small project. When a relatively unimportant project comes up, ask your boss to grant you additional responsibility "just this once." If he or she agrees, put forth extraordinary effort to ensure that the project exceeds expectations.

If your boss micromanages your entire team, you can be confident that it's not just you. Your next step should be to sit down with your boss and talk about his or her overbearing supervision. Admittedly, initiating such a discussion is a difficult task. You may fear that your boss will take your criticism as an attack or otherwise identify you as an "enemy." Yet, as I mentioned in the previous chapter, many micromanagers aren't fully self-aware; they don't realize how intrusive their actions are. In my experience, bosses like these often respond well to constructive criticism from their subordinates.

After having this discussion, try to ease your boss away from his or her micromanaging tendencies. Many micromanagers have an underlying fear that something will go wrong if anyone is given managerial discretion. You can address this fear by frequently sharing information throughout the course of a project. Don't wait for your boss to ask how things are going; instead, send a daily email with status reports and next steps. This helps reassure your boss that, in fact, everything is under control.

Neglectful Boss

Some managers are on the other end of the spectrum. Instead of micromanaging their subordinates' projects, they fail to give any directions at all. In an extreme case, their subordinates may feel that their boss is ignoring them. As a result, they feel that they have to guess what their bosses want.

To fix this problem, you'll have to be very assertive to get your boss's attention. If you receive an assignment with unclear goals, ask for clarification right then and there. Don't leave your boss's office or hang up the phone until you are satisfied that you know what you need to do.

During the course of the project, you should also communicate more frequently with your boss. For instance, if you send your boss a key email every Monday, Wednesday, and Friday at 4 p.m., he or she will know that it's important—and be more likely to respond to it. If that doesn't work, try to speak face-to-face with your boss about getting more direction. Be specific about what you need and how your boss can be helpful. If your boss still ignores you at this point, look elsewhere in the organization for mentors who can provide you with some form of guidance.

Abusive Boss

A boss who gets angry and abuses his or her workers is probably the worst type of "bad boss." By yelling at or otherwise belittling his or her employees, an abusive boss fosters an environment of fear. There is no excuse for this behavior—yet abusive bosses can be found in all sorts of organizations.

The only way to deal with an abusive boss is not to take personally the fact that he or she regularly loses self-control. The boss's unacceptable behavior has nothing to do with you. It has everything to do with his or her own problems, which you can't fix.

Nevertheless, your behavior may unwittingly push your boss's "hot buttons" and trigger a stream of abuse. If you want to stick it out with such a boss, try to identify what those triggers are. Does your boss go ballistic if you arrive five minutes late or if your desk is slightly messy? If so, the simplest solution is to avoid behaviors that invite your boss's wrath.

But this strategy won't work if your boss plays the blame game and gets angry whenever a project turns sour. You can try to explain the key causes and suggest how you will address them in the future. You can try to brush off abusive behavior with a joke—as the comedian Bill Cosby said, "If you can laugh at it, you can survive it."[6] But if you stop laughing after repeated incidents, you should have a frank discussion with your boss about his or her behavior.

If you're lucky, your boss will not be aware of how outrageously he or she is acting. If you provide calm, constructive feedback, your boss might have an epiphany and change his or her ways. Unfortunately, many abusive bosses know exactly what they're doing. They'll push and push until they meet resistance, at which point they're likely to retreat. The only way to succeed with such a boss is to stand your ground. Insist that your boss treat you with respect. Be specific about how his or her abusive behavior is affecting your work and which particular actions are intolerable. But whatever you do, keep your cool; nothing good can come from a yelling match.

LAST RESORTS

If your attempts to deal with your "bad boss" fail, you may need to complain to the human resources (HR) department. This is a momentous step; yet, if your boss is truly preventing you from being productive, it is in your organization's interest to correct the situation. Before you go to HR, document the specific instances of your boss's misdeeds toward you and preferably others. If the organization decides to keep your boss in place despite all the evidence you have collected, ask for an internal transfer or look for a job in another organization.

If you decide you need to leave your job, don't do it like JetBlue flight attendant Steven Slater. In August 2010, he made a dramatic exit after his plane landed at Kennedy airport—he cursed at passengers over the PA system and then slid down the inflatable emergency exit chute, beer in hand. Indeed, we've all been tempted at some point to indulge in such cathartic behavior. But in today's ever-connected world, professionals need to quit without burning any bridges. You never know when you'll cross paths with your boss or your coworkers in a future job.

To leave with tact, make sure to give reasonable notice—a month at the bare minimum. This allows your organization to find a replacement or otherwise plan for your departure. During this notice period, you should not merely "run out the clock"; keep working hard until the very last day. In particular, offer to train your replacement, tie up any loose ends, and make yourself available to answer any questions, even after you leave.

The most difficult part of leaving a job may be explaining your decision to your boss. This is a moment when you need to swallow your pride and stress that you are leaving mainly because of a new opportunity. This is not a time to rehash your objections to your current job. (But feel free to be truthful in the HR exit interview—without the whole story, HR can't take steps to remedy the situation.)

TAKEAWAYS

1. Make sure that you and your boss agree on what assignments you need to do and the relative priority of each.

2. Match your communication style with that of your boss with regard to the phone, email, and in-person meetings.

3. Carefully observe your boss's personality traits. Make sure that your actions and habits are compatible with the way your boss manages.

4. Take the initiative to submit a list of your accomplishments to your boss, especially at bonus time.

5. Give plenty of warning if a project is running into trouble. Bosses hate bad surprises, and they may be able to solve the problem with enough advance notice.

6. Be loyal to your boss; make your boss look good to his or her superiors.

7. Don't jump the chain of command without giving advance notice to your boss.

8. Think hard about whether a disagreement with your boss is worth fighting about. If you decide to stand your ground, provide well-researched alternatives in a calm manner.

9. Have a frank discussion with your boss if he or she is severely harming your productivity. If that fails, complain to the firm or request a transfer.

10. Leave your job with tact. Give a month's notice and don't burn any bridges on the way out.

Part V

PURSUING A PRODUCTIVE LIFE

So far in this book, I have offered tools to help you to become more productive in the traditional sense of the word—getting more done each hour that you work. This part broadens the concept of productivity to discuss how to formulate and pursue your long-term goals over your entire career.

In chapter 12, I will outline what I believe is the most productive approach to career planning. Under this approach, you should consider your career as an ongoing process over many years with multiple steps, each yielding better information for taking the next step.

In chapter 13, I will expand this approach to productive career planning by helping you respond to the rapid changes in the broader world. I'll also show you how certain fundamentals of economics and personal integrity will endure over your whole career.

In chapter 14, I'll return to what may be your biggest reason for increasing your productivity: having more time for your personal life. I'll offer suggestions to help you remain productive at work while still spending quality time at home.

12

MAXIMIZING YOUR CAREER OPTIONS OVER A LIFETIME

Students and young professionals frequently ask me how I planned out my career to become president of Fidelity Investments. My answer has always been clear: "There was no grand plan. I backed into my career one step at a time." Most successful executives would give the same answer.

When I was attending college and law school, I never planned to become the president of a financial services giant. At the time, I thought I would become a professor or a federal regulator. Indeed, at the start of my career, I held positions as a law professor, a senior official at the Securities and Exchange Commission, and a partner in a law firm. During those fourteen years, I learned a lot about myself and the financial sector. I found that I really liked doing deals and managing people, rather than writing articles and drafting regulations.

That's why I accepted a job offer as general counsel to Fidelity Investments when it was a relatively small company in 1987. I was fortunate to be part of a company and an industry that were expanding rapidly. For almost a decade, I broadened my skills by developing new products, helping the company enter new markets and learning to manage people. For a complex set of reasons, including some related to the external pressures on the company, I was chosen in 1997 to be president of Fidelity Investments.

What does my history suggest about your career planning? That you don't control the trajectory of your career. There are just too many factors beyond your control that will shape your job opportunities—such as global economic trends, political elections, industry regulation, and company finances. So don't commit the hubris of thinking that you can determine your professional glide path.

On the other hand, you can increase your *probability* of success by approaching your career with the right mind-set. Career planning isn't a onetime event; it's a continual process that has to be actively managed over a lifetime. At each step, you need to ask yourself: What can I do next that will *maximize my options in the future*?

GETTING STARTED: FORMULATING TENTATIVE CAREER AIMS

The first step in this process is to formulate a list of a few jobs that you eventually hope to hold—these are your Career Aims. In order to create this list intelligently, you should critically evaluate three subjects: your interests, your skills, and market demand.

Assess Your Interests

To start thinking about your Career Aims, figure out what characteristics of a job appeal to you now. To jump-start that process, consider these questions.

- What topics—e.g., public policy, civil engineering—do you find most enjoyable and interesting?

- Do you prefer reading and writing or playing around with numbers?

- Do you like to focus on project details or analyze broad trends?

- Do you prefer to work with colleagues or by yourself?

- Do you want to work on your own schedule, or are you willing to keep regular hours?

- Do you want to travel as part of your work, or do you prefer to stay near your home?

- What values of your employer and colleagues are most important to you?

- What social or public purposes, if any, do you want to pursue in your career?

- How much do you care about a job's salary relative to these personal goals and values?

Your answers to these questions will suggest a broad list of jobs that you might like. If you're at the beginning of your career, don't make the mistake of considering only the most obvious professions: doctors, dentists, lawyers, consultants, bankers, and engineers. What about geologists, nutritionists, advertising sellers, or commodity traders? When you put together your wish list, look at a long list of occupations like the one compiled by the Bureau of Labor Statistics.[1]

For those of you in the middle of your careers, the list of potential jobs is likely to be narrower, as you have probably chosen a profession or general line of work. For you, Career Aims may include a more senior position within your organization, a job in a different industry, or owning your own business. Nevertheless, within this narrower set, you should still create a broad list of potentially appealing jobs. Or you may be in the midst of a career crisis, thinking of changing professions entirely. In that case, you should cast a wider net.

Your next task is to learn more about what these jobs actually entail. This will help you delete some jobs entirely and clarify which jobs you might like the most. To gather this information, start by searching the Internet and attending job fairs; those sources will give you a rough description of the main facts about a given career. Soak up as much career counseling as you can get your hands on, including professional advice if you can afford it. A good career counselor can open up avenues you never would have considered.

To get the best grip on the day-to-day details of a particular job, interview people in that line of work. Talk to your friends and neighbors to see who they might know, or ask your guidance counselor to arrange a job-shadowing program. Once you find the right person to interview, ask him or her questions such as:

- What is a typical day in this job like?

- What do you like best and least about this job?

- Does this job help you learn and grow?

- How did you get started in this job?

- What job do you hope to hold in five or ten years?

- What is the starting salary and average pay for this job?

Determine Your Aptitudes and Skills

After you have a long list of jobs that you might enjoy doing, think about what skills you can offer to the world—and whether they match any jobs on your list. Consider not only your formal credentials but also your intangible personal skills, such as the ability to think on your feet or empathize with the less fortunate.

In some occupations, the formal prerequisites are well known. To practice as a litigator, for example, you have to graduate from an accredited law school and pass the bar exam. For other occupations, you'll have to search harder for the job requirements. For instance, what are the educational requirements to become a physical therapist? I had to call a physical therapist friend of mine to find out: six years of university studies, including a significant period of practical training in a clinic.

Beyond these formal requirements, you will need a personal set of skills that match the demands of the occupation. To work at a nonprofit charity, you will need fund-raising skills, empathy, and patience to deal with its many constituencies—including donors, employees, and service communities. To work as a bond trader on Wall Street, you will need to be an instantaneous decision maker who can quickly absorb a lot of information and evaluate competing bids.

Sometimes, especially when you're young, it's tough to be honest about whether you really have the skills you need for a certain career. As a teenager, I wanted to become a professional basketball player. I used to shoot hoops at the playground for entire afternoons, working on my jump shot. Unfortunately, college scouts never gave me a call: they had no need for a six-foot forward with middling talent. If I had chosen a college based on its basketball team, that would have been an exercise in self-delusion.

To help you honestly assess what you have to offer to the world, this endnote[2] has a link to a long list of transferable skills. Go through the list and find the skills that you already have or could easily obtain.

Next, make sure that your skills match those required in your desired profession. To ascertain what skills a job really requires, you should start by searching the standard sources for relevant information. But, again, those sources will be of limited help. To get a good understanding of the necessary skills, you will have to talk with people already in these jobs.

Judge Market Demand

After reviewing your interests and skills, you should evaluate whether there is sufficient market demand for your desired career. Unfortunately, some people undergo hardship before they take market demand into account. Consider the story of Joe Therrien, a drama teacher from New York City.[3] After several years of teaching, Joe decided to get a master's degree in puppetry, a degree that cost him $35,000 to obtain. When he finished his degree, however, there were no puppetry jobs to be found. So he returned to his old teaching job—as a substitute, for about half his former pay.

Even if there are some jobs in your desired profession, there may be too much supply relative to the demand. Take sportscasting, for instance. Although radio and television stations certainly employ sportscasters, this modest demand is dwarfed by the number of young men and women who love sports and think they'd make good announcers. As a result, it's very difficult to get your foot in the door in that field.

Don't just look at market demand by taking a snapshot in time; find out where the industry is going. Is it expanding or contracting? To take a simple example, coal-fired power plants face long-run decline, while renewable sources of energy are a potential growth engine.

MAXIMIZE YOUR OPTIONS—ONE STEP AT A TIME

Now that you've formulated your tentative Career Aims, you're ready to think about your next step. Don't try to figure out the complete trajectory for your entire career. Instead, ask whether your next job will move you in the right direction—by maximizing your options in the future.

I recently mentored a young man just out of college who was trying to plan his entire career in one fell swoop. Almost every week he wanted my opinion on which jobs he should hold at every stage in his life. My answer was always the same: "Don't try to nail down your entire career path all at once. Instead, focus on what you can ascertain now: what would be a sensible next step to help you move in the right direction or put you in a better position to make more informed choices about your career in the future?"

To maximize your options at each step in your career, pursue a combination of formal classroom education and informal learning on the job. In both environments, seek knowledge and skills that would be transferable to many types of jobs in the future.

Get Education and Training

Formal education is a well-established way to expand your career options. From a purely practical standpoint, a formal education may provide you with a needed credential; for example, you can't legally be a doctor without going to medical school. But a good education is more than a passport: you gain valuable knowledge along the way. On average, an extra year of education will increase your lifetime pay by around 8 to 9 percent.[4]

Given the rapid pace of development in the business and political world, you should expect to continue your formal education even after you start working. Some large organizations, such as General Electric and the World Bank, have their own top-notch training programs. Other organizations will pay some or all of your costs to get a second degree at night or on weekends. Such part-time degrees may have a better cost-benefit ratio than taking several years off work to attend a full-time graduate school. In any event, members of many professions must meet continuing education requirements to retain their license to practice.

Regardless of the format your education takes, choose a subject that will lead to a broad range of careers. This might mean rethinking that degree in creative writing, even if you find it intellectually stimulating. Though the world needs some people to write novels, the career prospects in the field are extremely limited. And don't specialize too early. For instance, although a degree in fabric styling may seem practical, there are only a few different careers where this major would be useful.

In my view, you can increase your career options if you start by studying a "hard" subject instead of a "soft" one. A hard subject is one that is more rigorous, where there is generally a right answer and a wrong answer, such as physics. You should learn hard subjects first because they teach you the fundamental skills that are needed to evaluate softer subjects. For example, if you first obtain a rigorous education in statistical methods, you will have some of the tools necessary to analyze the impact of many public policies. Furthermore, softer subjects are easier to learn on your own. You might be able to pick up the main ideas of a certain field of sociology by reading some papers, but you probably can't learn the fundamentals of neurophysiology without formal instruction.

Learn on the Job

After you obtain your desired formal schooling, or perhaps while you're still obtaining it, choose a job in which you can develop new skills or areas of expertise. Learning by doing should not be an afterthought: economists have estimated that the lifetime value of on-the-job training is roughly equal to an additional four years in the classroom.[5] But just as with formal schooling, make sure the skills you are developing are transferable.

For instance, if you take a job putting together airplane leases, you could become the world's expert on that subject. But this expertise is so narrow that it's not likely to help you in any other line of work. By contrast, if you take a job that relates in any way to corporate taxation, you can acquire a lot of transferable knowledge. Although you may be working on tax issues that are relevant only to certain types of companies, you will be learning how to analyze tax problems and devise creative solutions. Since all businesses want to reduce their taxes, those skills will help you land future jobs in a variety of industries.

One important aspect of learning on the job is learning about yourself and your career options. At each job, find out more about what you actually enjoy doing and what you're good at. Furthermore, try to learn about other positions that you frequently interact with—what skills they require and what jobs they lead to. If you can gather all this information, you'll be in a much better position to decide the next step in your career.

CHOOSING YOUR NEXT JOB

When you're deciding on your next job, you should try to gain some skills or expertise likely to apply to a broad range of future jobs. Here are some examples.

Develop Leadership Skills

Leadership is a skill that is inherently transferable and will always be in demand, so try to choose a job that will allow you to lead others. Consider Sarah, a highly skilled securities trader. For her next promotion, Sarah may be given a choice: trade securities in a new sector for higher pay, or start managing some of the firm's traders at the same pay. Even though it may not feel like an advancement, Sarah should take the management position in order to gain leadership skills that will be invaluable later in her career.

But you don't need an official title of "manager" to gain leadership skills. The Israel Defense Forces (IDF) train officers by putting its young recruits into many different types of high-stress situations, with little direction from the top. This is a great way to force recruits to exercise creativity and judgment in resolving tough problems—exactly the skills required to be a leader in civilian and military life. As an example, one team was assigned to solve the problem of back pain in helicopter pilots, an issue that was baffling army doctors. Without guidance, the team had to learn how best to measure back pain and why piloting a chopper seemed to bring about sore backs. After completing their exploration, they redesigned the pilots' seats to solve the problem—again without guidance.

Any job that hones your leadership skills in challenging situations will help you prepare for more senior positions. But make sure the job allows you to fail occasionally—without career-ending consequences. The IDF, for example, is quite tolerant of young officers who fail as long as they have taken a well-designed risk—distinguishing, in the words of Professor Loren Gary, between "a well-planned experiment and a roulette wheel."[6] After the failure of a "well-planned experiment," the young officers debrief their superiors and try to explain how the project could be improved for next time.[7]

Learn About Other Cultures

Gaining experience outside your home country is a good way to maximize your career options in this increasingly flat world. I lived for almost two years in Africa and have spent considerable time in England, Japan, and China. Through those experiences, I learned to deal with different economic, cultural, and political environments—which later helped me evaluate or start business units throughout the world. Indeed, many multinational corporations won't consider you for top positions unless you've had this sort of international exposure.

Although there are potential drawbacks to foreign postings, you can minimize them with a little foresight. First, employees in foreign offices are sometimes neglected by headquarters. Before moving to a foreign office, try to spend time at headquarters so you can develop contacts—especially mentors—and learn how the organization operates. Second, it's often difficult for employees in foreign offices to find a good job when returning to headquarters. Having a mentor at headquarters will keep you plugged in to what is happening there and help you identify job openings at the right time. Finally, moving to a foreign country may place a large burden on your family, especially if your children are school age. So ask for special financial assistance to place your children into high-quality private schools in those foreign countries.

Expand Your Organizational Experience

There are many different types of organizations: corporations, partnerships, nonprofits, and government agencies. If you've worked in only one type of organization, finding a job in another type can expand your career options. For instance, employers at some for-profit companies are reluctant to hire people who have worked only in government agencies. The employers are concerned about whether such applicants can make the transition from government to business.

Similarly, I've seen employers at publicly traded companies refuse to consider top-quality executives who have worked only for private companies. Running a public company does require some specialized knowledge related to SEC mandates and quarterly earnings reports. But those skills can be learned quickly by talented executives; all it takes is a short stint at a public company. Once you complete this short stint, you will look more attractive to a wider range of companies.

Grow Your Network

In addition to developing your skills and knowledge, your next step should help you expand your web of personal relationships with peers. To paraphrase a slogan, "Organizations don't hire people. People hire people." The more people you know in your industry, the more people will think of you when a job pops open—even when it is not publicly advertised.

To some extent, you can develop your network even without taking a new career step. When you have the opportunity, attend conferences or participate in committees at trade associations. When you do, arrive early so you can chat with people and exchange cards; follow up with a polite email or a request to connect on LinkedIn. Then you will have a group of knowledgeable people with whom you can discuss industry trends.

But such event-driven networking pales in comparison with the networks you build simply by working with colleagues. This sort of networking within an organization is usually informal and can create deep bonds. If you're already in midcareer, you've probably met many fellow employees at internal meetings or client presentations. You've spent a day or more traveling with colleagues. You've used those occasions to get to know them well. Those deeper relationships have made your current work more enjoyable and might help you find an unadvertised job in the future.

As you ponder your next career step, then, think about the networking advantages you might gain from it. You can grow your network by accepting a job in another unit of the same firm or by heading an interdisciplinary project staffed by people from various units. If you're even more ambitious, you can expand your network by going to work for a new company or in a new industry.

REVISING YOUR GOALS

Your approach to choosing the next step will depend on where you are in your career—at the start, in the middle, or toward the end.

Beginning Your Career

In the best of all worlds, you would love your job, it would pay well, and you would perform it expertly. In effect, you would be paid well to do a job that you would choose to do anyway.

Unfortunately, the reality is that you may not be able to get a lucrative job that you love at every step in your career. Sometimes your expertise in a certain subject doesn't translate into jobs that are in demand. In other cases, taking a job doing what you love may not be the best career move to make. In the early years, you may need to take a job that you dislike because it is the only option available to you. Or you may choose an unpleasant job that helps you gain skills (or savings) that you will need later.

For instance, some people take an all-consuming job as an investment banker in the short term to gain industry knowledge, pay off student loans, or save up money to start a business on their own. Similarly, young doctors must endure the grueling schedules and stress of residency training in order to complete their education. And many future Hollywood stars, such as Marc Norman, the Oscar-winning director of *Shakespeare in Love*, get their start earning a pittance in the mail room of a movie studio. Though these individuals may not "like" their current jobs, they are willing to put up with them so that they can get a better job later on.

Conduct an Annual Checkup

Even after you're well established in a career path, you should periodically reevaluate whether your current job is best for you. Personally, I advocate treating this process like a routine physical: you should do it every year.[8]

Why so often? Because a lot can happen in a year. Your preferences may change. You may learn more about the pros and cons of your current job. There may be significant changes in your physical condition, your family situation, or your financial portfolio.

During the same year, external factors may change. You may get a new boss or new colleagues, or your firm may be acquired by another organization. The demand for your firm's goods and services may increase or decrease, along with the competition you face.

To help you perform an annual checkup on your Career Aims, consider the following questions:

- During the last year, have there been any major changes in what you want from your job? What caused those changes?

- During the last year, what external events significantly affected your current job? Were these changes at the level of your firm, your industry, your country, or the world?

- How do those internal and external changes impact your long-term Career Aims? What will you do differently in the next year as a result?

- Is your current job preparing you for the next step? What transferable skills have you learned? Are you receiving the guidance and opportunities that you were promised?

- Do you want to be in the same position in one year? Three years? Ten years?

When you answer these questions, you may feel satisfied with your current position or could be satisfied with only modest changes. Alternatively, you may realize that your current job is not right for you. If so, you should figure out what next steps are likely to move you toward the jobs you want to hold.

Plan for Retirement

Although I've geared most of this chapter to a professional's path toward the top, the transition from the top toward a relaxing and stimulating retirement is no less challenging.

Retirement used to be an all-or-nothing decision. In the past, most people worked full-time until a certain age, at which point they retired. Today, the transition to retirement is often a longer process. According to a study done by the AARP, 68 percent of those aged fifty to seventy plan to work into their seventies or beyond.[9] However, these individuals still want to reduce their workload.

I see these preferences when I speak to audiences on the subject of retirement. I frequently ask, "How many of you want to work full-time until age seventy-two?" I usually see only one or two hands in the air— the true workaholics. But when I ask how many individuals want to keep working part-time to age seventy-two, I see most hands raised; people want to stay connected to their place of work.

This trend, called "phased retirement," is driven partly by the financial problems caused by longer life expectancy and inadequate savings.[10] But phased retirement is also driven by many professionals' desire to continue working for its own sake. In a poll of phased retirees, 70 percent of those aged sixty-six and over cited the "desire to stay mentally active" and the "desire to remain productive and useful" when asked to explain why they were still working.[11] To those individuals, work is much more stimulating than an extra round of golf.

To plan for your retirement career, you need to try out new roles and develop relationships during the decade *before* you retire. So while you're still working, look around your community for organizations that could use a helping hand. Consider offering your expertise to local teenagers by joining a mentorship organization or by teaching a class at your local school. See if there are any local businesses that could make use of your accumulated wisdom.

I personally faced this challenge when I turned sixty-five and left the chairmanship of MFS. In anticipation of my retirement, I started teaching at a business school, joined another board, and took a few chess lessons. I started to write articles and books on financial topics. I even tried my hand writing a book about personal productivity! In this way, I have created an array of possible options for a satisfying retirement.

Many of my friends have taken a more relaxed approach toward generating retirement options. A doctor friend of mine prepared for retirement by honing her skills as an amateur playwright. Once she retired, she would write a scene of a new play on days when she was not playing golf. Another friend of mine joined the board of a local opera company as his working days were winding down. During the final years at his firm, he successfully positioned himself to become chairman of the opera company's board after his retirement.

TAKEAWAYS

1. Don't try to formulate one trajectory for your career. Instead, think of your career as a series of steps—with you gaining knowledge and skills at each step.

2. Assess your own characteristics, skills, and preferences when considering a job or career change. Be honest about what's important to you.

3. Research your desired careers in various ways: interview people in the field, attend conferences, and read related articles.

4. Look carefully at external demand before focusing on one career or industry. Does the world want many more people in this profession?

5. When making each step along your career path, try to maximize the number of options you will have for your next step.

6. Don't overspecialize too early. Choose jobs that will teach you skills that will transfer to other careers.

7. Pick a job that will teach you how to lead, how to operate in different types of organizations, or how to navigate another country's business environment.

8. You may have to accept an unpleasant intermediate step in order to reach your ultimate Career Aims.

9. Revise your goals annually throughout your career; that will help you identify the right time to move forward or stay where you are.

10. In order to have an active retirement, get involved with local organizations and try out new activities while you're still working.

13

EMBRACE CHANGE
BUT STAY THE SAME

Most people strongly prefer stability to change. However, I believe that change is the rule, not the exception, in most aspects of the economy. My step-by-step approach to career planning recognizes this high degree of economic dynamism. To make productive choices in the working world, you need to learn how to embrace change at each step and take advantage of the opportunities change presents.

At the same time, certain aspects of the working world have remained the same over the years. These include the fundamentals of profit and loss and the ethical values of honesty and integrity. To succeed in the working world, you need to recognize these constants and act consistently with them.

LOOKING FOR STABILITY

Many people fear change at work, for good reason. Change requires employees to spare vital time and energy to meet new colleagues, learn new procedures, and develop new skills. It also requires employees to face the unknown. If there's a significant organizational shake-up, employees worry: How will I get along with my new boss? How will the new organization value my performance?

Sometimes, entire industries get caught up in trying to protect the status quo. Back in 1982, the Motion Picture Association of America (MPAA) lobbied Congress to protect its industry from a newfangled piece of technology, the VCR, due to the fear that the rise of home recording would substantially reduce TV viewership. Jack Valenti, the head of the MPAA, made the following bold claim: "The VCR is to the American film producer and the American public as the Boston Strangler is to the woman home alone."[1]

The MPAA's lobbying failed, and the VCR became a staple in the American home. However, instead of destroying the movie industry, VCRs created a huge new market for that industry to develop. Today, the motion picture industry makes more money selling DVDs—the successor to videotapes—than it does at the box office.

WHY WE FEAR CHANGE

Most people prefer stability because they fear the negative effects of a change more heavily than they welcome the positives.[2] In fact, it's possible that this disparity has evolutionary origins.[3] For our hunter-gatherer ancestors, a change in environment usually meant one of two things: either they had achieved a modest gain, say by finding a tree that bore more fruit; or they faced disaster in the form of a predator coming to kill them. As a result, our ancestors became very cautious in the face of any significant change. Through the process of natural selection, that instinct may have been hardwired into our brains, making us fear the downside of a change more than we appreciate the potential upside.

THE PERVASIVENESS OF CHANGE

Despite the inherent preference for stability, change at work occurs frequently at several levels. At the individual level, people change jobs more often than ever. In a study of U.S. workers, the Bureau of Labor Statistics found that individuals in their sample held an average of eleven jobs between ages eighteen and forty-four—meaning that their subjects moved to a new job roughly once every thirty months.[4] Even highly educated workers and older workers often changed jobs, though not as often as less educated and younger workers.

At the organizational level, leadership and strategy change constantly. So even if you stay at the same organization for a long period, you're likely to get a new boss more often than you might think. In the past decade, the world's 2,500 largest firms have changed CEOs an average of roughly once every seven years.[5] As a result, workers throughout companies must adjust frequently to significant reorganizations or major changes in strategic direction.

Over a longer time horizon, your organization's standing will not remain the same. Consider *Fortune*'s list of the fifty largest U.S. companies. Of the fifty companies on the list in 1970, only thirteen remained there in 2011, including such stalwarts as Boeing and IBM. The rest declined in importance, went bankrupt, or were swallowed up in acquisitions—all of which significantly impacted the employees of each organization.

RECOGNIZING EXTERNAL CHANGE

At the global economic level, your career prospects are likely to be adversely affected—and perhaps derailed—by short-term crises. For instance, the financial meltdown of 2008 was not a "once-in-a-century flood," as many commentators have proclaimed. Although the 2008 mortgage debacle probably caused the most damage of any recent financial crisis, there have been five other crises since 1986: the stock market crash of 1987, the real estate recession of 1990–1991, the Asian crisis of 1997–1998, the bursting of the Internet bubble in 2000–2001, and the euro currency crisis of 2011–2012. Each of those upheavals destroyed many companies and professional careers.

Though such individual crises cause short-term disruption to your economic environment, long-term trends will also shape your employment opportunities.[6] One of the most powerful long-term trends is technological innovation. Consider the recent explosion of computing power. Between 1986 and 2007, general computing power increased at an annual rate of 58 percent—meaning that computers in 2007 were more than nine thousand times as powerful as those in 1986.[7] This exponential increase has transformed the way most firms do business and has reshaped the entire economy.

However, technological innovation doesn't just affect what we usually think of as "high-tech" sectors. For instance, roughly 12 percent of Americans in 1950 were farmers, and each one produced enough food to feed about 15 people. Today, as a result of new technologies, roughly 2 percent of Americans farm—and each one can feed 155 people.[8] This dramatic shift has not only affected the agricultural industry; it has also made food cheaper and freed up labor for other pursuits.

Demographic trends are another huge driver of economic change. For example, Japan is shrinking as an economic power in large part because of its graying citizenry—the result of a low fertility rate, high life expectancy, and tough restrictions on immigration. The percentage of Japanese citizens over age sixty-five has gone from 4.9 percent in 1950 to 23.1 percent in 2010. By 2050, four in ten Japanese citizens are projected to be over the age of sixty-five.[9] These demographic changes imply slower growth in consumer demand and larger pools of retirement investments.

By contrast, the demographics of China have been very favorable to that country's economic growth. During the last decade, the working-age group in China has constituted a large percentage of the total Chinese population. However, the tide is beginning to turn: currently, the ratio of workers to retirees is facing a steep decline—by 2050, retirees are projected to make up one-third of the Chinese population.[10] This trend reversal is being caused by China's policy of allowing only one child per family, together with the population's rising life expectancy. As a result, in the future China will have fewer workers and more pressure on its fledgling retirement system.

EMBRACING CHANGE

In this fluid environment, my step-by-step approach to career planning is all the more relevant. With so much changing in the world around you, it would be foolish to cast one trajectory for your career in concrete. How would you adapt if your firm went bankrupt? What would you do if a new technology made your specialized knowledge obsolete? By maximizing your options at each step in your career, you will put yourself into a good position to react to whatever changes come your way.

However, you shouldn't be satisfied with merely being able to *react* to change. It's much better to be in a position where you can take advantage of the opportunities it presents. By that I mean identifying real trends and exploiting them, while avoiding market fads, bubbles, and other fantasies.

Your Next Career Step

When you start thinking about your next career step, pay close attention to long-term trends. Do you need to change jobs to benefit from a demographic shift? Do you need more training to keep pace with the latest technologies?

There are many ways to turn demographic trends to your advantage. For example, you can try to work in countries where the economic pie is expanding, or you can choose to work for firms in your own country that export to those expanding nations. Russia is a bad bet because of its declining population, while Brazil has excellent prospects because of its growing population.[11] Within any country, you can gear your career choices toward products or sectors that are attractive to the largest demographic group. For example, more retirement communities will be needed in Japan to serve the growing cohort of people over age sixty-five.

You also need to stay on top of technological trends. In the broadest strokes, this starts with your Career Aims. For instance, a career in traditional journalism will face headwinds because the Internet is making it harder for established news organizations to conduct business as usual. By contrast, the continued expansion of computing power means that programmers and software engineers will see a growing demand for the foreseeable future.

In particular, I would encourage you to consider jobs that combine two well-established disciplines, such as bioengineering. Interdisciplinary fields can offer great potential for breakthrough changes—for example, communicating with doctors through microchips embedded in implanted medical devices. However, you will have to push hard to overcome the parochial inbreeding of most fields. When Robert Langer, the most famous bioengineer in the U.S. today, received a doctoral degree in engineering from MIT, he initially could find jobs only in engineering—instead of ones that applied engineering techniques to human biology. Fortunately, he was eventually hired by an iconoclastic medical researcher.

Even while you're working at your current job, you can start looking for assignments with a high upside potential, such as taking over a unit with existing fast growth or heading a new initiative to advertise through social media. The key is to get there first: if you spot the new opportunity before others in your organization, you will have a better shot at leading the new initiative.

For example, when I was president of Fidelity, we had a large fund of small-company stocks run by a terrific manager. Responding to the trend toward more specialized funds, one analyst suggested expanding our product line to include a broader range of "style" funds for small-company stocks, such as "small-cap value" and "small-cap growth" funds.[12] Since that analyst developed the idea for the style-specific funds, he was an obvious choice to run one of them.

More broadly, don't be afraid to try out a career that you might later abandon. Carly Fiorina studied medieval history in college, then dropped out of law school, switched to marketing, and ultimately became the

CEO of Hewlett-Packard. Vikram Pandit, the CEO leading the Citigroup turnaround, started off in electrical engineering before moving to finance. Richard Branson launched a magazine to become a journalist but became fascinated by the business side and went on to found the Virgin series of companies (Virgin Airlines, Virgin Records, Virgin Finance). I doubt that any of those leaders considers their early career steps a failure. I certainly don't regret having gone to law school or practiced law, even though I ultimately discovered I liked business and finance better.

If you try out a new job or a new project, you may soon decide that it's not right for you. Cut your losses quickly by going in another direction and learning as much as you can from your mistakes. Many successful people have said that they learned the most from their failures, but to obtain that benefit, you need to carefully and honestly consider why you failed. Did you lack certain skills or expertise? Were your expectations unrealistic? Or did you run into an unforeseeable spate of bad luck? After carefully considering these questions, adopt whatever changes are necessary for your next step in your career. As John Wooden, the legendary coach of the UCLA basketball team, said, "Failure is not fatal, but failure to change might be."[13]

Strategic Planning for the Future

In designing a new strategy at your current organization, recognize that the future is inherently unknowable. Any prediction of the future is based primarily on data about the past. But our personal beliefs about the past are highly biased. As the philosopher and author Nassim Taleb put it, we each form a "narrative fallacy" in our head, placing events in the past within a convenient storyline that neglects the role of luck.[14] If we use our narrative fallacies of the past to make predictions about the future, we are likely to overemphasize known facts and fail to account for unforeseeable random events.

I see lots of people succumb to this narrative fallacy when they unquestioningly extrapolate past trends into the future. I've often been presented with what I call a "hockey stick" chart—which projects the future growth of a product or business that has seen some success in the past (see figure 6). The projection invariably takes this historic record of success and continues it into the future—at the past rate or even a better one. So, like magic, a small business is projected to become a big business!

Figure 6: HOCKEY STICK CHART

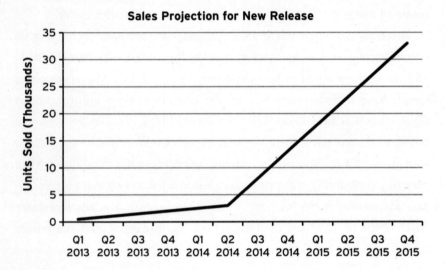

Sales Projection for New Release

However, these hockey-stick projections fail to recognize the inevitability of material changes over time. In most cases, the growth rate of a successful small business will slow down as it gets larger. The demand for the products of the business may not be that deep, or its success may attract the entry of strong competitors. Although the business may enjoy the benefits of economies of scale, those will eventually reach a plateau. At some point, the business may even face diseconomies of scale.

In the same vein, you should not take complicated mathematical models at face value—despite their facade of sophistication, they are only as good as their key assumptions. Consider the models supporting mortgage-backed securities (MBS) in the 2003–2006 era. Some of the models relied on default rates from a prior decade of home mortgages, even though many of the current mortgage products were new and un-known. Other models neglected to take into account potential liquidity events—what would happen if MBS could not easily be refinanced. As everyone knows, those models for MBS failed spectacularly in 2008.

So if you are formulating or reviewing a business projection or math-ematical model, focus on what could change in your business or in the broader world. At the minimum, identify a few potentially adverse fac-tors and run your model as if one of these factors will materialize. But that won't be enough; invariably, you will come across adverse factors that you didn't even consider—"unknown unknowns," in the words of former U.S. secretary of defense Donald Rumsfeld.

To try to discover the unknown unknowns, run a pilot project that helps you identify the full range of potential problems. When we were considering launching a fund at Fidelity, we used to make projections of its returns based on historic data. But it quickly became clear that this back-testing on paper did not accurately predict what would happen in the real world. Instead, we began to create pilot funds run by young ana-lysts. Through those pilots, we discovered a lot about the problems a fund would actually face: its trading costs and liquidity constraints as well as the precise coverage of its investment objective.

THE WORLD IS NOT NORMAL

Another problem with many mathematical models is that they are implicitly based on a normal distribution curve. Because normal distributions are shaped like a bell curve, most events are assumed to occur near the middle of the distribution, and seemingly uncom-mon events (say, a nationwide decline in home prices) are assumed to happen very infrequently.[15] But many economic and political phe-nomena are more dispersed than a normal distribution curve would predict. For instance, if the Dow Jones Industrial Average (DJIA) moved in line with a normal distribution curve, it would have gone up or down by more than 4.5 percent only six days between 1916 and 2003. In fact, the DJIA has moved that much 366 times during that period.[16]

Don't get snowed by fancy mathematical models with the key assumptions based on historic data. When designing new products or managing risk exposure, take a close look at the changes that would impact those assumptions. And don't automatically go along with models based on normal distribution curves. Reality is often abnormal, as reflected by "fat" tails at both ends of the curve.

STAYING THE SAME

Although you need to adapt to rapid change, there are some principles that have remained the same over centuries, with good reason. I'll focus on two of them: economic fundamentals and personal integrity. Whatever path you take in developing your career, you should abide by these precepts.

Economic Fundamentals

A company must generate profits as well as revenues to remain a viable business, and stock prices ultimately reflect a company's expected stream of future profits. Despite the simplicity and obviousness of these economic fundamentals, they seem to be challenged in each generation as some people get carried away with new business paradigms.

During the late 1990s, many investors were mesmerized by dot-com companies with innovative ideas but no profits. The stock prices of some dot-com companies, like the stock prices of today's social media companies, achieved mind-boggling valuations because their revenues were growing so quickly. Nevertheless, revenues create only the *potential* for profits. In order to earn profits, the company's expenses must be lower than its revenues.

I clearly remember the day when the executives of Pets.com—a company that sold pet food over the Internet—made a presentation to Fidelity analysts. The executives were boasting that their revenue on average had reached $30 per order. However, knowing that the company had been offering free shipping, one analyst asked how much it cost to mail those heavy containers of pet food. The answer was $32 per order! With that flawed business model, it was not surprising that the company went out of business before the end of 2000.

In the short term, companies without sound fundamentals can capture the public's imagination and command high stock prices. Although those companies' stocks have the momentum to deliver strong returns over short time periods, researchers have shown that their returns decline sharply over time. Over longer periods, such "momentum" stocks do not perform as well as those of value companies with stronger profit streams.[17]

In other words, fundamental economics win out within a few years. So don't hitch your wagon to a passing fad. To be successful, your firm will have to deliver economic value over time, as reflected by a steady stream of profits rather than just a growing volume of revenues.

Your Personal Integrity

Like economic fundamentals, personal integrity should be a constant North Star during your career. Personal integrity includes not only complying with applicable laws but also following your own ethical code on standards of business conduct. My code includes honest communications to all stakeholders, fair treatment of employees, and no misuse of corporate information.

Think about both your ethical strengths and any areas where you know you need to do better. Do you stretch out the time it takes to complete an assignment so that you can increase your billable hours? Do you pad your requests for expense reimbursements by a few dollars? Are you willing to shade the truth to make a sale?

Although most people believe they are ethical, few have actually written down their own code of ethics. Don't rely solely on the mission statement or compliance manual supplied by your firm. Instead, identify three or four main principles that will guide your personal behavior over your professional career—and write them down. For each principle, think about why you believe it is important. Then think about a situation in which you would find it difficult to abide by that principle, and consider how you would address the challenge.

Based on your own code of ethics, you should work continually to build up your reputation for personal integrity. A favorable reputation will help your career in many ways. It will make employers more willing to hire and promote you. It will encourage your colleagues to be open with you about their issues and problems. It will make customers more likely to do business with you and your organization. But if you fail to adhere to ethical standards, you will alienate your peers, bosses, and customers.

TESTING ETHICS IN THE LAB

Laboratory experiments have repeatedly demonstrated that people are willing to incur personal costs to exact revenge on those who have violated their trust. One well-known experiment is called the "Ultimatum Game," an exercise in which two people must divide an amount of money. Let's call the players Allen and Beth. At the beginning of the game, the experimenter gives Allen $10. Allen then decides how to divide the $10 and makes a "take-it-or-leave-it" offer to Beth. Beth has the power to accept or reject it. Let's say

Allen decides to keep $7 for himself and offer $3 to Beth. If Beth accepts the offer, the $10 is divided as proposed. But if Beth rejects it, both players go home empty-handed.

Traditional economic theory states that even if Allen offers only one cent to Beth, she should take the deal, because one cent is still more than nothing. In fact, offers under $2.50 are often rejected; players would rather give up the money in order to exact revenge on a partner who violates their notion of fairness.[18]

This observation has been replicated even when researchers increase the stakes substantially. For instance, Professor Lisa Cameron of the University of Melbourne performed the same experiment in a poor village in Indonesia.[19] That meant that the money involved represented a significant chunk of the subjects' yearly income. Nevertheless, subjects still placed a high value on fairness; one player even gave up an amount equal to his monthly income in order to punish his partner for making an "unfair" offer.

Unfortunately, a good reputation for personal integrity, developed over many years, can be lost quickly. Warren Buffett was exactly right when he said, "It takes 20 years to build a reputation and five minutes to ruin it."[20] The psychologists John Skowronski and Donal Carlston have demonstrated that people don't evaluate someone's integrity by observing all of her actions and taking some sort of "average."[21] Rather, people place a heavier weight on negative actions. For a person to be a "liar," he needs to tell a lie only occasionally; for a person to be "honest," he must tell the truth all the time.

Economists have supported this conclusion through evidence from eBay. When a seller on eBay receives his or her *first* instance of negative feedback—even if hundreds of other buyers had reported only positive experiences—his or her weekly sales growth is reduced by an average of 13 percentage points.[22]

Similarly, one thoughtless act can cause major damage to your organization, even if you're a small fish. Consider the story of a lazy FedEx deliveryman in California. In December 2011, a home surveillance video captured him casually tossing a computer monitor over the recipient's fence, breaking it. The homeowner then uploaded the video to YouTube. In less than two weeks, the video garnered 8 million views and caused significant damage to the FedEx brand.[23]

Of course, an ethical transgression at your job probably won't result in a viral YouTube hit. But misguided attempts to push through a deal or perform a favor can be quite harmful to your organization; they could open your firm to potential legal liability or cause it to lose a major customer.

So don't cross the line, or even come close, on ethical issues you confront during your career. Be prepared to sacrifice immediate benefits in exchange for maintaining your integrity throughout your career— indeed, it is this very willingness to forgo short-term gains that shows you really have a code of ethics. If you're ever in doubt about whether a course of action is appropriate, use the *"New York Times* test": would you feel comfortable if your actions were reported on the front page of the *New York Times*?

TAKEAWAYS

1. Recognize your subconscious bias toward stability. Evaluate new options on their merits, regardless of your starting point.

2. Accept that you will frequently change positions and bosses; holding a job for life is the exception, not the rule.

3. Observe technological and demographic trends so that you can position yourself in an expanding pie.

4. Don't use simplistic facts from the past to extrapolate wildly into the future. New problems and challenges will inevitably surface.

5. Challenge the assumptions behind complicated mathematical models. A model is only as good as its underlying assumptions.

6. Look for new opportunities for your organization. If you come up with the idea for an initiative, you might get the chance to lead it.

7. Don't get caught up in a fad or a bubble; in the end, the economic fundamentals of generating profits will always matter most.

8. Guard your personal integrity closely. The short-term gains of an ethical lapse will be dwarfed by the long-term costs of tarnishing your reputation.

14

BALANCING HOME
AND WORK

I end this book with a reminder of the goals of productivity. Why are you reading this book? What's the point of getting more done in less time? In my view, the point is not just to build a more rewarding career but to enjoy a more rewarding *life*. The more efficient you are at work, the more time you'll have for your family, your friends, and other aspects of life that you care about.

When I was a child in the 1950s, the relationship between home and work was quite traditional: a man was expected to be his family's breadwinner, and a woman was expected to take care of the children and the home. Today, the gender balance at work has roughly equalized,[1] but traditional gender roles still persist to some degree. Although many men have assumed a broader role at home, women often face unrelenting demands on their time from their children, their spouse, and their career. Moreover, there has been a sharp rise in households with only one parent, who must earn a decent living while still caring for his or her children.

At the same time, advances in telecommunication have made it possible to stay connected to the office while at home. This has brought its own mixture of good and bad news.[2] On the one hand, greater flexibility in work location can help you resolve practical home issues, such as caring for a sick child. On the other hand, you may resent the constant pressure to check your email or make a phone call while tending to your family at home.

WHAT WOULD YOU DO WITH AN EXTRA FIVE HOURS A WEEK?

Below is a short exercise to gauge how you value different types of activities. I have listed fourteen activities and put them into four categories: Work, Family, Community, and Yourself. To start with, estimate roughly the number of hours you spend each week on each activity.

Work

    Working at your workplace ☐
    Working from home ☐
    Commuting ☐

Family

    Spending time with your children and grandchildren ☐
    Spending time with your spouse or significant other ☐
    Caring for your parents ☐
    Preparing meals and doing housework ☐

Community

    Participating in schools or other programs related to your children ☐
    Participating in other charitable, civic, or political groups ☐
    Participating in faith-based or religious activities ☐

Yourself

    Engaging in sports or exercise ☐

Socializing with friends and relatives   ☐
Nurturing yourself through hobbies and personal activities   ☐
Sleeping   ☐

Total = 168 hours

    Now imagine that suddenly you have five extra hours to spend each week. Please estimate how much of that extra time you would devote to each of the activities listed above.

The answers to this exercise can be quite telling. Suppose you would spend most of that extra five hours per week spending time with your children. That means that extra time with your children is more valuable to you than extra time at work. Or suppose you would spend most of the extra time on yourself. That choice implies that you feel you have given up too much of your personal life to tend to your job and your children.

On the other hand, if you would spend most of your extra time at work, that may mean that you're generally satisfied with your family life and would like to make a larger commitment to work. Although some of you would choose that, most professionals—even those without children—come to the opposite conclusion. In a survey, 68 percent of professional women without children said that they would choose more time over more money, roughly the same percentage as professional women with children.[3]

To shift the balance from work to personal activities, there are two areas you should focus on: your employer's attitude toward flexible work schedules and your own style of working.

FIND A FLEXIBLE EMPLOYER—OR TRY TO CREATE ONE WHERE YOU ARE

As you know from earlier chapters, I've always emphasized results over hours. As a boss, I was comfortable if a brilliant analyst worked from 5 p.m. to midnight, as long as he or she identified good investment ideas.

Fortunately, I'm not alone: many employers allow workers to choose when to work to some degree. According to the 2012 National Study of Employers, almost 80 percent of employers permit some workers to periodically change their starting and quitting times within specified ranges.[4] In particular, many high-tech companies and customer service firms allow employees to work from home.[5]

There will be times in your life when you have special needs for flexible working hours, such as when you or your spouse gives birth or your child falls ill. Fortunately, more than half of the employers in the United States offer paid maternity leave to female workers. And almost half of those firms allow employees to take a few days off, with pay, to care for sick children.[6]

So investigate your employer's policies on paid leave and flextime *before* you accept a job. If, however, you don't happen to work for a flexible employer—and if you don't want to change jobs—you can still try to persuade your organization to change its work-life policies.

Start your campaign with the officials in your organization's human resources department, who will likely be sympathetic to your concerns. In a survey of two hundred HR managers, two-thirds said that family-supportive policies such as flexible hours are the single most important factors in attracting and retaining employees.[7] Employees agree: in a survey, a plurality of workers said that their employer's policies on work-life balance were the most important factor they considered when mulling a job offer.[8]

THE CASE FOR FLEXIBLE HOURS

Once employees are hired, flexible policies on hours and place of work can help reduce the costs associated with employee turnover. When the Detroit Regional Chamber of Commerce began allowing various flexible scheduling options in 2000, retention rates increased from 75 percent to 90 percent.[9] And many economists have showed that paid maternity leave significantly increases the probability that a new mother will return to her previous job.[10]

Similarly, flexible workplace arrangements help reduce absenteeism. Back in the 1980s, a large public utility in the western United States agreed to help researchers confirm that hypothesis. The company temporarily adopted a flexible work schedule (allowing its employees to distribute their working hours during the day as they wished) in only one of its subunits, while maintaining rigid schedules in similar subunits. In the following year, the subunit with the flexible schedule reported a 20 percent decrease in the rate of worker absences, while the rate in the other subunits remained essentially the same.[11]

CHANGE THE WAY YOU WORK

Though you should push hard to improve your organization's flexibility as a workplace, you can't dictate its policies. So use the tools within your control to achieve your personal goals as best as you can.

Go Home for Dinner

When our children were living at home, I tried very hard to be home for dinner every night at 7. During dinner, we usually talked about what had happened that day and sometimes about current events. When our children were small, I would play with them until their bedtime. When they became teenagers, I'd watch TV with them or discuss their homework. My wife and I would also chat about personal matters.

Unfortunately, I have seen many professionals work to 8, 9, or 10 every night and go into the office every day of every weekend. They always have a pile of work to finish and never seem to have enough time to do it during normal business hours. Although you may occasionally have to work late at night if there is a real emergency, there cannot be one every day. And on most weekends, you should be able to get away with (at most) a few hours of work at home when the babies are napping or the teenagers are sleeping late.

However, I acknowledge that in certain professions, such as consulting or investment banking, it is expected that every professional will work late six or seven nights every week. And for a variety of reasons, some organizations operate in a permanent state of crisis that keeps employees chained to their desks. Such a demanding job may make sense if it really turns you on or if it will dramatically expand your career options down the road. Nevertheless, if you really want to build a relationship with friends and family, you may want to leave the job after a few years.[12]

Assertively Protect Your Family Time

To keep a balanced schedule, you will have to be assertive and learn to say no. When I was an SEC official, I was offered the chance to cohead a special study on the then-fledgling topic of mortgage-backed securities. Although I found the subject fascinating, I initially turned down the offer because the task force was going to meet from 7 to 9 p.m. three times a week. When I explained that I was declining in order to make it home for dinner with my family, the initial response was shock and silence. But after a few days of standing my ground and tinkering with work schedules, we managed to reschedule the meetings from 5 to 6:30 p.m. And we had no trouble completing the special study and handling ordinary business during regular hours.

Hank Paulson, the former CEO of Goldman Sachs and later secretary of the Treasury, has written about how his long working hours began to take a terrible toll on his young family. In response, he had a candid discussion with his boss, who was receptive to a revised work schedule that let Hank arrive home in time to read a bedtime story to his children. Although his wife complained that he read the stories too quickly, his children soon embraced the "daddy style" of story reading.[13]

Paulson admits that when he subsequently became a boss at Goldman Sachs, he demanded that his subordinates meet project deadlines even if that meant working long hours in the evenings and on weekends. Yet when his subordinates criticized this demand, he clearly put the burden on them to assert their needs and insist on more flexible schedules: "It's not your boss's job to figure out your life. You spend so much time planning your work schedule and your career, you need to make that kind of effort to manage your private life, too. Learn how to say 'no.'"[14]

Depending on the culture of your organization and your boss's personality, you may be anxious about setting such limits with your boss. But remember: if you have shown that you are productive and trustworthy (see chapter 11, "Managing Your Boss"), your boss knows that you will get your work done with a more flexible schedule. When I first asked to leave early on Wednesday afternoons to watch my children's sports games, I was worried that my boss would get upset, so I offered to arrive early that day to make up the time. However, to my surprise, my boss saw it as an opportunity to show how much the company valued me and wanted to be flexible. When I became the boss and continued to leave early on Wednesdays, my example freed up other employees to attend the sports games, school plays, or violin recitals of their children.

Decide Who's the "Caretaker" in Your Marriage—or Hire Help if You Can

Even if you establish a routine that allows you to spend quality time with your family in the evenings, there aren't enough hours in the day for you to meet your obligations at work *and* spend the time it takes to raise children. So every successful professional with children needs one of two things: a spouse whose primary focus is child rearing or supportive outside child care.

Spouses who assume the child-rearing role don't need to be full-time homemakers; many "stay-at-home" partners have fulfilling part-time careers. While our children were in school, my wife, Liz, had a private practice as a psychotherapist, which allowed her to be flexible with her hours. Outside of her practice, Liz was also a talented oil painter. Nevertheless, she spent much more time with our children than I did.

Though Hank Paulson and I were each lucky enough to have a talented and compassionate wife whose main focus was caring for our children, there is no reason why this role should automatically fall on women. I'm glad to see more couples where the wife has a high-pressure job and the husband is the primary caretaker.

In my view, the decision about staying at home isn't about fulfilling gender roles at all. Consider the following: according to Census Bureau data, same-sex parents are just as likely as opposite-sex parents to have one partner stay at home.[15] Obviously, a same-sex spouse who takes on a child-rearing role isn't trying to satisfy antiquated gender expectations. Rather, those couples have decided *together* that the family is best off when one spouse stays at home while the other works. Those couples echo the sentiments of my wife, Liz, who says, "Every successful executive needs a wife—male or female."

Nevertheless, I freely admit that this approach will not work for everyone. If neither you nor your spouse can reduce your hours at the office, or if you are a single parent, you should get as much outside child support as you want and can afford. For those with deep financial pockets, a daytime nanny may be a partial answer. For those with nearby parents or other family members, those close relatives may be ready to supply child care. Other couples can sign up with a nearby day care center.[16]

Here are some additional tips that may be especially useful to working parents:

- Establish support networks at your job so you can give and get coverage for periodic events, such as doctors' appointments or school plays.

- Befriend other parents (at work, school, or elsewhere) with similarly aged children. These relationships can

be a tremendous resource for information, playdates for
your children, and emergency babysitting.

- Set up regular arrangements for carpooling, with
  friends or family members as backups for emergencies.

- If you can afford it, hire a housecleaner every week or
  every other week, and pay a local teenager to mow your
  lawn.

- Find a few healthy take-out restaurants that are on your
  way home from work. They can allow you to have a
  family dinner without having to spend time preparing
  the meal or cleaning the pots and pans afterward.

- If you choose to cook, prepare more food than necessary
  and freeze the leftovers—to be warmed up as needed
  on days when you have work emergencies.

Keep Your Home and Work Roles Separate—
Especially in Your Own Mind

When you finally arrive at home, you should concentrate your full attention on your family. This is not a place for multitasking of the sort I
extolled in chapter 3. First and foremost, avoid interruptions from work
such as phone calls and emails. If you really have to make a last-minute
phone call or send an email, do it before you open the front door. Once
you are with your spouse or family, they will justifiably become quite irritated if you are interrupted constantly by business messages.

The ubiquity of communications technologies does have its benefits.
If your boss can reach you on your cell phone, he or she might be more
willing to let you leave early for the day. Similarly, broadband technologies have opened up new opportunities for working from home, which
can be very helpful for new parents. But cell phones and email also cause

significant stress: they create a perceived need for constant accessibility and interrupt personal time.[17]

How can you avoid your family time being interrupted by constant calls from your office? The key, again, is to be assertive and set boundaries. Many professionals decide that they will not answer a call from work after hours, unless it's from their boss—and that's great! You can help yourself reinforce that boundary by assigning your boss's number a separate ringtone, letting you ignore most calls without even having to look at your phone.

Nevertheless, there are times—such as during the family dinner—when you really won't want to answer a call even from your boss. Here, you need to use a little bit more tact. Let your boss know about such "reserved" times and request that he or she avoid calling you during those times, if at all possible. If your boss repeatedly violates this request, it may be time for a frank discussion of the kind I advocated in chapter 11, "Managing Your Boss."

Similarly, if you are taking a much-needed holiday, ask your boss to respect the fact that you're on vacation. If you are fortunate enough to have an administrative assistant, you can also ask him or her to intercept incoming communication during this time. If something is truly important (say, the factory is on fire!), he or she can pass it along to you.

NOT EVERYTHING IS URGENT

Setting boundaries is absolutely necessary to maintaining a healthy family life. Professor Glen Kreiner of Penn State University led a team of researchers in a project to investigate how Episcopal parish priests set boundaries between their home and their work.[18] Priests, like many professionals, must deal with demanding expectations of access: a parishioner in distress expects to be able to talk to the priest at any time. Nevertheless, the researchers found that the priests were typically very clear about boundaries and expectations. As one priest said: "Thursdays are sacred time. . . . I am absolutely not available unless you have just been run over by an 18-wheeler. If you are headed to the emergency room, you call me, I'll be there, but don't you call me if you want to know whether something ought to be in the bulletin or not."

You may feel that many of your interruptions reach the level of importance of "getting run over by an 18-wheeler." Some interruptions surely do—that's why doctors are often on call at night, for instance. Nevertheless, many problems can wait until the morning to be resolved.

One priest in Kreiner's study described how he responded to a parishioner coming to his home seeking help one evening: "Oh, how long have you had this problem? Okay, you've been drinking for twenty years. Well, how about if we talk tomorrow morning?" In the same way, when confronted with a seeming crisis, you should step back and look at the big picture. Is this task so important that you should stop talking to your children and start working *right this minute*? In most cases, the answer is no.

The principle of avoiding interruptions illustrates a broader challenge: shifting your internal mind-set. When you get home, you need to be able to take off your "work hat" and put on your "home hat." This is not a trivial task. Between leaving work and arriving at home, your entire social structure changes. What was desired at work may be inappropriate at home. As one manager put it: "When I come home and try to get involved with my family I have a difficult time switching from my cognitive, directive management style to a more emotional, cooperative one. The very things I'm paid to do well at work create disaster for me at home."[19]

Sociologists have closely studied this challenge. They have observed how people change their various roles throughout the day—say, from mother to insurance agent to recreational tennis player and back to mother. A group of researchers from Arizona State University identified various "rites of passage," such as a regular morning routine or an evening commute, that help people make such daily transitions. Without those rites of passage, the researchers maintain, people have a very hard time switching among different roles.[20]

This is part of the difficulty of completing your day's work at home. It is easier to shift mental gears if you leave your work behind at the office; the act of leaving the physical space of your office helps to trigger subconscious changes in your mind. The reality, however, is that most professionals occasionally need to bring work home—at least 20 percent of managers do some work at home on a given day.[21] When you must bring work home, the key is to create a separate "mental space" for your work. This "mental space" includes separate dimensions of time and physical space, as well as your own mind-set.

On the time dimension, you should reserve certain times for your family every day, no matter what. For many professionals, that time is early evening, before the children go to bed. If you need to work after that, slip off to a separate physical space: your home study. A home study does not need to be fancy; it can just be a desk in your bedroom. The key is that it needs to be a *work* space, not a shared work-family space such as the kitchen table. You want the act of leaving this work space to help cue your subconscious mind to transition to your family role.

Just as you should establish a separate time and place for work activities at home, so you should separate your home and your office in your mind. The Canadian researcher Kiran Mirchandani observed the working habits of female professionals who do most of their work from home.[22] She noticed that they carefully differentiated between the work they did for pay and the tasks they did for their families. Even though family obligations, such as doing the laundry or watering the garden, seem a lot like "work," those individuals generally thought about their household chores as a "break" from work. In their minds, they constructed a rigid boundary between work and family activities.

In short, you cannot concentrate on your family if you're still thinking about work. So when you arrive home, don't lead off by complaining about something that happened at your office. That will just keep you mentally at work. Instead, ask your spouse and children about their day. Become an active listener, reacting empathetically and asking questions of your children. And save a little quiet time later in the evening for an intimate chat with your spouse. It is up to you to figure out how to shift out of work mode and devote your full attention to your family.

TAKEAWAYS

1. Look for employers that provide flexibility on when and where you work, and that offer paid leave for childbirth and other life events.

2. If you are in a position to influence your organization's policies, try to institute flextime policies to improve your organization's retention and productivity.

3. Commit every day to leaving work early enough to have dinner or spend time with your friends and family.

4. Be assertive to obtain more flexibility: assure your boss that you will get your work done even if you take an hour out of the day to take your child to the doctor.

5. If you are a busy executive, it really helps when your spouse is willing to spend more time with your children.

6. If neither you nor your spouse can reduce your office hours, hire a daytime nanny or make extensive use of child care.

7. Such couples should also get backup support at work and in the neighborhood to help out in jams.

8. When you are with your family, avoid all but the most critical interruptions from work. Most issues from work can wait until tomorrow morning.

9. Put your boss on a separate ringtone, but also encourage him or her not to call during private family time.

10. If you do have to bring work home, establish a separate time and place to do the work. Your mind needs to move from you as a professional to you as a family member.

EPILOGUE

As I've written this book, I have become more and more confident that professionals at all levels should focus on results produced rather than hours worked. It's the best way, in my opinion, for you to get more done at work while enjoying more time with your friends and family. However, I've also been impressed by how much your approach to productivity should depend on your own specific situation. In applying the lessons of this book, you should carefully consider your own stage in life and your organization's culture.

Your view of the appropriate balance between work and home will depend heavily on your stage in life. If you are a single college graduate working in an investment bank in New York City, you shouldn't worry about going home for dinner every night. There may even be days—or weeks!—when you don't get a full dose of sleep.

Nevertheless, once you and your spouse have children, your family life will require more of your time and attention. After you've reached this stage of your life, I do believe that you should make it home for dinner every night—and my advice on supportive child care and flexible scheduling at work becomes all the more critical. Once your children are enrolled in school, you may be able to spend less time on child care, but you will still want a flexible schedule so that you can be available for Little League games or piano recitals.

I have personally experienced this ebb and flow of the work-life dynamic. When I began my career as a law professor, I had no wife or family, so I tended to work most of the time. I was gung ho to succeed at all costs. Early in my career, the dean asked me to help out by teaching a first-year course, instead of my advanced seminar on financial institutions. I responded that I would love to teach property or torts, since they meshed well with my interest in economics. But I cautioned the dean that I had never gotten around to taking the second half of the contracts course at law school. Of course, what did the dean need? Another first-year section of contracts. Since I wanted to ingratiate myself with the dean, I accepted the offer. I spent the whole summer getting up to speed on the basic rules of contracts, instead of writing more stimulating articles on current financial issues.

By contrast, when I became chairman of MFS in 2004, I was married with adult children and had more say over my work schedule. Although I initially put in long hours to help stem the regulatory tide against MFS, by the end of 2007 I wanted to spend more time on public policy. MFS was kind enough to let me chair an SEC advisory committee and write two books on financial issues. During those years, I also developed more personal friendships, played more doubles tennis, and became more involved with charitable endeavors. As the years went by, I spent a larger and larger portion of the summer with my wife at our vacation home.

Similarly, to be successful, you have to be sensitive to your organization's unique trade-off between working long hours and getting results. Some organizations are very geared to producing good financial results with scant attention to how they are achieved. Other organizations give more weight to the hours you log at work than the results you produce and particularly value the time you devote to building a consensus within the organization.

I have learned to operate in both types of organizations. The Fidelity culture was very oriented toward concrete results. In that context, employees could have taken full advantage of my tips to productivity, such as dispensing quickly with small tasks and not attending time wasting meetings. However, this approach can be taken too far. For example, I've seen a CEO covertly assign the same project to two executives in the same company—who became unwitting competitors in getting results.

On the other hand, when I was secretary of economic affairs for Massachusetts, I found it virtually impossible to quickly make any major changes in budgets or programs. To be successful in that environment, I had to spend many hours touching base with relevant constituencies: community groups, labor unions, and industrial firms. Yet even within that difficult environment, I was able to organize my time efficiently and delegate certain tasks to my staff in developing support for those changes.

Since there is such a broad range of possible positions on the work-life balance and the results-time trade-off, it is often unclear where exactly an organization stands on these issues—or whether it is willing to make accommodations. I have often been amazed at the many failures of communication among well-meaning colleagues who don't ask one another really candid questions. As a result, professionals often misunderstand their organization's expectations on working hours or fail to take advantage of potential opportunities for scheduling flexibility.

For instance, I often see employees staying late at the office, even if it means missing their child's performance in a school play. They assume that their boss wouldn't tolerate their leaving early for the day. Yet in many such situations, the boss would have been willing to accommodate their needs. Believe it or not, most bosses understand your desire to spend time with your children or enjoy a romantic dinner with your spouse.

So don't be afraid to ask questions and voice your concerns to your peers and superiors. Your boss can't address your needs and desires unless you tell him or her what they are. Of course, some bosses might become defensive or even angry. However, if you politely raise specific points and propose constructive solutions, your boss and/or your organization may be able to help you achieve a more productive work schedule and a more satisfying personal life.

But regardless of your organization's constraints, remember that you have control over your own mind-set and behaviors on productivity. As

I've suggested, you can write down your goals, divided into time periods and ranked in order of priority. Then you'll be in a good position to spend the most time on your highest goals and minimize the time you devote to less significant matters.

Regardless of your employer's culture, you can adopt most of the specific techniques in this book. For example, you can still respond immediately to important emails and send out agendas before meetings. You can still read off the tops of the paragraphs and compose outlines before writing memos. And you can still plan your career with an eye toward maximizing your options and taking advantage of this changing world. Ultimately, it is within your power to boost your results and reduce your working hours.

APPENDIX 1
THE BIG IDEA: THE CASE FOR PROFESSIONAL BOARDS*

When the world's largest financial institutions had to be rescued from insolvency in 2008 by massive injections of governmental assistance, many blamed corporate boards for a lack of oversight.

This was a problem we had supposedly solved nearly a decade ago, when blatant failures of corporate governance (remember Enron?) prompted Congress to pass the Sarbanes-Oxley Act. The new rules had seemed promising. The majority of a board's directors had to be independent, which would, in theory, better protect shareholders. Senior executives were required to conduct annual assessments of their internal controls for review by external auditors, whose work would be further reviewed by a quasigovernmental oversight board.

The recent financial meltdown, however, has made it clear that the

* Modified from Robert C. Pozen, "The Case for Professional Boards," *Harvard Business Review* 88, no. 12 (December 2010): 50–58. Copyright © 2010 by Harvard Business Publishing. All rights reserved. Reprinted with permission.

new rules were insufficient. Most major financial institutions in 2008 were more than compliant with SOX. Indeed, at the banks that collapsed, 80 percent of the board members were independent, as were all members of their audit, compensation, and nominating committees. All the firms had evaluated their internal controls yearly, and the 2007 reports from their external auditors showed no material weaknesses in those controls. But that didn't stop the failures.

Why were the SOX reforms so ineffective? In my view, they merely added a new layer of legal obligations to the job of governance without improving the quality of people serving on the boards or changing their behavioral dynamics.[1]

I've been the president or chairman of two global financial firms, an independent director of several large industrial companies, and a long-time scholar of corporate governance. During my career, I've seen several chronic deficiencies in corporate boards—ones that will not be solved with another layer of legal procedures. Instead, corporations need to embrace an entirely new culture of governance, one in which professional directors view their role as their primary occupation. In this article, I will discuss the three main elements of a more professional board—size, experience, and time commitment. I will also address some of the difficulties in bringing about such a professional board.

A. SMALLER SIZE

Many of the financial institutions that failed in 2008 had very large boards, and all had a substantial majority of independent directors. Citigroup,* for example, had eighteen directors, of whom sixteen were independent. Boards as large as this are common in the financial sector. Industrial companies tend to have somewhat smaller boards—the average size for S&P

---

*To their credit, Citigroup has reformed their board in the period since I wrote this article. The board is now smaller, and more members are industry experts.

500 companies was almost eleven in 2009, according to recruitment consultants Spencer Stuart.

But even eleven directors are too many for effective decision making. In groups this large, members engage in what psychologists call "social loafing": they cease to take personal responsibility for the group's actions and rely on others to take the lead. Large groups also inhibit consensus building, which is the way boards typically operate: the more members there are, the harder it is to reach agreement, and so fewer decisive actions are taken.

Research on group dynamics suggests that groups of six or seven are the most effective at decision making.[2] They're small enough for all members to take personal responsibility for the group's actions, and they can usually reach a consensus in a reasonably short time. In my opinion, these advantages of small size outweigh the potential benefits of having extra generalists on a large corporate board.

The six independent directors called for in the new model are sufficient to populate the three key committees: audit, compensation, and nominating. Three different directors would serve solely as chairs of each of those committees, and the other three directors would each serve on two of them.

B. GREATER EXPERTISE

The Citigroup board was filled with luminaries from many walks of life—it boasted directors from a chemical company, a telecom giant, and a liberal arts university, for example. Yet in early 2008 only one of the independent directors had ever worked at a financial services firm—and that person was concurrently the CEO of a large entertainment firm. Of course, every board needs a generalist to provide a broad perspective on the company's strategy, and also an accounting expert to head the audit committee. The other members, however, should be experts in the company's main line of business.

Lack of expertise among directors is a perennial problem. Most directors of large companies struggle to properly understand the business. Today's companies are engaged in wide-ranging operations, do business in far-flung locations with global partners, and operate within complex political and economic environments. Some businesses, retailing, for one, are relatively easy to fathom, but others—aircraft manufacture, drug discovery, financial services, and telecommunications, for instance—are technically very challenging. I remember catching up with a friend who had served for many years as an independent director of a technology company. The CEO had suddenly resigned, and my friend was asked to step in. "I thought I knew a lot about the company, but boy, was I wrong," he told me. "The knowledge gaps between the directors and the executives are huge."

To close those gaps, large companies need independent directors who have the expertise to properly evaluate the information they get from managers. Perhaps more important, the directors must know what questions to ask about information they are not getting. Consider Medco, a pharmaceutical benefit manager (PBM). When it was owned by drug giant Merck, Medco recognized as revenue the drug copayments made by patients, although the company never owned those payments but merely processed them and passed them through to the health insurer. The distinguished directors on Merck's audit committee were generally unaware of this practice until Merck tried to sell some Medco shares to the public. If any of the independent directors had been experts in the field, they would have known that some PBMs recognize revenue this way and could have evaluated the appropriateness—and potential pitfalls—of the practice for Merck.

Indeed, a firm's audit committee should insist that the external auditors identify any significant accounting policies that depart from standard industry practice or for which the accounting literature allows alternative treatments. In either case, the external auditors should provide the committee with a careful analysis of the risks and benefits of available alternatives.

C. INCREASED TIME COMMITMENT

In the years before the financial crisis, the Citigroup board generally met in person seven times a year, for a full day each time. They also had a number of telephone meetings, each lasting a few hours. Factoring in some time for reading materials in advance of these meetings, let's estimate roughly that the independent director of Citigroup might have spent, on average, two hundred hours a year on board business, excluding travel time. Was this enough time to understand the operations of a complex global firm like Citigroup? The answer is obviously no.

Even a director with banking experience would need to spend at least two days a month, in addition to regular Citigroup board meetings, keeping abreast of company business if he were to contribute meaningfully to the board. And two days per month was, in fact, precisely the time commitment made by the head of the audit committee for one of Canada's largest companies, on whose board I also served. A retired accountant, this board colleague visited the company's offices relatively frequently. While he gave management advance notice of his visits, he talked informally with people at different levels in the finance function. He soon had a firm grasp of the company's financial operation and made sure that all material issues came before the audit committee. For the first time, the audit committee members began "to know what we didn't know," to paraphrase former U.S. defense secretary Donald Rumsfeld.

Independent directors of large companies sometimes assert that they have particular insight into the firms' operations because the board holds one meeting each year at one of the company's major facilities, rather than at headquarters. As a former company president who has hosted these field trips, I am skeptical. The employees interviewed by the independent directors on site are usually well rehearsed. If trips go as planned, the directors hear and see what management wants them to hear and see.

There's no way around it: directors must invest significantly more time than they currently do learning the business and monitoring internal developments and external circumstances that affect the company. Of course, more time spent on one company's business means less time available to devote to other boards. Independent directors, who are now allowed to serve on the boards of four or five public companies, should be restricted to just two. (This should not prevent them from serving on nonprofit boards.)

What this all adds up to is a new class of professional directors with the industry expertise and the time commitment necessary to understand and monitor large public companies effectively. Board service would not be a sideshow in their professional lives; it would be the main event.

D. THE LIKELY HURDLES FACING PROFESSIONAL DIRECTORS

A professional-director model is a significant departure from board process under current law. As a consequence, it is likely to elicit practical and legal objections. Let's look at the four most significant ones.

1. Professional Directors Would Be Hard to Find

Finding independent directors with relevant professional expertise will not be easy; the most-qualified people will be working for the company's competitors, making them unsuitable despite their expertise. Moreover, any executive running a large company will not have enough time to serve as a professional director.

As a result, most independent directors will be retired executives (but not former executives of the company in question). This pool of candidates is reasonably large: male and female executives often retire around age sixty in good health but want to continue to work, preferably on a part-time basis. For them, the role of professional independent director is a perfect fit. After all, who really wants to play golf every day for twenty-five or thirty years?

Recruiting professional directors primarily from the ranks of retired executives should go hand in hand with an end to mandatory retirement at age seventy or seventy-two. Mandatory retirement is simply a device that lets boards avoid the difficult process of evaluating directors; instead, they are automatically kicked out at a specified age. This is a terrible waste of talent—some directors do a great job at seventy-five, and others sleep through meetings at sixty-five.

2. They Would Be Too Expensive

Professional directors would be working a lot harder than directors do today—putting in roughly twice the hours. In addition, they'd be limited to serving on two for-profit boards. It is only reasonable, therefore, to accord professional directors a total compensation of approximately $400,000 a year—nearly double the current average annual compensation of $213,000 for directors of S&P 500 companies. Expensive as it sounds, this would not increase the company's total board compensation outlays by much, since there would only be six independent directors to pay, not ten, twelve, or even sixteen.

The more challenging issue is determining the composition of that $400,000. Directors of S&P 500 companies receive, on average, 58 percent of their compensation in restricted shares and stock options and the remainder in cash or benefits. I agree that professional directors should be paid more in shares than in cash to better align their interests with those of long-term shareholders; in fact, I recommend increasing the stock-based proportion to 75 percent.

3. They Would Not Want a Role That
Increased Their Legal Exposure

One could argue that because professional directors will actively supervise the company's operations, they will be subject to increased legal liabilities if something goes wrong. For example, if the head of the audit committee takes the lead in monitoring a company's financial function, will he or she be more liable than other directors if the financial statements contain material misrepresentations? The answer is definitely no, unless, of course, it can be shown that the audit head knew of the misrepresentations.

Under the business judgment rule, courts penalize independent directors only if they did not act in good faith: they did not carefully consider all the factual and legal issues; they neglected to obtain advice from independent experts if needed; or they deliberated for insufficient time to make a reasoned decision.[3] Because professional directors will spend more time on due diligence than today's norm, they will actually be in a stronger position to show that they acted in good faith.

4. They Would Meddle in Operations

Probably the most serious objection to my model is that it might blur the distinction between the roles of the board and management. A board of directors is supposed to set strategic goals for the company and monitor its progress against those goals. It has relatively well-defined duties in specified areas such as CEO succession, appointing the external auditor, and responding to takeover bids—but it is not supposed to get involved in day-to-day management.

Although the new model would entail some reallocation of power from senior executives to professional directors, it would not require directors to oversee day-to-day operations. Imagine an audit committee under the new arrangement. Like most audit committees today, it would meet quarterly to review financial filings and press releases. The committee would also meet to review the annual evaluation of internal controls. It would hold private discussions with the external and internal auditors, the chief financial officer, and the chief compliance officer. But under the new model, professional directors would also spend a significant amount of time gathering information throughout the year, engaging with company staff and others between board meetings. Through these discussions, professional directors would understand the company's financial issues much better than they could by sitting through a three-hour audit committee meeting each quarter. Far from telling employees what to do or not do, professional directors would simply be trying to identify material financial issues that should be brought before the committee for review and decision.

E. CONCLUSION

In short, my model of professional directorship directly responds to the three main factors behind ineffective decision making. In this model, all boards would be limited in size to seven people. Management would be represented by the CEO, and the other six directors would be independent. Most of the independent directors would be required to have extensive expertise in the company's lines of business, and they would spend at least two days a month on company business beyond the regular board meetings.

Those who agree that the new model is superior might be wondering how public companies could be persuaded to adopt it. Few CEOs would voluntarily embrace any scenario that shifts a significant degree of power from management to the board. One of three things, therefore, will have to happen if we are to get companies to adopt the new model.

First, government regulators could require large banks to adopt it as a matter of safety and soundness under banking laws. If bank directors are to constrain management from taking excessive risks, they must have extensive financial experience and spend considerable time between board meetings on bank business.

Second, shareholders could join together to pressure a company into adopting the new model. Large companies with records of chronic underperformance could benefit most from an influx of professional directors and would be a good place for shareholder campaigns to focus.

Finally, a few brave and confident CEOs of sound companies might actually be willing to try out the new model. We've seen important changes from the corner office before: the practice of majority voting started from the initiatives of a few enlightened CEOs. If experiments with the new model were to generate higher earnings or stock prices for the companies involved, then I would expect the new model to spread.

APPENDIX 2
SPEECH BY ROBERT POZEN TO THE BOSTON BAR FOUNDATION (2000)

Thank you very much, Joel, for your generous introduction. I'm deeply honored to be this year's recipient of the Boston Bar Foundation's Public Service Award. This award is particularly meaningful because it is given by an organization of lawyers who, despite being overworked and underappreciated, are reaching out to the community and supporting a broad range of public service projects.

I have been particularly impressed by the Foundation's programs for children in inner-city Boston. These children need the financial assistance and personal mentoring provided by the Foundation. I know the importance of role models from my own childhood; I had the benefit of a remarkable role model—my older brother Michael.

Let me tell you about Michael's difficult childhood and his remarkable career as a doctor. Next I will draw a few lessons from Michael's career as a doctor. Then I will draw a few lessons from Michael's life for the many children who must cope with difficult challenges at home and in school.

Before Michael was five years old, he had undergone several operations to reconstruct his mouth and palate. Because of Michael's birth defect, he had to attend speech therapy and contend with a facial scar. Both took a terrible emotional toll on him. I can remember, when he was seven or eight, other kids making fun of him because they couldn't understand what he was saying. I can remember, when he was sixteen or seventeen, his girlfriend's parents cutting off the relationship because they feared he might pass on his birth defect to their grandchildren.

Michael survived high school, went on to college, and then to medical school to pursue his dream of becoming a doctor. Michael had a hard time relating to the dry details of science courses during his first two years of medical school. But he became a star in the last two years when he did his clinical rotations. Michael was devoted to his patients and they loved him. He also found time to organize an ambulatory care program for migrant workers who picked vegetables in New Jersey during the summer. As a result of his outstanding work, Michael became a Robert Wood Johnson fellow and received a PhD in public health at Johns Hopkins while doing a cardiology internship there.

Michael then moved to Boston to teach and raise a family. In Boston, Michael was a whirlwind of activity. At Boston City Hospital, he established and trained a corps of paramedics to ride the ambulances to accident scenes. Every spring we still give out the Dr. Michael Pozen award to the paramedic of the year. Michael and another doctor launched a major research project on how emergency rooms should handle patients complaining of chest pain. Their work led to a computer program that helps doctors decide how to treat these patients most effectively. At the same time, Michael saw lots and lots of patients at the hospital. And he was one of the few doctors who would make home visits if one of his patients had a heart attack in the middle of the night.

Thus, it was a tragic irony that Michael, at the tender age of thirty-six, went to sleep one night and did not wake up because of a heart attack. The extensive autopsy was inconclusive—no heart disease, just sudden heart failure. My personal guess is that Michael had another birth defect that had not yet become evident.

Michael left a wife and two sons, ages three and seven. His widow devoted herself to raising the boys, and I tried to supply the boys with a male parental figure. Both are now young men, who have done very well personally and professionally, despite their father's premature death.

While Michael's story is a tragic one, I believe we can draw some lessons from his life.

The first is a message of hope for all those born with a disability or handicap. My brother was a person who could hardly be understood as a boy, yet he went on to deliver lectures regularly at medical school. Here was a person with a visible birth defect, yet he went on to marry and father two handsome sons.

The second is a message to all of us, to be more sensitive to children who lose a parent at an early age. The deck can be stacked against them at a time when support and encouragement are essential—when the measure of their lives is so dependent upon the adults around them.

In the U.S., children are "losing" parents and growing up in single-parent homes for many reasons, not only because of the early death of a parent. Unfortunately, it appears to be a growing trend. As recently as 1960, just 5 percent of all births in the U.S. were to unwed mothers. But by 1970, almost 11 percent of U.S. births were in that category. That category doubled again by the mid-1980s to 22 percent. And by 1996, almost one out of every three births in the U.S. were to unwed mothers.

Let's look at the issue from a different perspective. In 1970, 11 percent of children under eighteen lived in single-parent households. By 1998, 28 percent did—with the mother in the vast majority of cases. But it's not just single mothers. In fact, according to the Census Bureau, the number of single fathers grew 25 percent from 1995 to 1998, to over two million single-father families.

Many of these kids are doing just fine, thankfully. But many are not. We need to reach out to these children—whether they suffer from the emotional, educational, or financial handicaps that may result from growing up with just one parent.

Third, it's so easy to be consumed by the day-to-day pressures of our own lives, our own careers, and our own families. But we need to step back and look beyond our offices and neighborhoods, to consider what's happening outside of our own professions and industries. In the investment business, we seem to be obsessed with every major earning announcement and every utterance from the Fed, while other vital issues exist below our radar screens.

I applaud the Boston Bar Foundation for reaching out to the community to address children's needs. This is important work. In five, ten, or twenty years from now, the kids I've talked about this evening are likely to become our customers, our clients, and our employees. These are not children in some far off country; these are not children in some nameless institution; these are our children. And the work we do today, in mentoring them as children, will help their lives immeasurably.

I urge all of you to continue your generous support for the work of the Foundation.

NOTES

INTRODUCTION

1. Michael Kimmel, *Manhood in America: A Cultural History* (New York: Simon & Schuster, 1996).

1: SET AND PRIORITIZE YOUR GOALS

1. "McKinsey Global Survey Results: How Effectively Executives Use Their Time," McKinsey & Company, 2011.
2. "About Remember the Milk," www.rememberthemilk.com/about.

2: FOCUS ON THE FINAL PRODUCT

1. John Perry, "Structured Procrastination," www.structuredprocrastination.com.
2. Joseph R. Ferrari et al., "Frequent Behavioral Delay Tendencies by Adults: International Prevalence Rates of Chronic Procrastination," *Journal of Cross-Cultural Psychology* 38, no. 4 (July 2007): 458, doi: 10.1177/0022022107302314.
3. Laura J. Solomon and Esther D. Rothblum, "Academic Procrastination: Frequency and Cognitive-Behavioral Correlates," *Journal of Counseling Psychology* 31, no. 4 (1984): 503–509, doi: 10.1037/0022-0167.31.4.503.
4. Dan Ariely and Klaus Wertenbroch, "Procrastination, Deadlines, and Per-

formance: Self-Control by Precommitment," *Psychological Science* 13, no. 3 (2002): 219–224, doi: 10.1111/1467-9280.00441.

5. As a proportion of total revenue. Jennifer Smith, "Companies Reset Legal Costs," *Wall Street Journal*, April 8, 2012, http://online.wsj.com/article/SB10 001424052702304587704577331711808572108.html.

6. Stephanie Francis Ward, "The Ultimate Time-Money Trade-off," *ABA Journal*, February 21, 2007, www.abajournal.com/magazine/article/the _ultimate_time_money_trade_off1.

7. For further reading on this subject, see Cali Ressler and Jody Thompson, *Why Work Sucks and How to Fix It* (New York: Penguin, 2008).

8. Kimberly D. Elsbach, Dan M. Cable, and Jeffrey W. Sherman. "How Passive 'Face Time' Affects Perceptions of Employees: Evidence of Spontaneous Trait Inference in Context," *Human Relations* 63, no. 6 (2010): 735–750, doi: 10.1177/0018726709353139.

9. These researchers specifically used what's called a "false recognition" experimental procedure. They provide a subject with a few sentences that describe a certain type of behavior (but does not use the specific word). A few minutes later, subjects are asked to identify whether various words were actually in the description. For instance, the sentences could say, "Today, I went out and bought a car. I don't need it, but it struck my fancy. I like doing things this way—I hate to spend too much time mulling over a decision." If the subject mistakenly thinks that the explanation included the word "spontaneous," it is evidence that the subject subconsciously associates the idea of "spontaneity" with the description that he or she was given. This example sentence is from Donal E. Carlston and John J. Skowronski, "Savings in Relearning of Trait Information as Evidence for Spontaneous Inference Generation," *Journal of Personality and Social Psychology* 66, no. 5 (May 1994): 840–856, doi: 10.1037/0022-3514.66.5.840.

3: DON'T SWEAT THE SMALL STUFF

1. For more, see Robert D. Knapp, *The Supernova Advisor: Crossing the Invisible Bridge to Exceptional Client Service and Consistent Growth* (Hoboken, N.J.: Wiley, 2008).

2. For more, see Leslie A. Perlow, *Sleeping with Your Smartphone: How to Break*

the 24/7 Habit and Change the Way You Work (Boston: Harvard Business Review Press, 2012).

3. See, e.g., Joshua S. Rubinstein, David E. Meyer, and Jeffrey E. Evans, "Executive Control of Cognitive Processes in Task Switching," *Journal of Experimental Psychology: Human Perception and Performance* 27, no. 4 (August 2001): 763–797, doi: 10.1037/0096-1523.27.4.763.

4. Kenneth Lovett, "Ousted Majority Leader Malcolm Smith Fiddled with BlackBerry While Senate Burned," *Daily News*, June 10, 2009, http://articles.nydailynews.com/2009-06-10/news/17925247_1_thomas-golisano-republicans-independence-party.

5. Maralee McKee, "Seven Ways to Text with Graciousness and Savvy," www.mannersmentorblog.com/only-at-work/seven-ways-to-text-with-graciousness-and-savvy.

6. Marsha Egan, "Meeting Manners: Keep the Phone Off and Away," April 20, 2011, www.nationalmortgagenews.com/on_features/keep-phone-off-1024418-1.html.

7. Thom Shanker, "Gates Takes Aim at Pentagon Spending," *New York Times*, May 8, 2010, www.nytimes.com/2010/05/09/us/politics/09gates.html.

8. Viola Gienger, "Gates Says Defense Bureaucracy Swollen, Declares Cuts," Bloomberg.com, August 10, 2010, www.bloomberg.com/news/2010-08-09/gates-says-defense-bureaucracy-bloated-declares-cuts-in-contractor-jobs.html.

9. For more, see Russell Bishop, "Don't Let Bureaucracy Ruin Your Day," *New York Times*, April 2, 2011, www.nytimes.com/2011/04/03/jobs/03pre.html?ref=bureaucraticredtape. Also see Leisha DeHart-Davis, "Green Tape: A Theory of Effective Organizational Rules," *Journal of Public Administration Research and Theory* 19, no. 2 (2009): 361–384, doi: 10.1093/jopart/mun004.

4: YOUR DAILY ROUTINE

1. Quoted in Rachel Emma Silverman, "Where's the Boss? Trapped in a Meeting," *Wall Street Journal*, February 14, 2012, http://online.wsj.com/article/SB10001424052970204642604577215013504567548.html.

2. Bharat Mediratta, as told to Julie Bick, "The Google Way: Give Engineers

Room," *New York Times*, October 21, 2007, www.nytimes.com/2007/10/21 /jobs/21pre.html.

3. Carl Nielsen, as quoted in Josiah Fisk and Jeff Nichols, *Composers on Music: Eight Centuries of Writings* (Ann Arbor, Mich.: Pantheon Books, 1997), 216.

4. Roy F. Baumeister et al., "Ego Depletion: Is the Active Self a Limited Resource?," *Journal of Personality and Social Psychology* 74, no. 5 (May 1998): 1252–1265, doi: 10.1037/0022-3514.74.5.1252. Also see Kathleen Vohs et al., "Making Choices Impairs Subsequent Self-Control: A Limited-Resource Account of Decision Making, Self-Regulation, and Active Initiative," *Journal of Personality and Social Psychology* 94, no. 5 (2008): 883–898, doi: 10.1037/0022-3514.94.5.883.

5. See, e.g., Ernesto Pollitt and Rebecca Mathews, "Breakfast and Cognition: An Integrative Summary," *American Journal of Clinical Nutrition* 67, no. 4 (suppl.) (2008): 804S–813S.

6. Craig Lambert, "Deep into Sleep," *Harvard Magazine*, July–August 2005.

7. See, e.g., Masaya Takahashi, Hideki Fukuda, and Haihachiro Arito, "Brief Naps During Post-lunch Rest: Effects on Alertness, Performance, and Autonomic Balance," *European Journal of Applied Physiology and Occupational Physiology* 78, no. 2 (1998): 93–98, doi: 10.1007/s004210050392.

8. Corry Schiermeyer, "IBOPE Inteligência Poll: Two-fifths of Employees Would Take Naps at Work if Allowed," June 30, 2011, http://zogby.com /news/2011/06/30/ibope-zogby-poll-two-fifths-employees-would-take -naps-work-if-allowed.

9. Joseph Carroll, "Workers' Average Commute Round-Trip Is 46 Minutes in a Typical Day," August 24, 2007, www.gallup.com/poll/28504/workers -average-commute-roundtrip-minutes-typical-day.aspx.

10. See, e.g., Suzanne M. Bianchi et al., "Is Anyone Doing the Housework? Trends in the Gender Division of Household Labor," *Social Forces* 79, no. 1 (2000): 191–228.

11. Bureau of Labor Statistics, "American Time Use Survey Summary," June 22, 2011, www.bls.gov/news.release/atus.nr0.htm.

12. Hans P. A. Van Dongen et al., "The Cumulative Cost of Additional Wakefulness: Dose-Response Effects on Neurobehavioral Functions and Sleep

Physiology from Chronic Sleep Restriction and Total Sleep Deprivation," *Sleep* 26, no. 2 (2003): 117–126.

13. The three tests were a psychomotor vigilance task (measuring sustained attention), a computerized digit symbol substitution task (measuring working memory capacity), and a serial addition/subtraction task (measuring cognitive throughput).

14. Performance relative to the control group. Van Dongen et al., "The Cumulative Cost of Additional Wakefulness."

15. Yvonne Harrison and James A. Horn, "One Night of Sleep Loss Impairs Innovative Thinking and Flexible Decision Making," *Organizational Behavior and Human Decision Processes* 78, no. 2 (May 1999): 128–145. For a review of this and other related studies, see: William D. Killgore, "Effects of Sleep Deprivation on Cognition," *Progress in Brain Research*, 185 (2010): 105–129, doi: 10.1016/B978-0-444-53702-7.00007-5.

16. William D. Killgore, Thomas J. Balkin, and Nancy J. Wesensten, "Impaired Decision Making Following 49 H of Sleep Deprivation," *Journal of Sleep Research* 15, no. 1 (2006): 7-13, doi: 10.1111/j.1365-2869.2006.00487.x.

17. It is unclear whether two nights of ten hours' sleep is sufficient to recover from a week's worth of six hours' sleep. One study (Siobhan Banks et al., "Neurobehavioral Dynamics Following Chronic Sleep Restriction: Dose-Response Effects of One Night for Recovery," *Sleep* 33, no. 8 (2010): 1013–1026) suggested this to be the case, but another study (Alexandros Vgontzas et al., "Effects of Recovery Sleep Following Modest Sleep Restriction for One Workweek on Daytime Sleepiness and Performance: Gender Differences," paper presented at the annual meeting of the Associated Professional Sleep Societies, June 15, 2011) disagreed. In any case, the long-term effects of such deprivation and recovery are not well understood.

18. Andy Pringle et al., "Cost-effectiveness of Interventions to Improve Moderate Physical Activity: A Study in Nine UK Sites," *Health Education Journal* 69, no. 2 (June 2010): 211–224, doi: 10.1177/0017896910366790.

19. For example, one study divided adults randomly into three groups by exercise level: low intensity, moderate intensity, and no exercise. Each week, the researchers examined the level of energy or fatigue that the subjects

in all three groups felt. Both low- and moderate-intensity exercisers reported feeling more energy and less fatigue than the no-exercise group. See Timothy W. Puetz, Sara S. Flowers, and Patrick J. O'Connor, "A Randomized Controlled Trial of the Effect of Aerobic Exercise Training on Feelings of Energy and Fatigue in Sedentary Young Adults with Persistent Fatigue," *Psychotherapy and Psychosomatics* 77, no. 3 (2008): 167–174, doi: 10.1159/000116610.

20. Leon Watson, "The App That Tells You When You're Happiest (Unsurprisingly, It's 1.50pm on Christmas Day)," *Daily Mail*, www.dailymail.co.uk /sciencetech/article-2058228/Sex-makes-Appy-know-iPhone-study-reveals -satisfied.html.

21. For a specific example, see Emma E. A. Cohen et al., "Rowers' High: Behavioural Synchrony Is Correlated with Elevated Pain Thresholds," *Biology Letters* 6, no. 1 (2010): 106–108, doi: 10.1098/rsbl.2009.0670.

5: TRAVELING LIGHTLY

1. In one survey, 85 percent of executives stated that they consider teleconferences to be significantly inferior to personal contact with potential customers or partners. See "Business Meetings: The Case for Face to Face," *Forbes Insights*, 2009, http://images.forbes.com/forbesinsights/StudyPDFs/Business _Meetings_FaceToFace.pdf.

2. The average wait time from plane to baggage claim is seventeen minutes, according to http://doubletakemarketing.com, and it also takes several minutes to check the bag at your point of departure.

3. A. N. Nicholson and Barbara M. Stone, "Influence of Back Angle on the Quality of Sleep in Seats," *Ergonomics* 30, no. 7 (1987): 1033–1041.

4. "Difference Between Business Class and Economy Class," January 23, 2011, www.differencebetween.com/difference-between-business-class-and -economy-class.

5. Karl Doghramji, "The Effects of Alcohol on Sleep," Medscape Education, 2005, www.medscape.org/viewarticle/497982.

6. Here's one idea: Carry packets of oatmeal and tea in your luggage. That way, you have a quick and easy breakfast that requires only hot water!

7. See, e.g., Arne Lowden and Torbjörn Åkerstedt, "Eastward Long Distance Flights, Sleep and Wake Patterns in Air Crews in Connection with a Two-Day Layover," *Journal of Sleep Research* 8, no. 1 (March 1999): 15–24, doi: 10.1046/j.1365-2869.1999.00129.x.

8. For more, see Jim Waterhouse et al., "Jet Lag: Trends and Coping Strategies," *Lancet* 369, no. 9567 (2007): 1117–1129, doi:10.1016/S0140-6736(07)60529-7.

9. See, e.g., Anna Wirz-Justice et al., "No Evidence for a Phase Delay in Human Circadian Rhythms After a Single Morning Melatonin Administration," 32, *Journal of Pineal Research*, no. 1 (2002): 1–5, doi: 10.1034/j.1600-079x.2002.10808.x.

10. C. M. Espino et al., "International Business Travel: Impact on Families and Travellers," *Occupational & Environmental Medicine* 59, no. 5 (2002): 309–322, doi: 10.1136/oem.59.5.309.

6: EFFICIENT MEETINGS

1. Nicholas Romano and Jay Nunamaker, "Meeting Analysis: Findings from Research and Practice," paper presented at the 34th Hawaii International Conference, January 2001.

2. Oriana Bandiera et al., "What Do CEOs Do?" Social Science Research Network, February 2010, http://ssrn.com/abstract=1758445.

3. For more, see Charlan J. Nemeth et al., "The Liberating Role of Conflict in Group Creativity: A Study in Two Countries," *European Journal of Social Psychology* 34 (July–August 2004): 365–374, doi: 10.1002/ejsp.210.

4. E.g., Optimum = 7: Marcia Blenko, Michael C. Mankins, and Paul Rogers, *Decide & Deliver: Five Steps to Breakthrough Performance in Your Organization* (Boston: Bain & Company, 2010). Optimum ~=5: J. Richard Hackman and Neil Vidmar, "Effects of Size and Task Type on Group Performance and Member Reactions," *Sociometry* 33, no. 1 (March 1970): 37–54, doi: 10.2307/2786271.

5. A. H. Johnstone and F. Percival, "Attention Breaks in Lectures," *Education in Chemistry* 13, no. 2 (March 1976): 49–50.

6. "Cabletron Systems, Inc.," www.fundinguniverse.com/company-histories /Cabletron-Systems-Inc-company-History.html.

7. Joan Middendorf and Alan Kalish, "The 'Change-up' in Lectures," *National Teaching & Learning Forum* 5, no. 2 (1996): 1–5.

8. The line, of course, is from *Network*, directed by Sidney Lumet, Metro-Goldwyn-Mayer, 1976.

9. "'When We Understand That Slide, We'll Have Won the War:' US Generals Given Baffling PowerPoint Presentation to Try to Explain Afghanistan Mess," *Daily Mail*, April 28, 2010, www.dailymail.co.uk/news /article-1269463/Afghanistan-PowerPoint-slide-Generals-left-baffled -PowerPoint-slide.html.

10. This is the strategy of Ori Hadomi, the CEO of Mazor Robotics, based in Israel. He makes sure that there's a devil's advocate appointed in every meeting, so that the company does not rely on overly optimistic assumptions. See Adam Bryant, "Every Team Should Have a Devil's Advocate," *New York Times*, December 24, 2011, www.nytimes.com/2011/12/25/business/ori-hadomi-of-mazor-robotics-on -choosing-devils-advocates.html?pagewanted=all.

11. See, e.g., Michael I. Norton, Daniel Mochon, and Dan Ariely, "The IKEA Effect: When Labor Leads to Love," *Journal of Consumer Psychology* (2011), doi:10.1016/j.jcps.2011.08.002.

7: READING EFFECTIVELY

1. The study defined readers as "proficient" if they could gather content from different parts of a text, analyze when and if they fit together, and make inferences based on the text. See Statistics Canada, *Learning a Living: First Results of the Adult Literacy and Life Skills Survey* (Ottawa and Paris: Statistics Canada and OECD, 2005), www.statcan.gc.ca/pub/89-603-x/2005001 /pdf/4200878-eng.pdf; and Lois Romano, "Literacy of College Graduates Is on Decline," *Washington Post*, December 25, 2005, www.washingtonpost .com/wp-dyn/content/article/2005/12/24/AR2005122400701.html.

2. For more on adoption of online news, see Chee Youn Kang, "Communication Technologies: Diffusion of Online News Use and Credibility Among Young Web Users in the Information Age," master's thesis, University of Nevada Las Vegas, 2009.

3. Corey Binns, "Slow Down: Speed Reading Is Bunk, Studies Say," March 20, 2007, www.msnbc.msn.com/id/17705002/ns/health-livescience/t/slow-down -speed-reading-bunk-studies-say.

4. Jukka Hyönä, Robert F. Lorch, Jr., and Johanna K. Kaakinen, "Individual Differences in Reading to Summarize Expository Text: Evidence from Eye Fixation Patterns," *Journal of Educational Psychology* 94, no. 1 (March 2002): 44–55, doi: 10.1037/0022-0663.94.1.44.

5. Three of their subjects fit into a third category, nonselective rereaders (i.e., those who reread portions of text, but not in a way that reflected the structure of the text).

6. Jukka Hyönä and Robert F. Lorch, "Effects of Topic Headings on Text Processing: Evidence from Adult Readers' Eye Fixation Patterns," *Learning and Instruction* 14, no. 2 (April 2004): 131–152, doi: 10.1016/j.learninstruc.2004.01.001.

7. I've edited this article significantly for length and clarity. So if you're an expert on corporate governance and think that this article misses some key points, I kindly direct you to the original version here: Robert Pozen, "The Case for Professional Boards," *Harvard Business Review* 88, no. 12 (December 2010): 50–58, http://hbr.org/2010/12/the-big-idea-the-case-for-professional-boards/ar/1.

8. Suzanne E. Wade, Woodrow Trathen, and Gregory Schraw, "An Analysis of Spontaneous Study Strategies," *Reading Research Quarterly* 25, no. 2 (1990): 147–166, doi: 10.2307/747599.

9. The study had a very small sample size (sixty-seven total and only six "Good Strategy Users"); the improvement in test scores was not statistically significant.

10. Barbara J. Phillips and Fred Phillips, "Sink or Skim: Textbook Reading Behaviors of Introductory Accounting Students," *Issues in Accounting Education* 22, no. 1 (February 2007): 21–44, doi: http://dx.doi.org/10.2308/iace.2007.22.1.21.

11. Ibid., 14.

12. See, e.g., Ana Taboada et al., "Effects of Motivational and Cognitive Variables on Reading Comprehension," *Reading and Writing* 22, no. 1 (2008): 85–106, doi: 10.1007/s11145-008-9133-y.

13. See, e.g., CarolAnne M. Kardash and Roberta J. Scholes, "Effects of Preexisting Beliefs, Epistemological Beliefs, and Need for Cognition on Interpre-

tation of Controversial Issues," *Journal of Educational Psychology* 88, no. 2 (June 1996): 260–271, doi: 10.1037/0022-0663.88.2.260.

14. Teachers often use summarization as a technique to teach primary school children how to read. In one summarization strategy, the teacher reads a story one sentence at a time. After hearing each sentence, students must compose a summary—of no more than fifteen words—for the entire story up to that point. As students summarize longer and longer portions of text, they are forced to prioritize what is really important. In an experiment, researchers found that this strategy significantly increased comprehension. See Thomas W. Bean and Fern L. Steenwyk, "The Effect of Three Forms of Summarization Instruction on Sixth Graders' Summary Writing and Comprehension," *Journal of Literacy Research* 16, no. 4 (December 1984): 297–306, doi: 10.1080/10862968409547523.

8: WRITING EFFECTIVELY

1. National Commission on Writing, "Writing: A Ticket to Work . . . or a Ticket Out," September 2004, www.collegeboard.com/prod_downloads/writingcom /writing-ticket-to-work.pdf.

2. Ronald T. Kellogg, "Competition for Working Memory Among Writing Processes," *American Journal of Psychology* 114, no. 2 (2001): 175–191, doi: 10.2307/1423513.

3. Ronald T. Kellogg, "Attentional Overload and Writing Performance: Effects of Rough Draft and Outline Strategies," *Journal of Experimental Psychology: Learning, Memory, and Cognition* 14, no. 2 (April 1988): 355–365, doi: 10.1037/0278-7393.14.2.355.

4. In chapter 6, I mentioned that bringing people together to brainstorm may not be productive unless accompanied by debate. But here I'm talking about brainstorming by yourself, which is still quite valuable.

5. Paragraph 1 is a summary, whereas paragraph 2 is a conclusion.

6. Though these rules should guide your writing style, none of them is absolute; the situation sometimes calls for you to violate these principles, as I do occasionally in this book.

7. "Don't Forget the Spell-Check," http://officeteam.rhi.mediaroom.com /index.php?s=247&item=811.

8. Bob Boice, "Which Is More Productive, Writing in Binge Patterns of Creative Illness or in Moderation?," *Written Communication* 14, no. 4 (October 1997): 435–459.

9: SPEAKING EFFECTIVELY

1. *Seinfeld*, season 4, episode 63, first broadcast May 20, 1993, NBC, directed by Tom Cherones and written by Larry David.

2. Geoffrey Brewer, "Snakes Top List of Americans' Fears," March 19, 2001, www.gallup.com/poll/1891/snakes-top-list-americans-fears.aspx.

3. For fascinating reading on this subject, see Deborah A. Small, George Loewenstein, and Paul Slovic, "Sympathy and Callousness: The Impact of Deliberate Thought on Donations to Identifiable and Statistical Victims," *Organizational Behavior and Human Decision Processes* 102, no. 2 (2007): 143–153, doi: 10.1016/j.obhdp.2006.01.005.

4. " 'You've Got to Find What You Love,' Jobs says," *Stanford Report*, June 14, 2005, http://news.stanford.edu/news/2005/june15/jobs-061505.html.

5. Scott Berkun, *Confessions of a Public Speaker* (Sebastopol, Calif.: O'Reilly Media, 2010), 16.

6. Ralph R. Behnke and Chris R. Sawyer, "Patterns of Psychological State Anxiety in Public Speaking as a Function of Anxiety Sensitivity," *Communication Quarterly* 49, no. 1 (2001): 84–94, doi: 10.1080/01463370109385616.

PART IV: MANAGING UP AND DOWN

1. Of course, the support of your peers may also be crucial. Nevertheless, I decided not to include a chapter about "Managing Sideways" for two reasons. First, I believe the relationships between you and your boss and you and your subordinates are most critical to your productivity. Second, various parts of each chapter apply just as well to your equals as they do to your boss or your subordinates.

10: MANAGING YOUR TEAM

1. Teresa Amabile and Steven Kramer, "Inner Work Life: Understanding the Subtext of Business Performance," *Harvard Business Review* 85, no. 5 (2007): 72–83, 144.

2. Ibid. If you're curious, managers tended to rank "recognition for good work" as most important.

3. Adam Bryant, "In a Big Company, Make Everyone an Entrepreneur," *New York Times*, October 29, 2011, www.nytimes.com/2011/10/30/business/lynn -blodgett-of-acs-on-entrepreneurship-in-a-big-company.html?pagewanted=all.

4. Malcolm Gladwell, *Blink: The Power of Thinking Without Thinking* (New York: Little, Brown and Company, 2005).

5. Toby D. Wall et al., "Advanced Manufacturing Technology, Work Design, and Performance: A Change Study," *Journal of Applied Psychology* 75, no. 6 (December 1990): 691–697, doi: 10.1037/0021-9010.75.6.691.

6. The study also made conclusions about such job characteristics as task variety and effective feedback. See J. Richard Hackman and Greg R. Oldham, "Motivation Through the Design of Work: Test of a Theory," *Organizational Behavior and Human Performance* 16, no. 2 (August 1976): 250–279, doi: 10.1016/0030-5073(76)90016-7.

7. Rosanne Badowski, *Managing Up: How to Forge an Effective Relationship with Those Above You* (New York: Currency, 2003), 46.

8. Such as Alison Doyle, "Interview Questions and Answers," http://jobsearch .about.com/od/interviewquestionsanswers/a/interviewquest.htm.

9. For example, looking at data from forty-three automotive firms in the United States, researchers found that managers who had more trust in their lieutenants were much more likely to delegate tasks to them. See Gretchen M. Spreitzer and Aneil K. Mishra, "Giving Up Control Without Losing Control: Trust and Its Substitutes' Effects on Managers' Involving Employees in Decision Making," *Organization Management* 24, no. 2 (June 1999): 155–187, doi: 10.1177/1059601199242003.

10. "Maritz Research Hospitality Group 2011 Employee Engagement Poll," June 2011, http://maritzresearch.com/~/media/Files/MaritzDotCom/White%20 Papers/ExcecutiveSummary_Research.ashx.

11. If you want to learn more, start here: Steven A. Melnyk, Douglas M. Stewart, and Morgan Swink, "Metrics and Performance Measurement in Operations Management: Dealing with the Metrics Maze," *Journal of Operations Management* 22, no. 3 (June 2004): 209–218, doi: 10.1016/j.jom.2004.01.004. Also

see Steve Kerr, "The Best-Laid Incentive Plans," *Harvard Business Review* 81, no. 1 (January 2003): 27–33.

12. Sue Shellenbarger, "Better Ideas Through Failure," *Wall Street Journal*, September 27, 2011, http://online.wsj.com/article/SB1000142405297020401060457 6594671572584158.html.

13. Ibid.

14. Gretchen Spreitzer and Christine Porath, "Creating Sustainable Performance," *Harvard Business Review* 90, no. 1–2 (January–February 2012): 92–99.

15. Roy F. Baumeister et al., "Bad Is Stronger Than Good," *Review of General Psychology* 5, no. 4 (December 2001): 323–370, doi: 10.1037//1089-2680.5.4.323.

16. Andrew G. Miner, Theresa M. Glomb, and Charles Hulin, "Experience Sampling Mood and Its Correlates at Work," *Journal of Occupational and Organizational Psychology* 78 (June 2005): 171–193, doi: 10.1348/096317905X40105.

11: MANAGING YOUR BOSS

1. For more on this topic, see *Managing Up: Expert Solutions to Everyday Challenges* (Boston: Harvard Business School Press, 2008); and Michael and Deborah Singer Dobson, *Managing Up!: 59 Ways to Build a Career-Advancing Relationship with Your Boss* (New York: Amacom, 2000).

2. Peter Drucker, *The Practice of Management* (New York: Harper & Brothers, 1954).

3. This is inspired by Yael S. Zofi, *TOPS: Managing Up. How to Identify Your Manager's Style and Build a Stronger Relationship* (Brooklyn, N.Y.: AIM Strategies, 2008).

4. "Thoughts on Disagreement," http://thoughts.forbes.com/thoughts/quotes /disagreement.

5. Kenny Rogers, "The Gambler," United Records, 1978, LP.

6. Dan Bobinski, "Using Humor to Deal with Workplace Stress," Management-Issues, September 16, 2003, www.management-issues.com/2006/5/25/ opinion/using-humor-to-deal-with-workplace-stress.asp.

12: MAXIMIZING YOUR CAREER OPTIONS OVER A LIFETIME

1. "Occupational Employment and Wages—May 2010," Bureau of Labor Statistics, May 17, 2011, www.bls.gov/news.release/pdf/ocwage.pdf, table 1.

2. http://hrweb.mit.edu/system/files/Skills+Exercise.pdf. This list was compiled by MIT's Human Resources department.

3. Richard Kim, "The Audacity of Occupy Wall Street," *Nation*, November 2, 2011, www.thenation.com/article/164348/audacity-occupy-wall-street?page=full.

4. This is actually quite difficult to measure. You can't simply look at people who have twelve years of schooling and people who have thirteen years and look at the difference between their wages. People who choose to get an extra year of education might be systematically different, so simply comparing the wages of the two groups of people would confound multiple effects. For a review of this and other related issues, see George Psacharapoulos and Harry Anthony Patrinos, "Returns to Investment in Education: A Further Update," *Education Economics* 12, no. 2 (2004): 111–134, doi: 10.1080/0964529042000239140. The more mathematically inclined can refer to David Card, "Estimating the Return to Schooling: Progress on Some Persistent Econometric Problems," *Econometrica* 69, no. 5 (2001): 1127–1160.

5. This is even more difficult to measure than the wage-schooling relationship. Much of the research on this question was developed by the "father of labor economics," Jacob Mincer. In 1962, he made a rough estimate that on-the-job training (OJT) was roughly as valuable as formal schooling. In 1974, he revised that estimate downward, suggesting that OJT is worth about three to five extra years of school. For further reading, see Jacob Mincer, "On-the-Job Training: Costs, Returns, and Some Implications," *Journal of Political Economy* 70, no. 5 (1962): 50–79; Jacob A. Mincer, *Schooling, Experience, and Earnings* (New York: Columbia University Press, 1974); Barry R. Chiswick, "Jacob Mincer, Experience and the Distribution of Earnings," paper presented at the Conference in Honor of Jacob Mincer's 80th Birthday, New York, 2002.

6. Loren Gary, "Right Kind of Failure," Harvard Business Publishing Newsletters, January 1, 2002.

7. Dan Senor and Saul Singer, *Start-up Nation: The Story of Israel's Economic Miracle* (New York: Hachette Book Group, 2009).

8. All professionals should make an annual checkup of their Career Aims, regardless of their particular situation—but professionals in the middle of their careers are the most likely to forget this step.

9. Sixty-eight percent of those who had yet to retire. AARP, "Staying Ahead of the Curve 2003: The AARP Working in Retirement Study," 2003, http:// assets.aarp.org/rgcenter/econ/multiwork_2003_1.pdf.

10. At age sixty-five, an individual can expect to live an additional nineteen years. In 1950, a similar individual would have expected to live an additional fourteen years. See Centers for Disease Control and Prevention's "Health, United States, 2010: With Special Feature on Death and Dying" (Washington, D.C.: U.S. Government Printing Office, 2010), www.cdc.gov/nchs /data/hus/hus10.pdf, p. 132, table 22.

11. AARP, "Attitudes of Individuals 50 and Older Toward Phased Retirement," March 2005, http://assets.aarp.org/rgcenter/post-import/phased_ret.pdf.

13: EMBRACE CHANGE BUT STAY THE SAME

1. Testimony to Congress: "Home Recording of Copyrighted Works," 1982, http://cryptome.org/hrcw-hear.htm. Josh Barro, "Thirty Years Before SOPA, MPAA Feared the VCR," *Forbes*, January 18, 2012, www.forbes .com/sites/joshbarro/2012/01/18/thirty-years-before-sopa-mpaa-feared-the -vcr/.

2. This rough idea forms the basis of Prospect Theory, a recent development in the field of behavioral economics. For a good introduction to this subject, read chapters 25 through 28 of Daniel Kahneman, *Thinking Fast and Slow* (New York: Farrar, Straus and Giroux, 2011).

3. For a more rigorous explanation of this theory, see Rose McDermott, James H. Fowler, and Oleg Smirnov, "On the Evolutionary Origin of Prospect Theory Preferences," *Journal of Politics* 70, no. 2 (2008): 335–350, doi: 10.1017/S0022381608080341.

4. Bureau of Labor Statistics, "Number of Jobs Held, Labor Market Activity, and Earnings Growth Among the Youngest Baby Boomers: Results from a Longitudinal Survey," September 10, 2010, www.bls.gov/news.release/nlsoy .nr0.htm.

5. Ken Favaro, Per-Ola Karlsson, and Gary L. Neilson, "CEO Succession 2000–2009: A Decade of Convergence and Compression," *Strategy & Business* 59 (Summer 2010): 1–14.

6. Both of the trends that I'm about to discuss—technological and demographic change—are immensely complicated subjects. Here, I'm painting a picture with only the broadest brush.

7. Martin Hilbert and Priscila López, "The World's Technological Capacity to Store, Communicate, and Compute Information," *Science* 332, no. 6025 (2011): 60–65, doi: 10.1126/science.1200970.

8. See: "Growing a Nation: The Story of American Agriculture." http://www .agclassroom.org/gan/index.htm; America's Farmers Campaign, "Did You Know? Facts About American Farmers," http://www.americasfarmers .com/about/facts/did-you-know.aspx; World Bank, "Employment in agriculture (% of total employment)," 2011, http://data.worldbank.org/indicator /SL.AGR.EMPL.ZS.

9. Statistics Bureau, "Statistical Handbook of Japan," 2011, www.stat.go.jp /english/data/handbook/index.htm.

10. Howard French, "China Scrambles for Stability as Its Workers Age," *New York Times*, March 22, 2007, www.nytimes.com/2007/03/22/world /asia/22china.html?pagewanted=all.

11. Of course, countries are defined by more than their demographics: Russia is also facing challenges because of its concentration of wealth, while Brazil's future is also buoyed by progrowth economic policies.

12. According to Lipper, a U.S.-based growth fund invests (on average) in companies that are at least one-fifth of a standard deviation more "expensive" (relative to earnings, cash flow, and book value) than similarly sized companies. A U.S.-based "value" fund invests in companies that are at least one-fifth of a standard deviation "cheaper" relative to the same metrics. See "Worldwide Holdings-Based Fund Classification Methodology," April 30, 2010, www.lipperweb.com/docs/Research/Methodology/Worldwide _HBC_Methodology_1.12.pdf.

13. "Failure Quotes: Failure Leads to Success," www.motivatingquotes.com /failure.htm.

14. Nassim Taleb, *The Black Swan: The Impact of the Highly Improbable* (New York: Random House, 2007).

15. This is admittedly a simplification. A normal distribution is characterized by a particular family of probability distribution functions, which results in a bell curve shape.

16. "In Plato's Cave," *Economist*, January 22, 2009, www.economist.com /node/12957753.

17. "Why Newton Was Wrong," *Economist*, January 6, 2011, www .economist.com/node/17848665.

18. See Ernst Fehr and Urs Fischbacher, "The Nature of Human Altruism," *Nature* 425 (2003): 785–791, doi: 10.1038/nature02043.

19. Lisa A. Cameron, "Raising the Stakes in the Ultimatum Game: Experimental Evidence from Indonesia," *Economic Inquiry* 37, no. 1 (January 1999): 47–59, doi: 10.1111/j.1465-7295.1999.tb01415.x.

20. Anne Fisher, "America's Most Admired Companies," *Fortune*, February 21, 2006, http://money.cnn.com/2006/02/17/news/companies/most admired_fortune_intro/index.htm.

21. John J. Skowronski and Donal E. Carlston, "Caught in the Act: When Impressions Based on Highly Diagnostic Behaviours Are Resistant to Contradiction," *European Journal of Social Psychology* 22, no. 5 (September– October 1992): 435–452, doi: 10.1002/ejsp.2420220503.

22. Luís Cabral and Ali Hortaçsu, "The Dynamics of Seller Reputation: Evidence from eBay," *The Journal of Industrial Economics* 58, no. 1 (March 2010): 54–78, doi: 10.1111/j.1467–6451.2010.00405.x. The 13 percentage point result comes from the ThinkPad portion of the experiment.

23. "FedEx Guy Throwing My Computer Monitor," December 19, 2011, www.youtube.com/watch?v=PKUDTPbDhnA.

14: BALANCING HOME AND WORK

1. See U.S. Census Bureau, *Statistical Abstract of the United States*, 2012, table 616, "Employed Civilians by Occupation, Sex, Race, and Hispanic Origin: 2010," www.census.gov/compendia/statab/2012/tables/12s0616.pdf.

2. According to the Bureau of Labor Statistics, the average employed worker spends four hours per week working at home; for managers, that number jumps to seven hours per week. See U.S. Bureau of Labor Statistics, "Work-at-Home Patterns by Occupation," March 2009, www.bls.gov/opub/ils/pdf/opbils72.pdf.

3. *More* magazine survey of five hundred college-educated professional women over age thirty-four, as cited by Sue Shellenbarger, "Single and Off the Fast Track," *Wall Street Journal*, May 23, 2012, http://online.wsj.com/article/SB10 001424052702304791704577420130278948866.html.

4. Kenneth Matos and Ellen Galinsky, "2012 National Study of Employers," April 2012, http://familiesandwork.org/site/research/reports/NSE_2012 .pdf.

5. For instance, Cisco Systems has instituted an extensive telecommuting program, allowing its employees to work from home and keep flexible hours by use of broadband technology. According to one estimate, this program saved the company $195 million in 2003 as a result of higher worker productivity. See Council of Economic Advisers, "Work-Life Balance and the Economics of Workplace Flexibility," March 2010, http://www.whitehouse.gov/files /documents/100331-cea-economics-workplace-flexibility.pdf, page 22.

6. Ellen Galinsky, James T. Bond, and Kelly Sakai, "2008 National Study of Employers," May 2008, www.familiesandwork.org/site/research/reports /2008nse.pdf.

7. Joan Williams, *Unbending Gender: Why Work and Family Conflict and What to Do About It* (New York: Oxford University Press, 2000).

8. Hudson Worldwide, "In the Game of Hiring, Flexible Employers Win," February 12, 2008, http://us.hudson.com/in-the-game-of-hiring-flexible-employers -win.

9. Ken Giglio, "Workplace Flexibility Case Study: The Detroit Regional Chamber's Flexible Work Schedules," https://workfamily.sas.upenn.edu/sites/work family.sas.upenn.edu/files/imported/pdfs/detroit_regional_chamber.pdf.

10. See, e.g., Charles L. Baum, "The Effects of Maternity Leave Legislation on Mothers' Labor Supply After Childbirth," *Southern Economic Journal* 69, no. 4 (April 2003): 772–799.

11. Dan R. Dalton and Debra J. Mesch, "The Impact of Flexible Scheduling on Employee Attendance and Turnover," *Administrative Science Quarterly* 35, no. 2 (June 1990): 370–387, doi: 10.2307/2393395.

12. For a fascinating study of those in this line of work, see Sylvia Ann Hewlett and Carolyn Buck Luce, "Extreme Jobs: The Dangerous Allure of the 70-Hour Workweek," *Harvard Business Review* 84, no. 12 (December 2006): 49–59.

13. Henry M. Paulson, Jr., *On the Brink: Inside the Race to Stop the Collapse of the Global Financial System* (New York: Hachette Book Group, 2010), 31.

14. Ibid.

15. Ginia Bellafante, "Two Fathers, with One Happy to Stay at Home," *New York Times*, January 12, 2004, www.nytimes.com/2004/01/12/us/two-fathers -with-one-happy-to-stay-at-home.html?pagewanted=all&src=pm.

16. Some U.S. organizations do provide day care facilities for all employees, though they tend to be concentrated in large public and private employers. On this subject, the United States lags far behind many countries in northern Europe. Denmark puts the most money into child care, followed by other Nordic countries. In Finland, for example, every child under three is guaranteed a place in a local day care facility, free to low-income parents and at a reasonable cost to other families. The facilities, which are open from 7 or 8 a.m. to 5 or 6 p.m., serve breakfast and lunch. See "Baby Blues: A Juggler's Guide to Having It All," *Economist*, November 26, 2011, www.economist .com/node/21539925.

17. Here's one study that describes the harms of cell phones and emails after hours: Wendy R. Boswell and Julie B. Olson-Buchanan, "The Use of Communication Technologies After Hours: The Role of Work Attitudes and Work-Life Conflict," *Journal of Management* 33, no. 4 (August 2007): 592–610, doi: 10.1177/0149206307302552.

18. Glen E. Kreiner, Elaine C. Hollensbe, and Mathew L. Sheep, "Balancing Borders and Bridges: Negotiating the Work-Home Interface via Boundary Work Tactics," *Academy of Management Journal* 52, no. 4 (2009): 704–730.

19. Thomas J. DeLong and Camille Collett DeLong, "Managers as Fathers: Hope on the Homefront," *Human Resource Management* 31, no. 3 (Autumn 1992): 171–181, doi: 10.1002/hrm.3930310304.

20. Blake E. Ashforth, Glen E. Kreiner, and Mel Fugate, "All in a Day's Work: Boundaries and Micro Role Transitions," *Academy of Management Review* 25, no. 3 (July 2000): 472–491.

21. U.S. Bureau of Labor Statistics, "Work-at-Home Patterns by Occupation."

22. Kiran Mirchandani, "Protecting the Boundary: Teleworker Insights on the Expansive Concept of 'Work,'" *Gender & Society* 12, no. 2 (April 1998): 168–187, doi: 10.1177/089124398012002004.

APPENDIX 1: THE BIG IDEA:
THE CASE FOR PROFESSIONAL BOARDS

1. With one key exception: executive sessions. See Fred Wilson, "The Executive Session," April 30, 2010, http://articles.businessinsider.com/2010-04-30/strategy/29995759_1_executive-session-board-meeting-ceos.

2. See Marcia Blenko, Michael C. Mankins, and Paul Rogers, *Decide & Deliver: Five Steps to Breakthrough Performance in Your Organization* (Boston: Bain & Company, 2010); J. Richard Hackman and Neil Vidmar, "Effects of Size and Task Type on Group Performance and Member Reactions," *Sociometry* 33, no. 1 (March 1970): 37–54, doi: 10.2307/2786271.

3. For a review, see Clark W. Furlow, "Good Faith, Fiduciary Duties, and the Business Judgment Rule in Delaware," *Utah Law Review* 3 (2009): 1061–1095, http://epubs.utah.edu/index.php/ulr/article/viewFile/249/221.

ABOUT THE AUTHOR

BOB POZEN is a senior lecturer at Harvard Business School and a senior fellow at the Brookings Institution. Most recently, he was the chairman of MFS Investment Management. Prior to joining MFS, Bob was the vice chairman of Fidelity Investments and president of Fidelity Management & Research Company.

In late 2001 and 2002, Bob served on President Bush's Commission to Strengthen Social Security; he developed a progressive plan to make the system solvent. In 2003, Bob served as a moderate Democrat in the cabinet of Massachusetts governor Mitt Romney. In 2007, he served as chairman of the Security and Exchange Commission's Advisory Committee on Improvements to Financial Reporting.

Bob is an independent director of Medtronic and Nielsen. He is also a member of the governing board at the Commonwealth Fund and the Harvard NeuroDiscovery Center.

Bob has written *Too Big to Save?: How to Fix the U.S. Financial System,* a book on the recent financial crisis, and a guide for investors titled *The Fund Industry: How Your Money Is Managed.*

Bob graduated summa cum laude from Harvard College and holds a law degree from Yale. He lives in Boston with his wife, Liz.